NCTE's Theory and Research into Practice (TRIP) series presents volumes of works designed to offer a teacher audience a solid theoretical foundation in a given subject area within English language arts, exposure to the pertinent research in that area, and a number of practice-oriented models designed to stimulate theory-based application in the reader's own classroom.

Volumes in the Series

Computers in the Writing Classroom (2002), Dave Moeller

Co-Authoring in the Classroom: Creating an Environment for Effective Collaboration (1997), Helen Dale

Beyond the "SP" Label: Improving the Spelling of Learning Disabled Writers (1992), Patricia J. McAlexander, Ann B. Dobie, and Noel Gregg

Illumination Rounds: Teaching the Literature of the Vietnam War (1992), Larry R. Johannessen

Enhancing Aesthetic Reading and Response (1991), Philip M. Anderson and Gregory Rubano

Expressions: Multiple Intelligences in the English Class (1991), Peter Smagorinsky

Unlocking Shakespeare's Language: Help for the Teacher and Student (1988), Randal Robinson

Explorations: Introductory Activities for Literature and Composition, 7–12 (1987), Peter Smagorinsky, Tom McCann, and Stephen Kern

Writing about Literature (1984), Elizabeth Kahn, Carolyn Calhoun Walter, and Larry R. Johannessen

Questioning: A Path to Critical Thinking (1983), Leila Christenbury and Patricia P. Kelly

Designing and Sequencing Prewriting Activities (1982), Larry R. Johannessen, Elizabeth A. Kahn, and Carolyn Calhoun Walter

Learning to Spell (1981), Richard E. Hodges

Code-Switching

Teaching Standard English in Urban Classrooms

Rebecca S. Wheeler
Old Dominion University
and
Christopher Newport University

Rachel Swords
Newsome Park Elementary School, Newport News, Virginia

National Council of Teachers of English
1111 W. Kenyon Road, Urbana, Illinois 61801-1096

Staff Editor: Bonny Graham

Interior Design: Doug Burnett

Cover Design: Joellen Bryant

NCTE Stock Number: 07028

Library of Congress Cataloging-in-Publication Data

Wheeler, Rebecca S., 1952–
Code-switching: teaching standard English in urban classrooms/Rebecca S. Wheeler, Rachel Swords.
      p. cm. — (Theory & research into practice)
Includes bibliographical references and index.
ISBN 0-8141-0702-8 ((pbk))
1. English language—Study and teaching—United States. 2. English language—
    Standardization. 3. Education, Urban—United States. 4. Urban dialects—United
    States. I. Swords, Rachel. II. Title. III. Series.
LB1576.W4858 2006
372.6—dc22
      2005030726

xi

xv

ch

nd: Old and New Perspectives in

3

out Language   5

st Knowledge of the Home Language   5

Build on Students' Existing Knowledge   8

A Whole New Language Arts Mind-set   11

What Makes Standard English Standard?   11

What Makes "Nonstandard" Dialects Nonstandard?   12

Language Attitudes in the Classroom   14

African American English: Who Speaks What Where?   16

Language Transfer and International Englishes   17

The Vexing Problem of Terminology   19

Writing Style and Other Nomenclature   24

Conclusion   25

2. Moving from Correction to Contrast: Code-Switching in
Diverse Classrooms   28

The Correctionist Lens   30

What Linguistics Tells Us   32

Method in the "Madness"   33

Teaching Standard English in Urban Classrooms   38

Attitudes toward Standard English   40

3. Linguistic Insights for the Language Arts Classroom   47

How Language Varies   47

      Vocabulary 47

      Sounds 48

      Grammar 49

   Varieties of English 50

   Registers, Formality, and Dialects 50

   Standard English, Vernacular English, and So-Called
   "Nonstandard" English 52

      African American English: *Not* Standard English with
      Mistakes 53

4. Code-Switching Succeeds in Teaching Standard English 55

   Home Speech in the Classroom 55

      Caribbean Students in Canada: Déjà Vu 55

      Trinidad and Tobago 56

   How to Talk the New Walk 57

   The Top Ten Patterns 59

   When Students Speak Informal English 59

   Contrastive Analysis 61

      Research from Chicago 61

      Research from New York 62

      Results from Georgia 62

   Conclusion 63

II. Classroom Practice

5. Diversity in Language 67

   Variation Is Natural 67

   Language Variation Is Natural 70

   Recognizing Formal and Informal Patterns 71

   Exploring Language Variation in Literature 72

   The Next Steps 74

6. Teaching Noun Patterns: Possessives 75

   Understanding Possessive Patterns 76

Applying the Scientific Method 76

Discovering the Pattern in Student Writing 76

Formulating the Grammar Rule 77

Testing Your Hypothesis 77

Refining Your Hypothesis 79

What If You Don't Know the Answers to Students' Questions? 79

Teaching Possessive Patterns: Lesson 1 80

Anchor in Your Students' Writing 80

Start by Focusing on One Informal Pattern per Sentence 80

Create a Contrastive Analysis Chart 81

Begin Your Lesson on Possessives 81

Work with the Contrastive Analysis Charts 82

Help Students Discover the Informal Pattern 83

Help Students Discover the Formal Pattern 83

Let Students Practice New Understanding 84

Teaching Possessive Patterns: Lesson 2 87

7. Teaching Noun Patterns: Plurals 91

Plural Patterns in Informal English 91

Using Contrastive Analysis to Teach Plurality 91

Start with One Informal Pattern per Sentence 92

Create Contrastive Analysis Chart for Plurals 92

Leading Students to Discover Plurality 92

Discover the Plural Pattern inside Formal English 94

Discover the Plural Pattern in Informal English 95

Reviewing Plural Patterns 97

Reviewing Plural and Possessive Patterns 99

8. Teaching Subject-Verb Agreement 102

Building Your Contrastive Analysis Chart 102

Reviewing Subjects and Action Verbs 103

Teaching Subject-Verb Agreement: Lesson 1   104

   Discovering the Pattern in Formal Language   104

   What Subject-Verb Agreement Really Means   105

   Discovering Subject-Verb Agreement in Informal
   Language   106

Teaching Subject-Verb Agreement: Lesson 2   107

Teaching *Was/Were* Patterns for Subject-Verb Agreement   109

   Lesson 1: *Was/Were*   109

   Discovering the *Was/Were* Pattern in Formal Language   110

   Discovering the *Was/Were* Pattern in Informal Language   111

Reviewing *Was/Were*   111

Teaching *Is* and *Are* Patterns   114

   Lesson 1: *Is/Are*   114

   Discovering *Is/Are* Patterns in Informal and Formal
   Language   115

   Lesson 2: *Is/Are*   117

Reviewing Subject-Verb Agreement   117

9. Teaching Past Time   121

   Discovering Patterns for Past Time   121

   Teaching Time/Tense Contrasts   122

      Discovering the Informal Pattern for Showing Past Time   122

      Discovering the Formal Pattern for Showing Past Time   124

   Reviewing Past Time in Informal and Formal English   124

10. Teaching *Gonna/Going to*   126

   Finding the Pattern: *Gonna*   126

   Lesson 1: *Gonna/Going to*   127

   Discovering and Naming the Patterns: *Gonna* v. *Going to*   127

   Lesson 2: Reviewing *Gonna/Going to*   129

11. Code-Switching with More Complex Patterns   132

   Multiple Patterns in a Single Sentence   132

One-Many Relation between Form and Meaning 134

    Habitual *Be* 134

    Teaching Habitual *Be* 135

    "*Be* Understood" 137

    Teaching "*Be* Understood" 137

12. Code-Switching in the Reading and Writing Classroom 143

    Language Diversity and Reading 143

        Perceiving Language Differences in Literature 143

        Selecting and Teaching Grammar Patterns through Literature 146

        Using Literature to Enhance Contrastive Analysis Lessons 146

        Class Discussion 147

        Practice: Switching from Informal to Formal Language 148

    Language Diversity and Writing 148

        Using Language to Build Characters 148

        Reflecting on Language Differences in Personal Journals 149

        Editing and Conferencing 150

        Publishing 152

13. Encountering New Patterns 154

    Drawing on the Top-Ten Patterns 154

    Working through a New Pattern on Your Own 155

    Drawing on Existing Dialect Resources 157

14. Conclusion: How to Talk about Code-Switching with Others 158

Appendix A: Selected African American English Structures 163

Appendix B: A Literary Grammatical Concordance 179

Bibliography 185

Index 193

Authors 197

Foreword

This is a long overdue and tremendously welcome book. Linguists have argued, at least since the 1960s, that teachers could help speakers of vernacular varieties master Standard English more successfully if they pinpointed the contrasts between the vernacular and the standard and taught their students to bridge them. Some linguists and educators even created detailed manuals to help teachers do this. But these manuals were never published and made available to the general public in the way that Wheeler and Swords's excellent *Code-Switching* is now about to be. In the meantime, speakers of African American Vernacular English (AAVE) and other vernaculars have continued to be misunderstood, misdiagnosed, underrespected, and underassisted in their efforts to add Standard English to their linguistic repertoire. And they've also been limited in their school success and occupational mobility. This book will, I think, help to dismantle these barriers, enabling teachers to "reach out to the students of urban America" in ways they weren't able to do before.

One of the great features of this book is that it was jointly authored by an academic linguist (Rebecca Wheeler) and a classroom teacher (Rachel Swords). Teachers sometimes complain that while linguists have potentially valuable insights and suggestions for them, they don't convey them in sufficiently nontechnical language, and they don't have sufficient classroom experience to translate them into effective practice. Wheeler and Swords's collaboration helps to solve this problem. And the fact that the authors have successfully implemented the strategies they present in this book in classrooms and teacher training workshops augments the book's authority. The writing style is clear and conversational throughout, making it accessible to teachers, administrators, and parents.

The division of the book into two parts, one theoretical and the other practical, is appealing. The theoretical part (approximately the first third of the book) is devoted to a survey of relevant research on dialect variation, language attitudes, and contrastive analysis. Among other things, it indicates that the haphazard correction of student "errors" (the modus operandi of most teachers) generally fails to help students become effective users of Standard English, while teaching contrastive analysis and code-switching (virtually unknown among teachers) has been shown to be effective in several research studies. Of the informal varieties of English considered in this book, AAVE occupies a central place, as it does in research on American dialects over the past half century. But the book's approach—including its "scientific method" of discovering grammar patterns in students' speech and writing—is applicable to a wide range of dialects, including international ones. The essential insight here is that students who use nonstandard structures are behaving rationally and regularly, in accordance with the rules of their native vernacular. The importance of recognizing and respecting the integrity of students' language, and through it their families, their identities, and their culture, comes through loud and clear. Readers interested in learning more about any of the theoretical issues covered in the first part can follow up by consulting the works of linguists and educators cited therein.

The second and lengthier part of the book is devoted to classroom practice—and the ten chapters in this section will quickly become dog-eared as teachers turn to them again and again. Wheeler and Swords provide initial exercises for helping students recognize that varying one's self-presentation between formal and informal contexts (through conduct and dress, for instance) is normal, and the authors then provide tools for helping students master formal language (Standard English) by systematic contrasts with the more familiar patterns of informal language (vernacular English). Successive chapters focus on informal features that tend to show up in students' formal writing (possessives, plural nouns, and third-person singular present tense verbs without the -s suffix, for instance, or the use of *gonna* instead of *going to*). Appendix A summarizes the contrasts involved in the ten most common "informal" features (structures that are common in AAVE, but some also in other dialects), and Chapter 13 provides strategies for dealing with new patterns. Alternative analyses for some of the features discussed are certainly possible; what matters is that the analyses are accurate and that they work to help students develop linguistic versatility.

Chapter 12 ("Code-Switching in the Reading and Writing Classroom") and its related Appendix B ("A Literary Grammatical Concordance") will, I think, be a favorite of teachers interested in an integrated language and literature curriculum. Both segments of the book demonstrate how existing literary works can be used to enhance contrastive analysis lessons, and vice versa, and how students' personal journals and stories can contribute to their linguistic and literary development. Appendix B provides a list of children's books that employ the informal features discussed in *Code-Switching*, with specific examples and page numbers. One way in which this fine list could be expanded even further would be for teachers and other readers to send in to the authors information on other books that exemplify the key features, with the steadily expanding list being made available on a publicly accessible Web site. Interested readers can contact Rebecca Wheeler at rwheeler@odu.edu.

I also liked the authors' concluding chapter, which explores how to talk about code-switching with fellow teachers, parents, and administrators. Among the several good points in this chapter was their advice to start small and talk in general ways, as well as their observation that "with code-switching, the dynamics of the whole classroom change, from teacher as grammar police, to teacher as co-participant in the enterprise of crafting writing that fits the setting."

I have been asked many times for a book like this, by teachers and others. My belief and fervent hope is that this book will succeed in improving not only the dynamics of English language and literature classrooms, but also the performance of the students who pass through them, instilling in them a love of and excitement about the subject.

John R. Rickford
Stanford University
September 26, 2005

Acknowledgments

Each author offers her own acknowledgments.

Rachel Swords

Many people helped to make the writing of this book possible. First and foremost, I thank Dr. Rebecca Wheeler. During my time as a student in her linguistics course, Dr. Wheeler challenged my perception of language and helped me to embrace language differences. From the beginning, she applauded my efforts to find innovative ways to teach language in my own classroom. Later, she encouraged me to coauthor an article and then this book. I thank her for being a constant supporter and for always urging me to go one step further.

Newport News Public Schools has been the forum in which all of my work has taken place. I thank Susan Piland (director of staff development) and Pat Seward (language arts supervisor 6–12) for allowing me opportunities to share this work with my colleagues.

I have always been appreciative of the opportunities afforded me as a teacher at Newsome Park Elementary School. I thank Mr. Bender (former principal) for giving me the freedom to teach code-switching to my students. I also thank Dr. Teston (current principal) for taking an interest in my work and for allowing me to continue to teach language through code-switching.

From the onset of this project, my family has remained my constant support. They have taken great interest in this endeavor and readily share my work with anyone willing to listen. I thank my parents, Chet and Shari Sutphin, for believing in both me and my work. I thank my husband, Thomas Swords, for his support and patience during this lengthy project. I also thank my sister, Amy Howe, for sharing my frustration and excitement about this book and for being one of my biggest fans. I am grateful for my family's encouragement during the writing process.

Rebecca S. Wheeler

My first appreciation goes to my collaborator, urban elementary teacher Rachel Swords, whose insight, courage, and creativity in implementing code-switching and contrastive analysis in her classroom inspired me to initiate what has become a fertile, ongoing collaboration between us. I thank Christopher Newport University (CNU), especially Marsha Sprague, director of teacher education, and CNU's administration. Believing in this work, sharing the vision from the outset, Marsha has encouraged me through each step. CNU's Dean Douglas Gordon and Provost Richard Summerville provided me not only clear professional support in my research but also some release time from my 4–4 teaching assignment. Without that time, I would not have been able to complete this book. And I thank the students of CNU's MAT program, who helped me hone my own presentation of these materials and who have shown such openness to growing in understanding of language arts practice.

My relationship with the Newport News Public Schools (NNPS) has been one of the great gems of my professional life. Thank you Susan Piland (director of staff development), Pat Seward (language arts supervisor 6–12), Neil Stamm (director of research and evaluation), and Dave Blackburn (former grant writer for NNPS, now with Programs for Research and Evaluation in Public Schools of the Darden College of Education, Old Dominion University) for your continued interest and for affording me opportunities to work in our local elementary and middle schools.

It was Tim Grimes, Newport News director for GEAR-UP (Gaining Early Awareness and Readiness for Undergraduate Programs), who made possible my work in the middle schools from 2003 to 2005. Thanks to NNPS' GEAR-UP grant, I was able to work intensively with a local, urban eighth-grade team to bring code-switching to their language arts practice. While this book is directed toward elementary audiences, my experiences at Huntington with dedicated teachers and administrators have informed and deepened my own understanding of how to bring these research-based tools to the public schools.

I am grateful to Ray Jackendoff, 2003 president of the Linguistic Society of America (LSA), for his friendship, ongoing encouragement, and firm commitment to the importance of linguists partnering with teachers in the schools. I thank John Rickford, whose publications have been life changing for me. His clarion call for educators to abandon failing language arts techniques and adopt successful approaches from applied linguistics as we seek finally—finally—to reach African American students, this call has been my beacon and constant companion. To my linguist colleagues across the country, I greatly appreciate our discussions along my path of learning about language variation and bringing these insights to the schools. Thank you to Carolyn Adger, Anne Charity, Kirk Hazen, Julie Sweetland, Walt Wolfram, and all of the LSA Committee on Language in the School Curriculum. To Ralph Fasold, William Labov, Roger Shuy, Geneva Smitherman, and Walt Wolfram, thank you for the groundbreaking history of your scholarship and your collective voice.

Writing this book under the guidance and supervising eye of our NCTE editor, Zarina Hock, has been pure joy. Dr. Hock believed in our work from the outset and has helped us improve it consistently along the way. She's a dream of an editor. And to the eight reviewers of our work, we thank you for your detailed reading, affirmations, and challenges. Your comments have helped us deepen our work considerably. As always, remaining errors or shortcomings are on us alone.

Finally, I turn to my dear husband, Lou Seyler. Though at times he found unfathomable my journey of writing, rewriting, and constant editing and proofing, he affirmed me and my work all along the way. My life is blessed in our bounty.

I Theory and Research

1 The Lay of the Land: Old and New Perspectives in Language Arts

Rachel Swords works with her students, helping them learn the ins and outs of "proper," Standard English. In the margins of her students' essays, she pens the way the language "should be." In the halls, she prompts students to use the "right" grammar. But after many months, her students still seem to follow their old ways.

> *Student:* Janae need a marker.
>
> *Mrs. Swords:* Janae what?
>
> *Student:* She need a marker.
>
> *Mrs. Swords:* Tarik! We've talked about this. Janae what?
>
> *Student:* Janae *need a marker*!
>
> *Mrs. Swords:* We don't say, "Janae need a marker." We say, "Janae needS a marker."
>
> *Student:* Oh, OK.

The next afternoon, the story is the same; the child says, "My sister like to go to the playground." Swords has worked carefully with her students, but somehow they don't hear, can't hear what she is trying to teach.

Stories like this abound. Here's a similar tale from one of Rebecca Wheeler's teacher education students. The conversation is between an elementary teacher and student:

> *Student:* Can I go to da bafroom?
>
> *Teacher:* Can you what?
>
> *Student:* Can I go to da bafroom?
>
> *Teacher:* Can you WHAT?
>
> Student: *Can I GO TO DA BAFROOM! It's right there in front a you!*
>
> *Teacher:* We don't say "da bafroom." We say "THe baTHroom."
>
> *Student:* Whatever. Can I go?

These two scenarios are strikingly similar, yet these teachers don't know each other. Although they work in different schools, the way they talk with the children is nearly identical. In each instance, the child expresses himself or herself and the teacher challenges it, trying to get the child to rephrase from "improper" to "proper" English. In each scenario, while the teacher knows exactly what she wants the child to change ("Don't say, *Janae need*—say, *Janae needs*"; "Don't say, *da bafroom*—say, *the bathroom*"), the children just can't figure it out. Instead, each child keeps repeating the original comment exactly as he or she first expressed it. Ultimately, everybody got frustrated, and the children did not learn the Standard English (SE) forms the teachers were trying to teach.

Frustrating indeed.

Of course, as teachers, we also try to correct our students' writing, not just their speech. When we come across examples of "improper" English in our students' papers, we can't resist marking them. How else are we to teach our students the Standard English we know they need to succeed in school and in the world of work? With red pen, we circle errors, showing students—again and again—the "right" way to write English. So when a student writes *I be playing basketball all summer*, we circle *be playing* and jot what we believe to be the "correct" form in the margin—*am playing*. But does the student learn from these corrections? Not really—not any more successfully in writing than in speech. And so despite all our efforts, minority dialect students just don't seem to command Standard English, even though we have been teaching our hearts out.

Experts from applied linguistics can help us understand this surprising failure of our correction techniques. They explain that while "various strategies can be useful for learning Standard English equivalents[,] . . . [o]ne that does not work is correcting vernacular features" (Wolfram, Adger, and Christian, 1999, p. 122). By vernacular features, they mean those patterns in a student's speech or writing that are characteristic of the way the student talks with friends and family in the home community.

So the approach we teachers have tended to take—correcting student language—is the very approach that doesn't work. Dialectologists Walt Wolfram, Carolyn Adger, and Donna Christian point us to important research that confirms our own classroom experiences. They report on the work in the early 1970s by language researcher Anne Piestrup. Even thirty years ago, Piestrup "found that vernacular speakers who were corrected when they used vernacular features actually used more, not fewer, vernacular features over time" (Wolfram et al., pp. 122–23). Other educators have reached the same conclusion; simply correcting vernacular features doesn't work. For example, Keith Gilyard, an African American writing about his early life and education, points to the fact that "generations of Black English speakers have been subjected to 'correction' programs that haven't worked" (1991, p. 114).

We teachers have long charted a course of correction with our students, but our navigation plan isn't working. The students are not locking in the coordinates of the Standard English grammar we're trying to teach. Instead, they persist in using that "improper" language, and we persist in correcting what we see as their "bad grammar." It's time for a new plan.

That's what this book is about: helping teachers and students get off the correction treadmill and discover an approach to teaching Standard English that really does work—code-switching and contrastive analysis

Assumptions about Language

When we talk about "proper grammar" and "good English," we make a lot of assumptions about the nature of language. We assume that English *is* Standard English. We assume that Standard English is Right with a capital *R*, and that anything else is improper, bad, incorrect, and fractured. Indeed, we seem to believe that anything other than Standard English is pretty much *not* English.

These are the assumptions that lead us to correct our students' language. Various educators refer to this viewpoint in slightly different ways. Wheeler and Swords (2004) dub it the *correctionist model* of language. Both linguist John McWhorter (1998) and Sonya Nieto (2000), professor of language, literacy, and culture, speak of the eradicationist approach used by teachers who hope to repress or eradicate the language of the home and replace it with Standard English, the language of the school. Some even label students who come to school speaking the vernacular as "communication-deficient" (Chesebro, Berko, Hopson, Cooper, & Hodges, 1995, p. 149).

Students' Robust Knowledge of the Home Language

Yet, far from being communication deficient, minority dialect speakers are *communication robust*. Linguist William Labov, who pioneered research into the structure of African American English (AAE), affirms the communicative richness of the language many African Americans speak. In the African American community,

> we see a child bathed in verbal stimulation from morning to night. We see many speech events which depend on the competitive exhibition of verbal skills: sounding, singing, toasts, rifting, louding— a whole range of activities in which the individual gains status through his use of language. (qtd. in Wolfram et al, 1999, p. 87)

Also, accomplished writers such as Langston Hughes, Maya Angelou, and Toni Morrison (who won the Nobel Prize for Literature) use African American English to great advantage. We do not think of these authors as suffering from deficient communication skills or as writing in broken English.

Yet the language our students use is the very same language we find in the work of Hughes, Angelou, and Morrison. How can our society regard these authors so highly and yet be so concerned when our students' home language crops up in school writing?

One answer surely leaps out at us. We know that Hughes and Morrison are able to switch between their vernacular and a Standard dialect as their literary goals demand. So some of Hughes's poems are written in Standard English, while others use the cadences of his home language. Thus, in "Dreams," we read and hear Standard English: "Hold fast to dreams / For if dreams die / Life is a broken-winged bird . . ." But in "Mother to Son," Hughes draws on vernacular patterns:

> Well, son, I'll tell you:
> Life for me ain't been no crystal stair.
> It's had tacks in it,
> And splinters,
> And boards torn up,
> And places with no carpet on the floor—
> Bare.
> But all the time
> I'se been a-climbin' on,
> And reachin' landin's,
> And turnin' corners,
> And sometimes goin' in the dark
> Where there ain't been no light.
> So, boy, don't you turn back.
> Don't you set down on the steps.
> 'Cause you finds it's kinder hard.
> Don't you fall now—
> For I'se still goin', honey,
> I'se still climbin',
> And life for me ain't been no crystal stair.

This poem is filled with the speech patterns of African American English, but translating it into Standard English would rob the poem of its powerful voice.

Well, son, I'll tell you:
Life for me **hasn't been any** crystal stair.
It's had tacks in it,
And splinters,
And boards torn up,
And places with no carpet on the floor—
Bare.
But all the time
I**'ve** been **climbing**
And **reaching** landings
And **turning** corners,
And sometimes **going** in the dark
Where there **hasn't been any light**
So, boy, don't you turn back.
Don't you **sit** down on the steps.
Because you find it rather difficult.
Don't you fall now—
For **I am** still **going**, honey,
I am still **climbing**,
And life for me **hasn't been any** crystal stair.

Indeed, translating Hughes's poem into Standard English (see boldface) produces a pedestrian statement sapped of life and energy. Through this exercise, we see how important it is to hear the human voice in literature, and that voice often is not speaking Standard English. Clearly, Hughes is in control of his language. He chooses his language to suit his purposes.

Similarly, Morrison moves between Standard English and the people's vernacular to fit the setting. Her 1993 Nobel Prize lecture was in Standard English, an extremely refined version of Standard at that:

> Official language smitheryed to sanction ignorance and preserve privilege is a suit of armor polished to shocking glitter, a husk from which the knight departed long ago. Yet there it is: dumb, predatory, sentimental. Exciting reverence in schoolchildren, providing shelter for despots, summoning false memories of stability, harmony among the public. (2000, p. 14)

Yet, in her recent novel, *Love*, we find vernacular language and sentence fragments, both structures characteristic of comfortable conversation.

> "Then why ain't you smiling?"
>   Bill Cosey turned to look at Sandler. His eyes, though bright from drink, radiated pain like cracked glass. "What do they say about me?" he asked, sipping from the thermos.
>   "They?"
>   "You all. You know. Behind my back."
>   "You a highly respected man, Mr. Cosey." (2003, p. 42)

Here, Morrison strategically employs a range of voices and language styles: In the narrative description, she uses full sentences in Standard English. Then she chooses language that allows her characters to speak with contrasting voices—Mr. Cosey, a prominent citizen, uses the grammar of formal English, even though he speaks in sentence fragments, the usual pattern of conversation (*You all. Behind my back.*). Sandler, on the other hand, uses the grammar patterns of vernacular language (*[W]hy ain't you smiling? . . . You __ a highly respected man, Mr. Cosey.*). Readers never question that Morrison is in command of her language.

Build on Students' Existing Knowledge

Like Morrison and other literary greats, capable writers are able to choose language to fit the setting. We know that when our students write using double negatives (*I ain't got none*) or home speech possessives (*Mom_ jeep is out of gas*), they are often not consciously choosing these language patterns. Instead, they are writing as they speak. Yet our schools expect students to perform in Standard English and penalize them if they don't. Similarly, broader society often expects people to use a Standard dialect in daily exchanges. So as teachers, one of our goals is to help students develop and hone useful linguistic tools. Competence in Standard English is surely one such tool.

For a new approach, let's fast forward to Swords's third-grade classroom. Zoom in on the next school year, after she has fundamentally changed how she teaches language and how she responds to her students. Here we witness a very different exchange.

> *Student:* Mrs. Swords, Sydni want to know if she can work in my group.
>
> *Mrs. Swords:* Jawan, right now we're practicing talking formally, like we would with the principal or the mayor. Can you code-switch[1] to Standard English?
>
> *Student:* OK, Sydni wants to know if she can work in my group.
>
> *Mrs. Swords:* Is that okay with everyone else in the group?
>
> *Student:* Yes.
>
> *Mrs. Swords:* OK, then it's fine with me!

Swords is now engaging with her students in a very different way. She doesn't correct this student's language. Instead, she asks the child to *code-switch*—that is, to choose the language appropriate to the context. Here, the class is practicing how to switch from Everyday English to Standard English—from one language code to another. Given this context, Swords responds to the form of the child's language directly and with ease while mainly focusing on what the child wants and means. This exchange is much more successful than the one related at the beginning of this chapter. The child understands and responds to Swords's point about language, and nobody gets frustrated.

Of course, a lot has gone on in the classroom before Swords and the student can interact in this way. Indeed, based on what she had learned in Wheeler's Master of Arts in Teaching (MAT) English course on language varieties in the schools, Swords fundamentally changed how she approached her students' language, both spoken and written.

Through studying basic insights in applied linguistics, Swords had learned that students who write *My goldfish name is Scaley* or *I have two dog and two cat*[2] are not making mistakes in Standard English. Instead, they are following the grammar patterns of their everyday language. If they're not making mistakes, then correction isn't appropriate. In its place, Swords learned to use *contrastive analysis*, a well-established tool from second language acquisition studies (see Lado, 1957).

According to linguist Terry Odlin (1989), when a person learns a second language, we should expect to see the patterns of the first language transfer into what he or she says or writes in the new language. Of course, we all understand that the sounds of a person's first language will affect how that person sounds in a second language. When the sounds of a person's first language transfer into how she or he speaks a second language, we say that person has an accent. Likewise, the grammar patterns of a person's first language crop up as she expresses herself in a second language. But when the grammar of a person's first language transfers into his or her second language expression, we are not so understanding. We usually talk about a person's "grammatical errors" or "broken English" (even though when the sounds of a person's first language transfer into the second language, we don't refer to "sound errors" or "broken sound"). Perhaps we need a name for grammatical transfer that is more parallel to the name we have for sound transfer. Here's an initial attempt at a simple descriptive term: *grammatical echo*.

> *Grammatical Echo*: When the grammar patterns of a person's first language transfer into his or her expression in another language or language variety, we hear the grammatical echo of the first language.

Here are some examples of how grammar from a person's first language can transfer into his or her second language expression. Spanish speakers writing in English may well use "word for word translations from Spanish, as in *the porch of Carmen* from *el balcon de Carmen* instead of the more usual, idiomatic English, *Carmen's porch*" (Odlin, 1989, p. 96). More whimsically, Odlin quotes from an actor's manual designed to help actors sound like a recent Russian immigrant, by using characteristic Russian language transfers into English:

> Oh! I very good fellow! Why? Because I Cossack. I very big Cossack. . . . I be big mans. And women's, they love me lots. Nastia Alexanderovna—she big ballet dancer in Czar ballet—Countess Irene Balushkovna, she love me. (qtd. in Odlin, 1989, pp. 1–2)

By looking at the contrasts between the grammar patterns in this fictional character's speech and the grammar patterns of Standard English, we can learn a great deal about Russian itself. We can see that Russian does not use the verb *be* as a Standard English speaker would (*I very good fellow* v. *I am a very good fellow*; *I very big Cossack* v. *I am a very big Cossack*). Similarly, we can see that Russian does not use articles in front of nouns (*She big ballet dancer* v. *She is a big ballet dancer*). Among other fruits of our grammatical sleuthing, we might also recognize that third-person singular subjects do not take the distinct verb endings we find in Standard English (*She love me* v. *She loves me*).

What's happening is that the patterns (sound, word, grammar) of the home language transfer into the way a person expresses himself or herself in Standard English. In effect, we can see the echo of Russian grammar cropping up in our Cossack's Standard English expression.

This notion of "language transfer" also applies when we're talking about a person learning to speak or write in a new dialect (language variety). First, a few words about the word *dialect*. Wolfram and Schilling-Estes (1998) explain that "the term dialect . . . is a neutral label to refer to any variety of a language which is shared by a group of speakers" who live in the same place or belong to the same social or socioeconomic group (250). Just as sound or grammar traits of a person's first language transfer into his or her second language expression, so the traits of a person's first dialect transfer into that person's expression as he or she is learning a second dialect.

Here's how knowing about dialect transfer will help teachers with African American students who are learning formal English (i.e., Standard English as a Second Dialect [SESD]): In the same way that we know something about the home grammar of the Cossack by how the actor's manual showed him importing Russian grammar into Standard English, we know something about the home language of an urban African American student who writes *He a good man* or *She deserve a good man*. We know that African American English has no need for *be* in equative sentences (*He a good man*). We also know that the agreement patterns for third-person singular subjects require the bare dictionary form of the verb (*She deserve a good man*). Now, instead of thinking that our students struggle with broken English, we can see the grammar echoes of their first dialect cropping up in their Standard English expression. As teachers, we can draw on this information to help our students transition from home grammar to school grammar in the classroom.

A Whole New Language Arts Mind-set

Swords was struck by the implications of what she was learning in her graduate class. If the children were not making mistakes in Standard English but instead were transferring in the detailed grammar patterns of their home language, then a whole different approach to language arts opened up. From here, Swords saw her way clear to recognizing and respecting the language of the home while adding the language of the school to her students' linguistic toolboxes. No need to throw out the baby with the bathwater. The students could talk with friends and family in the community using the language their families chose, and they could use home language for writing narrative dialogue to make their characters real. That's what great writers such as Hughes, Morrison, Walker, and Angelou do. The trick for Swords was to help her students add Standard English to their linguistic repertoires.

With a linguistically informed approach to language arts, you will be able to move away from seeing your students' writing as deficient, filled with errors, and in need of correction. In its place, we will show you how to draw on your students' strengths in their home language as a springboard from which they can reach Standard English. This approach is based on forty years of research in applied linguistics (see Chapters 3 and 4). As John Rickford (1996) clearly says, "teaching methods which DO take vernacular dialects into account in teaching the standard work better than those which DO NOT." That's what code-switching is—a demonstrably successful method for teaching Standard English that does take vernacular dialects into account (Rickford, Sweetland, & Rickford, 2004).

What Makes Standard English Standard?

As teachers, we know that teaching our students to speak and write in Standard English is a key job of the schools. Perhaps it's time to define *Standard English* to see what makes it "standard."

We often talk about Standard English using a singular form, as if only one Standard exists. But linguists identify a range of regional U.S.

Standards (Northern Standard, Midlands Standard, Southern Standard, etc.; see Chapter 3) in addition to more than half a dozen major international Standard Englishes. These are all prestigious in their own right. Clearly, there is not simply one Standard English.

Wolfram, Adger, and Christian (1999) explain that the Standard dialect is the prestige dialect in an area. The Standard dialect is the standard simply because it is the language variety spoken by the educated, affluent, power-elite of the nation. Here's how the link between prestige language and prestige social groups works: When we hold a group in high regard (as we do with the educated, professional occupations in the United States), we unconsciously transfer that regard to the language the group speaks. So whatever language variety the professional, governing group speaks will be seen as "Standard." If the powerful of Britain had been centered in Liverpool, for example, the dialect the Beatles spoke would be Britain's Received Pronunciation, but since the leaders clustered in London, the speech of that region became British Standard English. Likewise, according to Geneva Smitherman,

> It is axiomatic that if Black people were in power in this country, Black English would be the prestige idiom. This is a point which cannot be stressed too often, for frequently we find even Black students themselves with a negative image of they speech [sic]. They too have been brainwashed about the "inherent and Absolute rightness" of white, middle-class dialect. (2000, pp. 128–29)

That's how a Standard variety gets its prestige status—it is the language spoken by the powerful of the nation.

You may notice that we have occasionally put the term *Standard* in quotation marks. That's because the term is problematic. The implicit contrast between Standard and nonstandard language evokes a whole range of truly troubling and unjust connotations—language that is "good" or "bad," "adequate" or "inadequate," "right" or "flawed." Each of these assumes that Standard English is well structured and grammatically "proper" in ways that the so-called nonstandard varieties are not. This is simply not true. Both Standard English and vernacular varieties have their full complement of grammar.

What Makes "Nonstandard" Dialects Nonstandard?

Just as Standard English is prestigious, vernacular dialects lack prestige. Indeed, we often hear them described as sloppy or broken, the language of lazy, uneducated speakers. But this assessment too reflects our social judgments, not linguistic or grammatical ones. Inverting and mirroring the case for Standard English, if we hold a group in low regard (e.g., speakers from poverty in urban areas or from the rural mountains), we hold their language in low regard. That is why vernaculars are disfavored language forms—they are the language varieties spoken by the disempowered, disenfranchised, disfavored of the nation. Indeed, how we see a language is a portrait of how we see the social group speaking that language, even though we often don't realize that these feelings and beliefs reflect social and cultural factors rather than anything inherent in the language itself.

So, while languages are all linguistically equal, they differ in social status and also in place and breadth of use. Vernacular varieties, nearly by definition, are used in casual, familial, community settings, whereas the Standard varieties are used as the lingua franca of the business and professional world, a fact reflected by the many names for Standard English: language of wider communication (LWC), business English, professional English, mainstream American English (MAE), Standard American English (SAE), and so on. In our work, we affirm the teaching of Standard English as a way to offer all children the linguistic tools they may need in the broader, professional world of work.

It's sometimes hard to believe that vernaculars like African American English have grammar and that one can make mistakes in AAE just as one can make mistakes in the Standard dialect. Yet for decades linguists have been clearly stating that vernacular dialects are fully regular, rule-governed language systems, just like any of the regional Standard Englishes (Labov, 1972; Wolfram, 1969). This means that when a southerner says *I might could carry you to the store,* she or he is successfully following the grammar of the regional Standard variety. Similarly, when an AAE speaker says *Mama jeep need gas,* the speaker is obeying the grammatical rules in his or her home language variety.

Once we recognize that vernacular dialects are just as regular and rule governed as Standard English, we open the door to recognizing that Standard English (or any of the regional Standards) is just one (albeit a privileged one) among the many language varieties of the United States. Just as Southern English or Ozark English are dialects of English, so Standard English is an American English dialect.

Since any language variety is like a fully stocked kitchen, any dialect (e.g., AAE, Appalachian, Midland, Standard English, Standard Southern English) has the wherewithal to express whatever the speakers need. The speakers of one dialect may use a phrase while speakers of another may use a single word, or the speakers of one language variety may follow one grammar pattern to signal a meaning while speakers of another may follow a different pattern to signal that same meaning (in Chapters 2 and 6, we'll contrast how AAE and SAE show possession). But in each case, all language varieties have the means to express an idea one way or another. Sometimes a feeling may seem to come across more poignantly in one dialect or another, but as you will see, while language varieties clearly differ, difference does not signal deficit.

Language Attitudes in the Classroom

A linguistically informed language arts speaks not only to the structure of language but also to our attitudes toward language in the classroom. Our attitude can make or break our relationships with our students. Labov (1995), quoting Rosenthal and Jacobson (1968), explains that the "main effect of a child speaking AAVE [is] to affect the teachers' attitudes toward the child, with a resultant negative expectation that affect[s] teachers' behavior toward the child in many ways" (p. 49). In other words, whether Black or White, a teacher is likely to consider a child speaking African American English as slower, less able, and less intelligent than the child who speaks Standard English. We call this attitude *dialect prejudice*. Nieto (2000) explains that as teacher expectations are reduced, so the child's classroom performance diminishes (pp. 8–49).

We have found that as teachers understand more about the integrity of vernacular dialects and the structure and regularity of student language, they step away from dialect prejudice in the classroom. Teachers come to see students as fully intelligent, capable, and worthy. Their expectations for student performance rise, bringing to the classroom a self-fulfilling prophecy for success as their students work to master Standard English (Nieto, 2000).

Teachers frequently suggest that Standard English is the one and only language appropriate to the school setting. Often, the argument for the use of Standard English is justified. Clearly, as a student writes a history, social studies, or science report, or makes a graduation speech, or talks with the school principal, SAE is the expected language of expression.

But what of student work in creative writing or poetry? In these venues, surely Standard English is only one of the choices available to students, and not always the appropriate one, at that. If students in the Ozark Mountains, for example, sought to write a story that accurately evokes local life, their characters would need to speak in the patterns of the local speech community. According to linguist Bethany Dumas (1999), if the students wanted to express the idea of being in a hurry, an authentic Ozark voice would require that they write *I lit a shuck for home* (p. 70)[3] instead of the Standard English *I'm in a hurry to go home*. Or, to render the sounds of Southern Mountain English (SME), students need to get the vowels and consonants right (writing *fahr* instead of the Standard English word *fire* and *hep* instead of SE *help*) (pp. 72–74). Not only is home speech *appropriate* in some school contexts, but it is also necessary if students are to accurately produce dialogue from a specific locale.

But what if some of the students don't know the local dialect and speak and write only the Standard? Is Ozark English relevant to these students? If majority language–speaking students were to fulfill the Ozark creative writing assignment, they would need to learn the salient contrasts between Standard English and Southern Mountain English in sound, vocabulary, and grammar. Indeed, doing so requires that all students (including majority language speakers) use critical thinking skills. As students act as sleuths, discovering the patterns of language, they follow the steps of the scientific method. This kind of systematic thinking helps all students develop important reasoning skills. Thus, not only is the home speech vernacular at times appropriate in assigned school writing, but also studying the contrasts between home and school speech may be necessary and academically valuable for those who do not natively speak the local dialect.

Beyond its usefulness in dialogue, authors may choose a community dialect for intentional rhetorical effect. That's surely what Geneva Smitherman was doing in her article "English Teacher, Why You Be Doing the Thangs You Don't Do?" The first paragraph displays her virtuosity with multiple varieties of English:

> Let me say right from the bell, this piece is not to be taken as an indictment of ALL English teachers in inner city Black schools, for there are, to be sure, a few brave, enlightened souls who are doing an excellent job in the ghetto. To them I say: Just keep on keepin' on. But to those others, that whole heap of English teachers who be castigating Black students for using a "nonstandard" dialect— I got to say: the question in the title is directed to you, and if the shoe fit, put it on. (1972, p. 59)

Smitherman is able to use language—and powerfully so.

Finally, as teachers lead students in the study of how grammar patterns contrast across dialects, majority language students learn important lessons about appreciating cultural diversity among their peers. Majority language students come to see that the language of their vernacular-speaking classmates is not broken, lazy English. Instead, the child who says *My dog name is Bark*, or *She ask could I go*, or *I be playing ball all summer* is also following specific rules of grammar, just as the child who says *My dog's name is Bark*, or *She asked whether I could go*, or *I play ball all summer* is following a set of grammar rules. The difference lies in *which* grammar rules the child is following. In the former instance, the child is following the rules of one vernacular variety, African American English. In the latter, she or he is following the grammar of Standard English. Only when our students understand these basic concepts of language diversity will we foster true respect for the multicultural and multidialectal diversity in our classrooms.

African American English: Who Speaks What Where?

> The fact is that most African Americans do talk differently from whites and Americans of other ethnic groups, or at least most of us can when we want to. And the fact is that most Americans, black and white, know this to be true. (J. R. Rickford & R. J. Rickford, 2000, p. 4)

Linguist John Baugh (2000b) conducted an experiment regarding our abilities to ascertain a person's race by the way she or he talks. He found that people can identify a person's race in just seconds of speech. How do we do this, and why does it matter in school? While a real answer would fill volumes, the simple answer is this: through the sounds, intonation, word choice, grammar, and rhetorical patterns of a person's discourse. Taken together, these language patterns as spoken by many African Americans constitute a distinct language variety known over time by a wide variety of names, such as Negro dialect, Nonstandard Negro English, Negro English, Black dialect, Black English, Black English Vernacular, African American Vernacular English, African American language, African American English (Green, 2002, p. 6). Currently, linguists refer to the variety by one of the last three terms.

Yet the name "African American English," or any of the other names for the variety, is almost a misnomer given its limitations. John Rickford characterizes who speaks AAE when

> [n]ot every African American speaks AAVE, and no one uses all of the features . . . 100 percent of the time. Although it is often said that 80 percent of African Americans speak AAVE (Dillard 1972: 229), this is a guestimate. . . . In general, [characteristic] phonological and grammatical features [of AAVE] . . . are used most often by younger lower- and working-class speakers in urban areas and in informal styles, but the extent to which this is true, and how often the features are used varies from one feature to another. (1999a, p. 9)

Indeed, speakers' use of African American English varies by class, style, age, gender, and linguistic environment. Wolfram's 1969 landmark study "A Sociolinguistic Description of Detroit Negro Speech" shows that how often a person uses a given trait will vary by social class of the speaker. Wolfram found, for example, that the degree to which a speaker used unmarked third-person present tense (*She walk . . .*) varied by social class, with lower classes using the feature more frequently and higher classes using it less frequently[4] (Rickford, 1999a, p. 10, quoting Wolfram, 1969).

Language Transfer and International Englishes

Although we center our discussion on Everyday English spoken by African American children, our work offers teachers insights on how to work with students speaking any language variety that contrasts with Standard American English. Our work is relevant to majority language students who import the patterns of spoken language (e.g., sentence fragments, informal word choice, e-mail abbreviations) into their written work, to students speaking diverse U.S. dialects (e.g., Southern, Ozark Mountain, Northern, Ocracoke), to students speaking in the language patterns of one or another international English (e.g., Singapore English, New Zealand English, South African English), and to ESL students whose English shows the influence of the patterns of their native language (e.g., native Spanish speakers, Thai speakers). Here we explore how our work connects to international students.

International students, nonnative speakers of American English, increasingly populate our classrooms. Some of these students speak a variety of English other than American or British English, and many others speak English as a second language. When these students speak or write Standard American English, first language patterns will likely transfer into their English expression.

David Crystal (1995) tells us that when students come from a country whose people speak one of the diverse world Englishes,[5] we should expect their expression in American English to show influences reflecting sound, vocabulary, and grammatical patterns of their first language (p. 111). A native speaker of South Asian English, for example, might say *I am understanding it* or *I am knowing it*. These are the grammar echoes of South Asian English cropping up in a student's Standard American English expression. By contrast, in Standard American English, "stative" verbs (verbs that refer to a state of being) such as *understand* and *know* are not used in progressive aspect (the *be + -ing* form of the verb) (p. 360). Instead, in Standard American English, we would say *I know it* or *I understand it*.

At the University of British Columbia, three elementary teachers did a class project dedicated to helping teachers meet the needs of students from Thailand (www.library.ubc.ca/edlib/worldlang/thai/index.htm). They found a range of recurrent "errors" in their Thai students' English. Specifically, teachers named "omission of tense" (*Yesterday, I go to the store already.*); "omission of plurals" (*I buy 5 mango, 7 banana, and 3 apple.*); "omission of articles" (*Teacher nice.*); and "no subject-verb agreement" (*Linda go to the store. Sylvie and Dana go to the store.*) (www.library.ubc.ca/edlib/worldlang/thai/ESLErrors.htm). These teachers astutely perceived that certain patterns crop up again and again as Thai natives learn to speak English. We can take their point one step further.

Instead of simply calling these students' work error filled, we can recognize echoes of Thai grammar in the students' American English speech and writing. We can then use contrastive analysis and code-switching to help the Thai speaker switch from Thai grammar patterns to the corresponding Standard English patterns. For example, while Standard American (or Canadian) English shows tense by changing the shape of the verb (*went*; *baked*), other languages (such as Chinese and Thai) show past time by using words and phrases in the sentence—*yesterday* or *last week*. Knowing this, the U.S. teacher can build a bridge from what the Thai speaker knows (in Thai, time is shown by adverbials) to new information regarding American English (in SAE, time is often shown by an ending on the verb or by change in the shape of the verb). In this way, as we contrast the Thai patterns for showing time with American English ways for showing time, we help students gain better, more conscious control of the American structure. The same kind of analysis applies to Thai students' patterns of usage for plurality, articles, verb agreement, and so forth.

Indeed, so common are second language intrusions into English speech and writing that Anne Raimes's *Keys for Writers* (1996) lays out a correspondence for two dozen languages (e.g., Arabic, Bengali, Chinese, Farsi, French, German, Greek, Hebrew, Hindi, Japanese, Portuguese, Russian, Spanish, Swahili, Tagalog, Thai, Turkish, Urdu, Vietnamese), showing how students transfer the grammar patterns from their first language into the language they are learning—spoken or written American English (http://college.hmco.com/english/raimes/keys_writers/3e/instructors/esl/transfer.html).

In sum, the core issue is that speakers of one language may transfer their home language patterns (sound, vocabulary, grammar, and conversational style) into what they say or write in a language or dialect they are newly learning. Whether we're talking about speakers of entirely different languages (e.g., Spanish, Russian, Thai, Chinese), speakers of different international Englishes (e.g., New Zealand English, British English, Indian English), or speakers of different American English dialects (e.g., Midland, Southern, Appalachian, Northern, African American English), in each case we should expect patterns from the home language to transfer into the student's Standard American English.

In *Code-Switching*, while we focus our discussion on and draw our examples from African American English, the insights and techniques we offer are relevant across the very broad range of students who speak minority dialects, as well as those who speak casual Standard American English, international Englishes, or English as a second language.

The Vexing Problem of Terminology

Appropriately naming the different styles of language we're talking about—the language that minority students may speak or write and the language the schools expect—has been an ongoing and vexing process. In the late 1990s, Wheeler (1999) started by using *home speech* versus *school speech*. Further reflection, however, revealed these terms to be problematic for a number of reasons. First, Standard English isn't the only language used in the schools (again, think of the work of Maya Angelou or Toni Morrison or Langston Hughes), so we can't equate school speech with Standard English. Further, as discussed earlier, it's not even true that children should always and only use Standard English in school. Then, some people's home speech is very close to school speech, so the two terms are not distinct.

Of course, we wouldn't use *nonstandard* versus *Standard* because of the negative (and erroneous) connotations of *nonstandard*. Further, the term *Standard* might be hard to teach to early elementary students (K–3) because it lacks concrete associations in children's lives. *Vernacular* versus *Standard* is too technical, as is *register*.

We considered *community English* versus *Standard English*, but our local school administrators commented that nobody would know what *community English* meant. And at the elementary level, the term *community* is problematic in reference to language. From the moment our students enter school, we teach them that they are part of a classroom community and a school community. So the term *community* could not single out the language of nurture for our students since it specifically refers to the communities of the classroom and school. Perhaps this is a fluke of our local setting, but it did influence which terms we could use in our district and in our work locally.

The term *professional English* might seem like a good idea, but it too was problematic. Young students in Swords's classes see all people who work as professionals. Bus drivers, taxi drivers, hairstylists, and carpenters are all professionals in their areas of expertise, yet they might not be speakers of Standard English. Perhaps we could reorient the children's understanding, pointing to only the white-collar professions, but we didn't want to unseat the children's understanding of bus drivers and hairstylists as professionals in their own right.

We considered *Everyday English* versus *Standard* as a good possibility but again ran into difficulties. Currently, we teach students that determining a time and place to use a particular language is much like deciding on the appropriate clothing to wear in a given situation, using an analogy that readily works to explore the naturalness of variation in our lives. So we were looking for terms that could be relevant to talking about both different styles of clothing and different styles of language. While *everyday* might seem to work, for many of our urban students everyday clothing does not differ from the clothing they wear in school or church, thus undercutting the distinction. This became apparent in Swords's classroom when the school held a special day on which children could wear jeans to school. Several children wore their dress code slacks, explaining that they did not own any jeans. Thus, their everyday pants and their school pants were one and the same. Since students spend the majority of their weekday in the school setting, the term *everyday* could be confusing to elementary children who wear their school clothes every day.

Reviewers of this book suggested that we call the variety we're talking about here *African American English*. While we are fully aware that the variety of language that urban African American students often use is called African American English, we do not suggest that teachers use this term with students or parents. Indeed, we avoid using this term in our work in the schools for both factual and practical/political reasons.

Factually, the limits of the term *African American English* end up hobbling it for useful classroom usage. First, among the youth culture, students of all races, not only African Americans, use the patterns of the language variety. Second, as Green (2002), Rickford (1999a, 1999b), and many others have observed, not all African Americans use all the forms all of the time. Third, while we focus on language that many African American students speak, the broader point of this book applies to any and all students producing language different from the language that standardized tests and schools expect students to use. These limitations suggest that we look for some other way to refer to urban student language different from the classroom English target.

While the factual reasons for finding a more appropriate term are compelling, far more important are practical and political reasons for avoiding the label *African American English* in the classroom. Our experience in the public schools is that to focus on race in talking about language is to evoke anger and resistance among teachers and public school administrators. In the words of one language arts supervisor in our local school administration, "that would be political suicide." And as Sweetland observes,

> race-neutral terminology seemed to have made it easier for at least some of the teachers to embrace the steps necessary in a contrastive analysis approach—the naming of distinct varieties, the recognition that both are rule-governed and systematic, and the affirmation of the validity of both varieties. . . . If . . . teachers can't be brought to embrace Black or Korean or East Indian ways with words but can be convinced to be more tolerant of Casual, Vernacular or Everyday language, then it is incumbent on those dedicated to educational equity to at least achieve the latter. (Chapter 4)

Actually, in Wheeler's work with teachers, she starts out by not labeling students' language in any way. She presents teachers with a range of student sentences like *My goldfish name is Scaley*, *Ellen Goodman essay say it all*, and *Mrs. Smith is a great teacher because she help us learn* and asks if these examples are familiar. Always the answer is a resounding "Yes!" Since her intent is to provide teachers with new linguistic tools, she doesn't want to lose her audience right at the starting gate. Accordingly, she leads off by talking about the language patterns themselves and then by naming the patterns with a generic label.

But eventually in the classroom, as in this book, we do need a name for the language urban children often speak and for the target language of the school tests. We wanted terms that were simple, positive, and intuitive. Finally, we considered *formal* versus *informal English*. Here's how we arrived at these labels: First, focusing on the target language, Standard English, we realized that children and vernacular speakers *experience* speaking Standard as a kind of dress-up. The experiences our students report are of being fancy and careful[7] when they try to speak with the principal or write presentations that they mount for the whole school. Indeed, sometimes, when children imitate teachers or "talking proper," we have found that they become hyper-proper, even imitating a British society accent. This led us to the term *formal English*.

We then wanted to make a clear, parallel contrast, to name the child's more natural, comfortable, unmonitored way of using language. That led us to *informal*. These (obviously) are not technical linguistic terms. Instead, with *formal* versus *informal English*, we seek to reach our diverse audience intuitively.

We are acutely aware of the drawbacks and limits of these terms—language varies along a complex array of axes: age, gender, region, socioeconomic group, racial or ethnic group, and so forth. And then *within* language varieties, we see further variation in how much any given individual uses a particular variety of English. Quantitative sociolinguists can track variation within a dialect, feature by grammatical or morphophonological feature. Thus, *formal* versus *informal* are not technically accurate linguistic labels for the contrast between the diverse languages of the community and Standard English.

We need terms, however, that speak to our diverse audiences—children in early childhood, teachers who have taken no linguistics at all, school administrators who need to close the Black/White test score gap *now*, politicians and journalists who watch how schools are serving our children, and the children's parents—parents who may or may not be literate but who want, in Lisa Delpit's (1995) terms, to be sure their children learn the codes of power required by broader society. To reach our audience, we need terms that capture key insights and defuse concern.

The key insights are these: Traditional techniques for teaching Standard English to urban minority students have failed because these techniques misdiagnose the linguistic situation. Teachers see children's language (*Put mama book on the table; Sara want some ice cream*, etc.) as Standard English with mistakes. But this diagnosis is mistaken. Linguistics correctly assesses the language facts. Children are not making mistakes in Standard English: they are following the patterns of the home language variety. In response, linguistics offers a two-pronged solution: contrastive analysis and code-switching. We contrast the grammar of the home language with the grammar of the school language so that children become conscious of the differences between the language they are using and the language the school requires. Then we enhance children's abilities to *code-switch*—to choose the language style to fit the setting. On school tests and in many job settings, this is Standard English. In the home, it will be the language of nurture or whatever the parents model and require.

This approach promotes deep respect for the child's home community and language. We lay aside the blame game and recognize what the child *does* know. Then we build on the child's existing knowledge as a springboard to Standard English.

In our experience, the terms *formal* and *informal* are intuitively accessible. They capture the simple and uncontroversial notion that we all vary how we present ourselves setting by setting. Both adults and children understand these terms. In the words of a Virginia supervisor for 6–12 English language arts,

> I can teach *formal/informal* and children will get it. Teachers will get it. They understand. I can use it with teachers, with students. Heck, I can stand up in front of the school board with TV cameras running and talk about helping our children change from informal to formal English and nobody will get upset. Nobody in the schools, nobody on the board, nobody in the community will get upset. And they will all understand the basic idea. Remember who your audience is—it's teachers K–12, and it's students in those years. Your book would do well to remember who your audience really is. . . . Those other terms point fingers and get people upset. Formal and informal does not single out any group. We ALL change our language to fit the setting; it's inclusive and unifying. With those terms, I don't owe anyone apologies, and I don't have to give any explanations. . . . (personal communication)

Indeed, *formal* and *informal* work really well with young children (and with middle school and college students and K–16 teachers). It is important for young children to have something concrete to relate new terms to. We get that with *formal/informal*. Students know about hangout clothes and about dress-up clothes. This fits their experience of comfortable language versus best-behavior language, so we can build an analogy from the concrete and familiar (clothing) to more abstract and less familiar (language). We have never had any parents question our use of *formal/informal*, quite a feat in these politically charged times. And Swords's second- and third-grade students accept and use the terms in discussions with their peers.

Recently, two teachers asked Swords how she teaches subject-verb agreement. They commented that their students were having a hard time understanding it, but Swords's students clearly "got it." Some of Swords's students had been with these other teachers while the class was reading out loud. Where the text showed a phrase like *he wants*, Swords's colleagues' students voiced *he want*. The teacher kept interrupting them, saying, "Say the sounds that are there! Say *-s* on *want*! Like this—*wantS*. You're leaving off the *S*!" Understanding this scene, Swords's eight-year-olds explained to the children, "Oh, you're using informal English. I know you understand the meaning of these words, but when you read out loud, you need say it the formal way—*wantS*." Swords's students went on to suggest that their schoolmates should use formal language in school. Clearly, *formal* and *informal* are tools that even early elementary students can grasp and use.

In discussing what terminology we ought to settle on, Swords commented,

> It is important to remember that the general public is much like I am—we are not linguists. For people like us, the terms *informal* and *formal* make sense, and they work. We want to promote the understanding that Standard is not better than vernacular English, only different. We will lose sight of our goal if we start alienating people with terms that they do not understand or terms that could be interpreted as negative. Teachers will not want to teach code-switching if they feel we are adding to their plate. For this reason, we must keep our approach simple and accessible to the general public.

Accordingly, in this book we use the terms *formal* and *informal* in our charts. For variety, in our discussions we draw on the full set of near equivalents (*formal/informal, Everyday/Standard, vernacular/Standard, home/ school, language of nurture/school English,* etc.) to refer to the language contrasts and choices we're exploring.

Writing Style and Other Nomenclature

Before moving on, we need to say a few words about the writing style we're using in this book as well as what we mean by *theory.*

First, *Code-Switching* is intentionally conversational in tone. This bears not only on the shape and style of individual sentences, but also on the pacing of the entire book. Our book, in the words of one of our readers, "is unique in providing lots of examples of what dialect-based instruction looks, feels, and sounds like in an actual classroom." That is exactly our intent—to give readers a tangible, hands-on feel for how code-switching and contrastive analysis play out in the language arts classroom. Of course, evoking what such instruction "looks, feels, and sounds like" means that we go into considerable detail, almost like a camera's zoom lens homing in on the details of particular classroom scenes. And since people don't learn an approach from seeing it just once, we illustrate core concepts (such as using the scientific method to discover grammar patterns in student writing) in a variety of classroom lessons. We see this as a strength of the book, as we try to meet the needs of public school teachers who probably have no background in linguistics.

Finally, we need to explain how we use the term *theory* in this book. Rather than using the term as a theoretical linguist would (very technically), our use of *theory* is specifically geared for the classroom teacher. By theory, we mean core insights, principles, and analyses of language structure and use as relevant to the language arts classroom. That is, by theory, we intend, first, the most basic insights and principles about language structure, the sort that might be outlined in introductory chapters of an introduction to language text (Fromkin, Rodman, & Hyams, 2002). Under the rubric of theory, we also intend to invoke and draw on technical linguistic scholarship in the areas of second language acquisition studies and the sociolinguistic literature analyzing the structure and use of African American English. As we draw out linguistic principles (e.g., language is patterned, language is rule governed, language is systematic, language varies, difference is not deficit) and as we employ specific analyses of vernacular grammar constructions, our purpose is to show classroom teachers how these insights can bring them a more effective language arts. In effect, when we talk about theory, we mean linguistic principles and analyses from linguistics and sociolinguistics. And when we talk about practice, we are talking about how these principles and analyses can play out in the language arts classroom to help teachers foster Standard English mastery among their students.

Conclusion

Traditional models of language have long sought to dismiss and repress the language our minority children bring to the table. Yet, ironically, these students' performance on standardized tests requiring Standard English remains in the doldrums. Our schools continue to fail our urban minority students.

In this book, we suggest that if we want to reach our African American urban students, we must respect—indeed, admire—the language strengths they bring to our schools. Only when we recognize the robust resource that our students offer can we begin to build bridges between cultures that may allow students to add Standard English to their repertoire.

Why students succeed or fail is a deeply complex matter. It may not be simply, or even primarily, a matter of teachers fostering children's abilities in Standard English. Nonetheless, we suggest that how we approach students' language and culture is crucial. As we bring the students' language and culture into the classroom, we invite the whole child in. Doing so contributes to "the trellis of our profession—and the most crucial element of school culture . . . —an ethos hospitable to the promotion of human learning" (Barth, 2002, p. 11). In this way, code-switching and contrastive analysis offer potent tools of language and culture for transforming the dialectally diverse classroom and closing the achievement gap in the United States.

Notes

1. While it may seem unusually advanced for a third-grade teacher to suggest that her students "code-switch" to formal English, children understand the concept given sufficient preparation. So, before the time of this interchange, Mrs. Swords had led the class in many discussions about how our clothing varies by setting (e.g., blue jeans for the weekends versus a suit or dress to attend a wedding), and that our language is like our clothes—we change language to suit the setting. After providing this background, Mrs. Swords explained to her third graders that to switch language style context by context is called "code-switching." In this way, even young children come to grasp an apparently sophisticated concept.

2. Note that we are talking about students *writing* the sentence *I have two dog and two cat*. While students quite readily use the everyday, informal possessive (*My goldfish name is Scaley*) or subject-verb agreement (*The Earth spin on its axis*) in speech *and* in writing, the everyday plural form tends not to occur very often in spontaneous speech. In our work on the Virginia peninsula, this plural form shows up when students read Standard English texts out loud or when they are writing their own essays. Swords regularly hears urban minority students voice informal English plural patterns when they are reading a Standard English plural in the text. That is, given a book that has the written sentence *I have two dogs*, urban minority students may voice it as *I have two dog*, thus following the grammar pattern of the home dialect (see also Fogel & Ehri, 2000; Smitherman, 2000, p. 170; Taylor, 1991, p. 106).

3. According to Dumas (1999), in the early twentieth century, "people did not own flashlights, and country roads were not lighted at night. When farm people walked home from a neighbor's at night, they carried a lighted cornstalk that had been soaked in kerosene—they literally *lit a shuck for home* when they departed, usually in a hurry" (p. 90).

4. For example, the likelihood that a person would say *She like ice cream* ranged from a high of 71 percent to a low of 1 percent as follows: lower working class (LWC: laborers and other unskilled workers)—71 percent; upper working class (UWC: carpenters and other skilled workers)—57 percent; lower middle class (LMC: high school teachers and many white-collar workers)—10 percent; and upper middle class (UMC: lawyers and doctors)—1 percent. But not all grammatical features show that kind of stark class gradation. For example, consonant cluster simplification (*test* → *tess*) occurs 84 percent, 79 percent, 66 percent, and 51 percent of the time respectively across LWC, UWC, LMC, and UMC (Rickford, 1999a, 1999b).

5. Crystal's *The Cambridge Encyclopedia of the English Language* (1995) lists eight major world Standard Englishes (East Asian; South Asian; Western, Eastern, and Southern African; Caribbean; Canadian; American; British and Irish; Australian, New Zealand and South Pacific Standard). Then, within each of these international Standard English categories, Crystal cites a partial list of between six and a dozen versions of the relevant standard (e.g., South Asian Standard English may be further divided into illustrative subgroups: Indian English, Pakistani English, Bangladeshi English, Nepalese English, Sri Lankan English, Burmese English, etc.), totaling nearly sixty popular varieties of international Standard Englishes (1995, p. 111). Clearly, when we speak of a single Standard English, we are oversimplifying the facts to a startling degree.

6. Dating back to the 1950s, Robert Lado (1957) claimed that by contrasting the structures of two languages, linguists could predict how hard it would be for a speaker of one language to learn the other language. This was called the contrastive analysis hypothesis. That hypothesis came under fire for some fairly complex reasons we won't go into here (Odlin, 1989, p. 15). But the criticisms leveled against contrastive analysis (CA) do not hold when the issue is people acquiring a second dialect. We are not trying to predict what features will transfer from students' home dialect into their expression in school, and we are not trying to assess how difficult it will be for a speaker of a minority dialect to learn a Standard dialect. Instead, we, and other scholars in second dialect work, use contrastive analysis as a teaching tool. With CA charts, we help students discover the systematic and detailed contrasts between the grammar of their home language and the grammar of the school dialect as a tool for learning SE more effectively.

7. Characterizing the switch to Standard English as feeling like dress-up or being fancy does not, of course, reflect the experience of all vernacular speakers. As is well documented, many minority students experience an extreme rift between themselves and the values of the school (Labov, 1995; Ogbu, 2003; Richardson, 2003), and they find that speaking Standard English violates their cultural heritage—indeed, their very identity. For these students, the term *formal* for Standard English does not feel particularly apt.

2 Moving from Correction to Contrast: Code-Switching in Diverse Classrooms

Twenty squirmy second graders wiggle on the autumn red carpet as Mrs. Swords takes a seat in the comfy rocking chair before them. It's reading time and the children can choose whichever book they wish to hear that day. *"Flossie and the Fox!" "Flossie and the Fox!"* the children call. Since Mrs. Swords brought Flossie to class, the children haven't been able to get enough of it. Never before have they experienced a story in which characters speak like they and their mom and dad and friends do at home. By the third time the children heard the story, they broke into a choral response at one particular point: "Shucks! You aine no fox. You a rabbit, all the time trying to fool me."

But the fox walks a different verbal path. In reply, he tells Flossie, "'Me! A rabbit!' He shouted. 'I have you know that my reputation precedes me. I am the third generation of foxes who have outsmarted and outrun Mr. J. W. McCutchin's fine hunting dogs. . . . Rabbit indeed! I am a fox, and you will act accordingly.'"

Soon the children *knew* the book. They absorbed fox-speak and Flossie-speak.

Now Mrs. Swords invites the children to role-play. "Who would like to talk like a fox today?" Hands shoot up all over the passel of second graders. "OK, Devon, you be the fox. And who wants to talk like Flossie?" Mrs. Swords inquires.

In her blue belted pants, with neatly tucked white shirt, Heather jumps up and down, "Me, I do! I do."

"All right, Heather, you play Flossie."

Back and forth, back and forth, Devon and Heather play.

Children in the class keep tabs. They have already learned that language comes in different varieties or styles and that language comes in different degrees of formality, just like our clothing. The children have already made felt boards and cutouts showing informal and formal clothing and have talked about when we dress informally and when we dress formally. And the children have taken the next steps. They have already looked at and discovered patterns in language—the patterns of informal language and the patterns of formal-speak. They have been primed.

Heather, stretching her linguistic abilities, banters with Devon. "My two cats be lyin' in de sun."

Wait a minute.

The class quickly checks the language chart on the classroom wall. Their chart shows how we signal plurality in both informal and formal English. Heather has stumbled. She has used the formal English pattern (*two cats*—in which plurality is shown by an *-s* on the noun) when she was supposed to be following the informal pattern (*two cat*—in which plurality is shown by the context or number words).

Mike hollers out, "Heather, wait a *minute*! That's not how Flossie would say it! You did fox-speak! Flossie would say 'My two *cat* be lyin' in de sun.'"

Heather stops. Hands on hips, she considers the wall chart. Mike is right! She regroups and recoups. "My two *cat* be lyin' in de sun!" Heather and Devon are back in their roles. Only one more minute till they swap sides.

In this way, the children practice choosing the forms of language appropriate to the time, place, setting, and communicative purpose. They code-switch between the language of the home and the language of the school.

Sometimes in writing a story, in order to develop a character, children choose the language of nurture, the language they learned on their grandma's knee. Other times, formal times, as when the children write up their research on the relative lengths of dinosaur teeth for their math storyboards, they know they'll choose the language of the professional world because they know that other teachers, the principal, and school visitors will see their work.

Throughout their classroom experiences, children learn to masterfully choose their language to fit the setting. And they do so with joy, verve, and command.

—Rebecca S. Wheeler

Excerpted from Brock Haussamen, with Amy Benjamin, Martha Kolln, and Rebecca Wheeler, *Grammar Alive! A Guide for Teachers*, Urbana, IL: National Council of Teachers of English, 2003. Reprinted with permission.

The children in Swords's class seem to hear a different tune when it comes to language. They live inside a confidence and know-how about what they're saying when. Freed of the bonds of "correct and incorrect," the children know which variety is Standard English and which is the vernacular, and they navigate the linguistic trail as sure-footed as mountain goats.

What's the secret of Swords's classroom? What does she know about language? What do the children know? In other words, how do these new language ways play out in the daily language arts classroom? This chapter offers teachers answers to these questions.

The Correctionist Lens

Before exploring how to move to a new language arts, let's look again at business as usual in the integrated language arts (ILA) classroom.

> *Student:* Mrs. Swords, why you be teachin' math in the afternoon?
>
> *Mrs. Swords:* Why do I WHAT?
>
> *Student:* Why you *be teachin'* math in the afternoon?
>
> *Mrs. Swords:* Why do I what?
>
> *Student:* Why you *be teachin' math* in the afternoon?
>
> *Mrs. Swords:* We don't say, "Why you *be* teaching math in the afternoon?" We say, "Why *are* you teaching math in the afternoon?"
>
> *Student:* Oh, OK.

But the next day the child would begin again, "Mrs. Swords, why we be havin' math in the afternoon?" And Swords would reply, "Why do we WHAT?" The exchange was always the same. She would attempt to "correct" the child's verb "error," but it was clear that no learning was taking place.

Rachel Swords, one of the authors of this book, began her career in an urban elementary school six years ago by correcting every sentence she deemed incorrect. As time went on, however, she noticed that her students were asking significantly fewer questions. She would call for questions and her students would begin: "Mrs. Swords, why you be . . . is you? Ain't you? Never mind." The students knew she was going to correct them. They tried to ask the question in the form the school system wanted, but they didn't know how. Rather than risk the embarrassment of being corrected in front of the class, students became silent.

Once Swords realized why the questions had stopped, she tried another, more passive approach. She would repeat a student's question in mainstream American English (*Why do I teach math after lunch?*) and then answer it, also in the same language variety. While this method didn't embarrass the children or hinder their questioning, their language did not change. Even though Swords consistently corrected their speech and writing, her students still did not learn the Standard English forms.

Swords and, we'd dare say, most teachers, take the same approach to student writing as in the following examples.

1. The dog name is Bear.

2. I have two cat.

3. Last year, he watch all the shows.

Seeing *I have two cat* and *The dog name is Bear*, Swords thought the children were struggling, having problems with these basic grammatical structures. In response, she tried to show students the "right" way to indicate plurality, possession, and tense, to teach them the way it "should be." So she red-penned the paper, "correcting" the "error."

Teachers envision a single "right way" to construct a sentence (Birch, 2001). The correctionist model diagnoses (or rather, misdiagnoses) the child's home speech as "poor English" or "bad grammar," finding that the child "does not know how to show plurality, possession, and tense," or the child "has problems" with these. A correctionist approach sees the student as having "left off" the plural marker, the apostrophe -*s*, and -*ed*. Teachers offer remedies: "That's not how you do it! That's not right! This is how you should do plural, possessive, tense."

When a teacher tells a vernacular-speaking child that he or she "shouldn't say it like that" or that "the right way" to show possession, plurality, past time, etc., is the Standard English way, the teacher effectively seeks to repress, stamp out, or eradicate student language that differs from the standard written target (Gilyard, 1991; McWhorter, 1998). This approach tries to subtract home language from the child's linguistic toolbox (Gilyard, 1991; McWhorter, 1998; Wheeler & Swords, 2004).

Swords's experience and approach is a common one. Concern with the vernacular dialects our children bring to school has been long-standing; Heath (1983) expressed it this way:

> In the late 1960s, school desegregation in the southern United States became a legislative mandate and a fact of daily life. Academic questions about how children talk when they come to school and what educators should know and do about oral and written lan-

guage were echoed in practical pleas of teachers who asked: "What do I do in my classroom on Monday morning?" (p. 1)

Now, almost forty years later, teachers remain concerned: Christenbury (2000) has observed that "[o]ne of the most controversial—and difficult—issues for English teachers is their responsibility to students who speak what is considered 'nonstandard' English, English that violates the usage rules we often mistakenly call 'grammar'" (p. 202).

Christenbury's comment, subtle and revealing, sets the stage for the central concern of our work. English teachers routinely equate Standard English with "grammar," as if other language varieties and styles lack grammar, the systematic and rule-governed backbone of language. Nothing could be further from the truth.

What Linguistics Tells Us

When teachers talk about language as "correct" and "incorrect" (or "proper" and "improper," "good" and "bad," etc.), they implicitly assume that the only real and grammatical language is Standard English. Often, teachers believe that students' home language is nothing but degraded, inferior, failing attempts at hitting the Standard English target. But this simply is not true. Christenbury (2000) aptly observes that "telling or teaching students that their language is wrong or bad is not only damaging, but false" (p. 203). Doing so presupposes that only one language form is "correct" in structure and that that form is "good" in all contexts. Martin Joos (1967) explains why this is not true as he talks about "the five styles of English usage":

> It is still our custom unhesitatingly and unthinkingly to demand that the clocks of language all be set to Central Standard time. . . . But English, like national languages in general, has five clocks. And the times that they tell are not simply earlier and later; they differ sidewise, too, and in several directions. Naturally. A community has a complex structure, with variously differing needs and occasions. How could it scrape along with only one pattern of English usage? (pp. 4–5)

In "scraping along" with only one English, we lose a profound resource, the language fluency children bring with them to school, fluency in the home language vernacular.

In this book, we show that when children come to school speaking a language variety different from Standard English, we can use the systematic structure of that language as a potent resource in teaching Standard English. Indeed, research shows that approaches that use the vernacular to teach the Standard are more effective than those that don't (see Chapter 4; Rickford, 1999a, 1999b).

To build on children's language strengths, we need to take a number of cognitive leaps. We have described the first—recognizing what we are assuming about children's language; namely, we often believe that children's home speech is broken and ungrammatical. Next, we ask teachers to let go of those assumptions, to *cease believing*, for a moment, that the children are making errors. For only then will teachers open sufficiently to be able to perceive *pattern* in student language. Only then will a whole new approach to language arts open up to them.

Method in the "Madness"

Let's begin by looking at two common language patterns often diagnosed as "broken" or "bad" grammar: AAE possession (*My dog name is Bear*) and habitual *be* (*He be happy*). By looking at these examples, we begin the linguistically informed process of recognizing pattern where convention diagnoses error. Recognizing the pattern in child language will suggest a powerful alternative for the language arts classroom.

The Grammar of Possession in African American English

Drawn from the writing of three urban third graders on the Virginia peninsula, examples 4a–c are representative of language patterns of a broad range of speakers, K–16[1] and beyond (Green, 2002; Rickford, 1999a, 1999b; Taylor, 1991; Wolfram, Adger, & Christian, 1999).

4. a. We have sweets on the weekend at <u>mom house</u>.

   b. My <u>goldfish name</u> is Scaley.

   c. <u>Christopher family</u> moved to Spain.

Teachers, parents, and administrators alike describe the sentences in 4a–c as "error filled," finding that the child has "left off" the apostrophe *-s* and "should be" producing the "correct" counterparts in 5.

5. a. We have sweets on the weekend at <u>mom's house</u>.

   b. My <u>goldfish's name</u> is Scaley.

   c. <u>Christopher's family</u> moved to Spain.

Yet linguistic research across four decades demonstrates that students who express themselves as in sentences 4a–c *do know* possession. How can that be?

Let's expand the data we just presented in order to discover the grammatical patterns at hand.

6. a. I go to <u>Justin house</u>.

   b. <u>My mom old jeep</u> is low on gas.

   c. <u>The dog name</u> is Bear.

   d. <u>Christopher family</u> move to Spain.

   e. <u>Michael birthday</u> is in March.

   f. <u>My goldfish name</u> is Scaley.

Instead of assuming that students are making errors, let's assume they are following a common pattern (Shaughnessy, 1977).

Using the Scientific Method in Language Arts

But if we think that students might be following a pattern, we'll need to collect enough samples of student language to be able to accurately figure out what the pattern is. That's why we call student writing "data"—because it is a set of sentences (data) that we will study to figure out what pattern happens again and again. When we figure out what pattern recurs, we will describe what we see, and that becomes a hypothesis we will check against other data.

Here are the steps to a linguistically informed approach to student writing:

- Collect data.
- Examine the data.
- Seek the pattern.
- Describe the pattern.
- Test your description of the pattern.
- Refine your description of the pattern.

If we can find a pattern, we may have found a grammatical rule.

The technique we are using with language data should sound familiar—it is the scientific method, applied to discovery of language structure. In code-switching, we use the scientific method to help us describe the structure of students' language, both written and spoken. As such, this approach takes grammar out of the realm of drill-and-kill, or memorization, and locates it squarely in the quadrant of critical, analytic thinking. It is even possible to use this style of language discovery and analysis to satisfy statewide standards for science that require that children apply the scientific method. Yes, even in the third-grade classroom. Swords has done so.

Returning to the data, just about any English speaker readily understands that these sentences convey possessive meaning: *Mom has a house*, *The goldfish has a name*, and *Christopher has a family*. The question, then, is how these sentences carry possessive meaning, in and of themselves. Or, given that we know these sentences signal possession, what arrangement of words (i.e., what structural pattern) happens in each and every one? That pattern will be the possessive rule in this language variety.

When Swords posed this question to her third graders, they found the answer to be obvious: "Why, Mrs. Swords, they sit side by side! *Mom* is next to *house* and *goldfish* is next to *name*." In this fashion, the children easily (and independently) named the grammatical rule for possession in AAE. At Swords's prompting, the children got more specific. They decided that each sentence shows the pattern of *owner + owned*.[2]

Let's summarize the children's process; it's an approach we follow throughout this book. When Swords gave her students a set of sentences (data), they scanned them, looking for what all the sentences had in common (of course, Swords led them through this process at the outset). Then, finding a pattern, the children articulated the regularity, stating it as a rule. In this way, students discovered the grammatical rule of possession in AAE. In technical terms, we say that in AAE, possession is signaled by adjacency, the trait of one word sitting next to another (Smitherman, 2000). In this book, we go with the more user-friendly description, *owner + owned*.

True to the scientific method, Swords then led her students to test their hypothesis to make sure it really covers all the examples. Here's how we run a scientific check with our examples. We begin with sentence 6a and check whether the owner occurs before the thing owned. Yes, *Justin* is indeed the owner and comes before *house*, the thing owned. Similarly, in 6b, *mom* is indeed the owner and comes before the thing owned, *jeep*. We proceed down our collection of data, verifying that our hypothesis captures all the facts. Then we check our hypothesis against any new data that come along, revising it as appropriate to capture the new language data.

We have now confirmed our hypothesis: in this language variety, we signal possession by *owner + owned*, or as they say in New Orleans, "alongside nouns."[3] In this way, we have discovered and named the grammar pattern the children are following.

Thus, sentences such as *My goldfish name is Scaley* do not lack grammar. The speakers have not "left off" the apostrophe *-s*; they are not making errors or failing to show possession. Instead, they have very precisely and successfully shown possession by following the systematic grammatical patterns of their language of nurture. This grammatical pattern simply stands in contrast to the pattern for possession in Standard English.

We can begin to represent the teacher's and students' understanding in a graphic organizer called a code-switching or contrastive analysis chart, as in Figure 2.1. Clearly, the chart is incomplete at this point. We haven't yet translated the informal English into formal English. We save the specific techniques of translation for the applied sections of this book. In the meantime, we want to give you a visual way to represent the understanding that AAE and Standard English use different patterns to show possession. Swords and other teachers put charts such as this one (with both columns completed) up on classroom walls to help students during editing.

Possessive Patterns

Informal English   *Formal English*

Taylor <u>cat</u> is black.
The <u>boy coat</u> is torn.
A <u>giraffe neck</u> is long.
Did you see the <u>teacher pen</u>?

Pattern

owner + owned

Figure 2.1. Contrastive analysis chart for informal v. formal English possessive patterns.

The Grammar of Habitual be *in African American English*

We now move to another common example of student home language that crops up in the school setting. Let's look at a student's use of *be* as in *She be at home*:

7. "Bobby, what does your mother do every day?"

   "She *be* at home!" Bobby said.

   "You mean, she is at home," the teacher corrected.

   "No, she ain't," Bobby said, "'cause she took my grandmother to the hospital this morning."

> "You know what I meant," the teacher said. "You are not sup-
> posed to say 'She *be* at home.' You are to say, 'She *is* at home.'"
>
> "Why you trying to make me lie?" Bobby said. "She ain't at
> home." (LeMoine, 1999, pp. 1–2)

The child draws a strong contrast between the forms of *be* in 8 versus 9.

   8.   She be at home.

   9.   She is at home.

When the teacher tells Bobby that he ought to say *She is at home*, the child
denies it twice and then becomes agitated, wondering why the teacher
is "trying to make [him] lie." Clearly, for the child, *She is at home* is not a
translation of *She be at home*.

In Bobby's language system, *She is at home* would mean his mother
was at home *at that very moment*. But Bobby knew that wasn't true. He
wanted to convey a different meaning. He wanted to signal that it was
"her habit to be home on a day-to-day basis" (LeMoine, 1999, p. 2). To
do so, he naturally chose to use the form of *be* that conveys habitual
meaning in AAE. Linguists call this form "habitual *be*." Not knowing the
grammar of AAE, the teacher not only utterly derails the conversation
but makes no progress in helping Bobby learn the patterns of Standard
English.

Baugh (1999) comments on habitual *be*, offering two examples, *He
be standin on the corner*; *He be talking when the preacher be talking*:

> From a linguistic point of view, this use of *be* performs grammati-
> cal work. In African American vernacular these sentences convey
> habitual activities. By contrast, the standard form *is* will be used
> instead of *be* to convey momentary actions. The difference between
> *He be happy* and *he is happy* is that the latter conveys a momentary
> state while the former refers to a state of perpetual happiness. (p.
> 6)

Baugh continues, talking about the perplexity the child who speaks African American English may experience in the classroom:

> Imagine the confusion confronting a black child in school who is
> trying to use Standard English to convey a habitual state or event.
> Under such circumstances it would be difficult for the child not to
> use his or her native grammar. *Be* provides a grammatical tool that
> is unavailable to speakers of standard English. In addition to all
> that AAVE shares with other dialects of English, it has unique gram-
> matical forms that serve important communicative functions; it is
> far from being an impoverished dialect. (p. 6)

Teaching Standard English in Urban Classrooms

Linguistics shows us that if you want to teach Standard English to speakers of other dialects, start by contrasting the home grammar with the school grammar, or SE. This way, instead of seeking to correct or eradicate home speech styles, we add language varieties to the child's linguistic toolbox, bringing a pluralistic vantage to language in the classroom (Gilyard, 1991; McWhorter, 1998). Such an approach allows us to maintain the language of the student's home community (see the Conference on College Composition and Communication's *Students' Right to Their Own Language* [1974]) while adding the linguistic tools needed for success in our broader society—the tools of mainstream American English. In doing so, we can work with students to help them switch between their different language styles—to code-switch, that is—choosing the language variety appropriate to the specific time, place, audience, and communicative purpose.

When we say that our goal is to help children both learn Standard English and honor the language and culture of the home community, we implicitly situate ourselves within the broader literacy movement in the United States. "Literacy" is no simple idea. Instead, we can identify a range of approaches in the United States today. Literacy scholars cluster into groups based on how they answer a constellation of questions. Scholars differ, for example, on what they mean by literacy and what they consider to be the language or languages of literacy. They take positions on whether we should or shouldn't teach Standard English. They ask whether we should teach only Standard English or whether we ought to draw on diverse language varieties from the natural language landscape. Scholars query what materials we should use in assessing literacy: do we count literacy as fluency only in the works of White middle-class European culture, or do we recognize a broader literacy base—all different kinds of writing and reading from diverse cultures of peoples of color and peoples of non-Western nationalities? Finally, literacy scholars and practitioners disagree about what it means for an African American to learn to speak the Standard dialect and work with cultural readings and writings of mainstream American culture.

We've described the usual classroom response in which teachers lament the "error-ridden" writing of their African American students. We've recognized this red-pen approach to be correctionist or eradicationist of student home language. Such approaches to student language constitute the meat and potatoes of traditional language arts.

Similar sentiment is powerfully expressed by well-known personalities who in turn influence and reflect how the American public understands student language. In 2004, for example, Bill Cosby, a prominent African American entertainer, became the poster child for popular views of language. According to an AP wire report, in "his remarks in May at a commemoration of the [50th] anniversary of the *Brown v. Board of Education* desegregation decision, Cosby denounced the grammar of some Black people" (May 20, 2004). Like Jesse Jackson before him, Cosby embodies the correctionist viewpoint, which seeks to eradicate home language. He assumes that all speakers (and all teachers) should excise, extract, repress, and supplant home language with "good grammar." He takes this not only as a truth, but The Truth.

Teachers also traditionally hold that the language of literacy is Standard English and that the materials students must command come mainly from White middle-class culture: "In the popular view, there is no choice of dialect at all in educational settings. In fact, Standard English and education imply each other" in this view (Adger, 1998, p. 152). The traditional approach expects Standard English to supplant or replace the vernacular language of the home and that students will fully assimilate to the norms of the dominant culture. This approach is also presumed by daily oral language exercises and by grammar and writing texts.

Yet other prominent African Americans would beg to differ with Cosby and Jackson and such traditional assumptions about English. African American university educators such as Geneva Smitherman and Denise Troutman praise the linguistic dexterity children show as they write rap or jump rope lyrics, or engage elaborately in the language sport of playing the dozens or signifying (Smitherman, 1977; Troutman, 1999). Far from deriding the language of the African American home, Smitherman and Troutman and other African American educators and linguists (Baugh, Perry, Delpit, Lanehart, Richardson, Rickford, etc.) recognize and affirm the robust dynamism of African American students' language.

These educators offer tangible ways to honor and draw on the rich language knowledge African American children already have from their home culture as the children carve a path to Standard English mastery (Delpit, 1995; Perry & Delpit, 1998; Smitherman, 2000). Each testifies to the impressive power of students' home linguistic culture. Theresa Perry recalls the power of the way "rhythm, rhyme, metaphor, repetition are and were used by Jesse Jackson, Martin Luther King, Jr., Rev. William Borders, and African-American preachers all over this country." She cites "Toni Morrison's use of the call and response sequence in her award winning novel, *Beloved*" (Perry & Delpit, 1998, p. 12).

In her groundbreaking *Talkin and Testifyin: The Language of Black America*, Smitherman similarly tells of the intricate ways African Americans verbally interact at home and in the community using "black modes of discourse." These modes are made up of "verbal strategies, rhetorical devices, and folk expressive rituals," part of the "'rich inheritance' of the African background" (1977, p. 103). Through examples from songs, sacred and secular, to church sermons in which the congregants interject their responses, affirming the preacher's word, to community banter in barber- and beauty shops (pp. 104–5), to humorous put-downs between friends where verbal acuity and wit are highly prized (pp. 118–19), Smitherman recounts the fast-moving, complex subtleties of African Americans' verbal engagement and repartee (see also Troutman [1999] for a vivid description of African American women's rhetorical devices and styles).

Thus, contrary to traditional assumptions, African American children do not arrive at school "linguistically impoverished." Instead, they arrive positively adept at intricate verbal exchange.

But the ways in which many African American children are pros at language are not recognized or valued by schools. Poignantly, Delpit (1995) wonders how many teachers would "relate [the rap songs and linguistic weavings on the playground] to language fluency" (p. 17). So Black children find themselves in a quandary in the schools. Highly verbal in their communities, they are seen by the school system they're required to attend as nonverbal or lacking English, even when that school system is itself predominantly African American.

Attitudes toward Standard English

Among the nontraditionalists, the next fork in the literacy road comes with practitioners' attitude toward Standard English. In *Other People's Children: Cultural Conflict in the Classroom*, Delpit (1995) talks about parents wanting to ensure that "the school provides their children with discourse patterns, interactional styles, and spoken and written language codes that will allow them success in the larger society" (p. 29). Delpit's focus is on African American students learning the skills necessary "to harmonize with the rest of the world" (p. 18), and she defines *skills* as "useful and usable knowledge which contributes to a student's ability to communicate effectively in standard, generally acceptable literary forms" (pp. 18–19).

By implication, Delpit suggests that the language forms students need to command are those of Standard English. She recounts the frustrations of African American parents who find that the liberal "process" writing approach to literacy does their children a disservice. While the process approach seeks to foster fluency, Delpit, like Smitherman and Troutman, tells us that African American kids have plenty of fluency in the home language, citing the "verbal creativity and fluency that black kids express every day on the playgrounds of America as they devise new insults, new rope-jumping chants and new cheers" (1995, p. 17). Delpit recognizes the potent language talents African American children possess outside the schoolhouse doors. Inside school, she seeks to steer classroom work toward meaningful engagement leading to skill in the Standard code. Indeed, she sees literacy in Standard English as but one aspect of the "culture of power," which she urges teachers to explicitly teach minority students (pp. 21–47).

Similarly, Smitherman asserts that "*[a]ll* students need to know this language [Standard English, or the language of wider communication] if they are going to participate fully in the global world of the twenty-first century" (2000, p. 161). (But see below, as Smitherman complicates the matter considerably—and rightly so—in discussing "multiliteracies.")

Thus, Delpit and Smitherman don't see Standard English as Grammar with a capital *G* or as "good" language, but instead as one key to the lock of participation in wider society. Perry goes even further. She equates learning to read, write, and speak the Standard code with freedom itself, citing the historic African American commitment to "freedom for literacy and literacy for freedom" (Perry, Steele, & Hilliard, 2003, p. 17). Paraphrasing Malcolm X, Perry says, "Read and write yourself into freedom! Read and write to assert your identity as human! Read and write yourself into history! Read and write as an act of resistance . . . so you can lead your people well in the struggle for liberation!" (p. 19).

Like Delpit, Smitherman, and Perry, John Rickford also affirms the importance of fostering Standard English mastery among African American students. A scholar of far-reaching academic achievement in technical linguistics, Rickford also works prolifically in language and education. During the Ebonics controversy of 1997, Rickford was one of the informed voices who helped unbind the media's misperceptions about what the Oakland, California, school board had sought to achieve with their African American students. His Web site (www.stanford.edu/~rickford) continues as a resource to anyone wanting an accessible, nontechnical, but scientifically accurate treatment of issues of language and literacy in education and the African American community (see also Rickford, 1996, n.d.).

Rickford points the way to success with African American students. Indeed, throughout his educational writing, he (and his collaborators) describe a range of research-based approaches from linguistics that have been shown to succeed in teaching Standard English to African American students (Rickford 1999a, 1999b, 2000; Rickford & A. E. Rickford, 1995; Rickford & R. J. Rickford, 2000). He outlines successful approaches used over the past three decades, including (1) a linguistically informed approach to teaching reading, (2) contrastive analysis, and (3) dialect readers that "introduce . . . reading in the vernacular, [and] then switch . . . to the standard" (Rickford, 1999a, pp. 338–44; Rickford, Sweetland, & Rickford, 2004; Redd & Webb, 2005).

Practitioners such as teacher Carrie Secret and linguist John Baugh show us how to use African American language styles to help African American children learn Standard English. Talking about the Standard English Proficiency program (SEP) of Oakland, California, Secret (1998) describes how central language and culture are to the success of children's learning: "If you don't respect the children's culture, you negate their very essence" (p. 80). In describing how the SEP program "uses culture to enhance reading achievement," Secret draws on "nine cultural aspects that permeate African-American life: spirituality, resilience, emotional vitality, musicality and rhythm, humanism, communalism, orality and verbal expressiveness, personal style and uniqueness, and realness" (pp. 80–81). She reiterates that her "mission was and continues to be: embrace and respect . . . the home language of many of our students, and use strategies that will move them to a competency level in [Standard] English. We never had, nor do we now have, any intention of teaching the home language to students. They come to us speaking the language" (p. 81).

Baugh, in his probing work *Out of the Mouths of Slaves: African American Language and Educational Malpractice* (1999), also offers ways to make literacy studies culturally relevant for African American students. He found that "although . . . children wanted to become educated, they didn't want to 'act white.'" (p. 32). Baugh noted that motivation is a key element in students' ability to gain literacy skills, and that "many inner-city students are, frankly, bored by traditional reading materials." In response to children's needs, he developed the "Lyric Shuffle Games," "a series of games that can introduce and reinforce literacy through highly motivational exercises incorporating popular lyric music" (p. 32). In Lyric Shuffle, students select lyrics as reading material. Baugh noted that contrary to popular expectation, many African American musicians use Standard English in their lyrics, so students can study the Standard forms through this medium. Students transcribe the lyrics, make word lists, and use flash cards, rearranging the words to form "new sentences, new poems or lyrics, or an original short story (p. 35). They do a Sentence Shuffle, a Poet Shuffle, a Song Shuffle, a Grammar Roulette, and Story Shuffle, integrating reading and writing in ways that tap into students' core interests (Baugh, 1981).

In sum, traditional English teachers and many linguists are united in affirming the importance of students learning the codes of power. The key difference lies in how each group conceives of the learning enterprise.

Other scholars, however, make quite clear their opinion that teaching Standard English is a form of hegemonic repression in which the White supremacist establishment continues to dominate and demean African American language and culture. Linguist Elaine Richardson (2003), for example, speaks of an "ideology of White supremacist and capitalistic-based literacy practices" that "reproduce stratified education and a stratified society," an approach that "attempts to erase [African Americans], culturally, word by word" (pp. 8–9). She and others she cites (e.g., Macedo, 1994) call on us to recognize that when we teach the "academic essay," we are not teaching "'neutral skills' needed to succeed in the corporate educational system," but instead are foisting on African Americans a "culturally biased education . . . [that] trains them to sever ties with Black communities and cultural activities" (Richardson, 2003, p. 9).

In partial remedy, Richardson (2003) has articulated an African American curriculum for her college students. She believes that "[l]iteracy acquisition is not a set of skills to be mastered. It is a looking inward into one's own thought and cultural/language patterns and history, while looking outward into the world's, seeking to intervene in one's own context" (p. 116). In doing so, students "deserve an education that locates them within their history and encourages them to define their futures" (p. 117). Richardson sees "African American Vernacular English as a discourse, not simply a set of grammatical features to be eradicated from speech and writing" (p. 115), but more broadly, she argues that "African American rhetorical and discursive practices [ought to be] the center of the curriculum" (p. 120). Thus, she offers an intricate, culturally relevant curriculum for African American students.

Finally, scholars increasingly interrogate the very notion of literacy itself. They are clear that there is no single literacy, no single way of handling a single written code. In his foreword to Smitherman and Villanueva's *Language Diversity in the Classroom: From Intention to Practice*, Suresh Canagarajah explains that we are surrounded by "multiple versions of English" and that all "of us are required to navigate different discourses in everyday domains, such as the mass media, communication, and work. These fluid social and communicative environments have motivated some educators to speak of a basic need for multiliteracies to be functional in today's world" (2003, pp. ix–x). He invokes the complex skills required to be literate on the Internet (e.g., "multiple modalities of communication (sound, speech, video, and photographs, in addition to writing) and multiple symbol systems (icons, images, color and charts, in addition to words) but also multiple registers, discourses and languages" (p. x). Most forcefully, Canagarajah asserts that "teaching literacy in a single language (English) or a single dialect of that language ('Standard English') fails to equip our students for real world needs" (p. x).

Also recognizing multiliteracies is Rebecca Rogers (2003), who reports that the family she studied (the Treaders) are "extremely proficient with the literacies of their daily lives" (p. 144). Drawing a contrast between "neighborhood proficiencies with language and literacy" (p. xiv) and "schooled literacy," she suggests that "inner city residents who are labeled as 'illiterate' are in fact using highly complex linguistic and social resources," resources "that are neither called upon nor recognized within institutional contexts" (p. xiv). Rogers recounts that the mother in the Treader family "negotiated a petition for traffic conditions" and was able to "read strategically, and [think] critically" (p. 3). The daughter "critically read the newspaper" (p. 3) and generally "demonstrated many of the same proficiencies with literacy as her mother" (p. 144). Yet, Rogers notes, the mother, who had an eighth-grade education, was assessed as reading at a fourth-grade level. The daughter was put into special education, labeled by the school as "low literate" with serious language disabilities. Rogers suggests that a "more equitable schooling would . . . [recognize] these literacies in the school and the classroom" (p. 156).

Now, having gotten a bird's eye view of how to move from correction to contrast in the language arts classroom, having glimpsed how to apply the scientific method in analyzing your students' language, and having touched on the complex terrain of literacy studies, it's time for us to move on—time to explore some basic insights from linguistics that will help you in the language arts classroom.

Notes

1. These patterns are not restricted to the language of young children, as is seen in the following examples of the same grammatical pattern drawn from eighth graders and community college students:

   a.   I don't understand my <u>little sister work</u>. (eighth grader)

   b.   <u>Ellen Goodman essay</u> tell all about violence. (community college)

   c.   There is a link between violence on TV and violence in <u>children behavior</u>. (community college)

2. To say that *–'s* signals possession oversimplifies the facts. For example, *Anne Rice's book* could mean that Anne Rice owns the book, but it also could refer to the book Anne Rice wrote. Here, *-'s* signals association but not ownership. Thus, *-'s* signals a broader range of meaning than just possession (e.g., *the city's improvement, in a month's time, today's session, for simplicity's sake*).

3. This analysis too oversimplifies the facts, although not irrecoverably. For example, *floor lamp* and *coffee table* are phrases containing nouns sitting side by side, but these do not convey possession. Instead, they convey meanings such as "a lamp for the floor" or "a table intended or used for serving food or beverages such as coffee." If students bring up such examples during class discussion, the teacher should be pleased, not concerned. A bit of sure-footedness and use of the scientific method will come to the rescue. Actually, the solution is implicit in our fuller description of possession in AAE. The nouns refer to *owner + owned*. On confronting such examples, the teacher might praise the student for good and clear thinking. She might say something like this:

> *Teacher:* That's a great example! You're absolutely right, *Mom jeep* and *coffee table* do seem to follow the same sort of pattern. Each has two nouns sitting side by side—*mom* and *jeep, coffee* and *table*. Do you think that *coffee table* has possessive meaning like *Mom jeep* does?
>
> *Students:* No . . . it don't.
>
> *Teacher:* I agree with you. So what's the difference between the two? How do we know that *Mom jeep* is possessive but *floor lamp* or *coffee table* is not?

From this point, the students are likely to realize and voice that Mom owns the jeep but that the coffee clearly does not own the table. Again, ownership is a simplification of what's going on with the genitive marker (apostrophe *-s* in Standard English), but it is a fairly good approximation for elementary and middle school students. So when the students figure out that "possession = owner + owned" (or *possessor* + *possessed*) in AAE, the teacher can take that as the latest hypothesis about the AAE grammar for possession. She then will check—"Yes, we can rule out *coffee table* because coffee does not own a table." She can ask the children for other examples to check. Perhaps they'll come up with examples such as *telephone pole* or, if children are studying American history at the time, they might think of *wagon train*. In each instance, the teacher should lead the students through checking their hypothesis—that in AAE, we signal possession by "owner + owned" and so none of these examples fits the pattern. They're not possessive in AAE, and the class has confirmed that their hypothesis for the grammar rule of possession covers all the data they've come across or thought up so far. In this way, the teacher turns a potentially awkward moment into a grammar discovery.

3 Linguistic Insights for the Language Arts Classroom

In this chapter, we share basic insights from linguistics that support teachers understanding and responding to the different ways of talking and writing that students bring from home to school.

We draw from current writings in dialectology to explain basic questions such as "How do dialects vary?" and "Why do we have dialects?" We explore issues of register and review why some dialects are seen as Standard and others as "nonstandard." Knowing that English varies in sound, vocabulary, and grammar from North to South to East to West, from this to that social group or age group, and from this to that professional or economic enclave, teachers will not be surprised that their African American students' language may vary from Standard English. As they recognize and understand so much variety in English, they will feel more comfortable responding to the language of their own students.

How Language Varies

Basic insights from linguistics help the classroom teacher make sense of the often dizzying array of ways students talk and write, ways often different from what the school system requires.

Vocabulary

The most obvious ways in which students' language differs from school speech may lie in vocabulary. Each generation of young people has its own special words that set it off from older generations. This language, of course, is *slang*. According to linguist Geoffrey Pullum (1997), "[s]lang, in any language, consists of a finite list of words or idiomatic phrases, highly vivid and informal, in the most casual stratum of its lexicon." According to Pullum, slang is "the ephemera" of the street—our most casual words, which come and go relatively quickly. Slang words from the 1960s (e.g., *dig* or *groovy*) are so far out of date that they sound no better to contemporary ears than slang from the twenties (e.g., *baloney*, *bee's knees*, *big cheese*, *spiffy*, or *swell*), and we can bet that the slang of today's youth will soon sound just as out of date.

So English (like all languages) offers different types of vocabulary. We've glanced briefly at slang, the vocabulary of youth. Vocabulary also differs by speaker's occupation and region. Jeffrey Eugenides, in *Middlesex*, his Pulitzer Prize–winning novel about a Greek immigrant family, illustrates the specialized vocabulary of bootlegging during the U.S. Prohibition:

> So began my grandfather's life of crime. For the next eight months he worked in Zizmo's rum-running operation, observing its odd hours, getting up in the middle of the night and having dinner at dawn. He adopted the slang of the illegal trade, increasing his English vocabulary fourfold. He learned to call liquor "hooch," "bingo," "squirrel dew," and "monkey swill." He referred to drinking establishments as "boozeries," "doggeries," "rumholes," and "schooners." He learned the locations of . . . the churches that offered something more than sacramental wine, and the barbershops whose Barbicide jars contained "blue ruin." (2002, 112)

Different regions of the country have different words too: *bourré* is a "card game played with trump suits and tricks," a word chiefly used in Louisiana (Cassidy, 1985). No surprise that a word of French origin (*bourrer*—"to stuff") should be found in Louisiana, given its French heritage. Or *bugle*, meaning "the nose; also the mouth, the head," as a term used chiefly in the Atlantic region and the upper Mississippi Valley (*I wish he'd shut his bugle*) (Cassidy, 1985).

Sounds

Language varies not only by vocabulary but also in its sounds, or pronunciation. We call this *accent*. Accent varies fairly predictably from region to region in the nation. Whole regions of the United States can be defined, in a technical way, by pronunciation. Linguists William Labov, Sharon Ash, and Charles Boberg, for example, "define the South linguistically as that area which monothongizes /ay/" in certain word environments (Feagin, 2003, p. 128). That is, words such as *sigh*, *sign*, and *side*, which speakers from other regions say like [sahee], [saheen], and [saheed], come out in southern speech as approximately [sah], [sahn], and [sahd]. This way of speaking has "long been recognized as a hallmark of Southern speech"—at least since the 1920s (Thomas, 2003, p. 150).

Or, moving west, when we see a sign on a Utah bulletin board reading *bike for sell*, we may or may not realize that the writer has written the word *sale* as it sounds in the local dialect, [sell]. Contemporary dialectologists have written articles tracking how the vowels of Utah are systematically pronounced one degree lower than in other parts of the country. The effect is, for example, that the vowel in *feel* is pronounced [fill] and the vowel in *fill* is pronounced as [fell] (Bowie, 2003, p. 46). This is an example of sound change, one of the many ways that language naturally changes. Thus, language varies by sound—speaker accent or pronunciation. While speakers' pronunciation also varies by age, occupation, and socioeconomic bracket, we'll leave the details of this to other books on sociolinguistics and language variation (see especially Fromkin et al., 2002; Wolfram, Adger, & Christian, 1999; and Wolfram & Schilling-Estes, 1998).

Grammar

In addition to language varying by vocabulary and sound, language varieties contrast in grammar. Dennis Preston illustrated this point in his 2003 presidential address to the American Dialect Society: "When people in Milwaukee say *by Aunt Mary's* (while nearly everyone in the United States says *at Aunt Mary's*), they borrow the semantics of the preposition *by* from German, a hardly surprising fact considering Milwaukee's dominant early German population" (p. 235). In Pennsylvania, if a car is dirty, locals will say *The car needs washed*, whereas people in other locations will say *The car needs washing* or *The car needs to be washed*. Wolfram and Schilling-Estes (1998) explain:

> In another case of dialect differentiation based on the types of structures that can co-occur with particular verbs, we find that the verb *need* may co-occur with either *-ing* or *-ed* verbs, depending on the dialect area. In most of the US, *need* takes an *-ing* complement, as in *The car needs washing*. However in some areas, most notably Western Pennsylvania and Eastern Ohio, *need* takes an *-ed* verb, as in *The car needs washed*. The *need* + verb + *-ed* pattern is also found in some areas of the British Isles, particularly Scotland. Although using an *-ed* verb with *need* may sound awkward or even "wrong" to speakers who use *-ing* with *need*, there is nothing intrinsically more "correct" or more logical about using the *-ing* form. (pp. 78–79)

Finally, a grammatical highlight from the South. In the South, you may hear speakers saying *It was so cold, I liketa froze*. Wolfram and Schilling-Estes (1998) explain the grammar rule involved: *Liketa* is counterfactual, conveying a meaning that something possibly could have happened (it was not impossible) but in fact did not happen. Thus, if "speakers of standard varieties wish to convey the meanings indicated by these special auxiliaries, they must resort to complex constructions such as . . . *It was below freezing outside, so I could have frozen in theory, but I was in no real danger*" (p. 78). We think that *liketa* is a subtle and powerful word—look how much it can convey!

In sum, different groups of people may speak English differently. Their language will differ at least by sound, vocabulary, and grammar.

Varieties of English

Our descriptions so far have explored differences in sound, vocabulary, and grammar from all over the United States. When dialectologists study one region or group, they discover a constellation of traits (patterns of sound, vocabulary, and grammar) that hold together as a distinct way of speaking American English. A distinct way of speaking a language is called a *dialect*, or *language variety*.

When linguists talk about dialect, they do so in a technical way and mean simply a coherent cluster of linguistic traits. So a *dialect* is a "variety of the language associated with a particular regional or social group" (Wolfram and Schilling-Estes, 1998, p. 350).

Since everyone is associated with a particular regional or social group, everyone speaks a dialect. This means that so-called "Standard" English is a dialect of English. Also known as language varieties, dialects vary in structure (sound, vocabulary, grammar, and social conventions for holding conversations) on the basis of speaker "age, socioeconomic status, gender, ethnic group membership, and geographic region" (Wolfram, Adger, & Christian, 1999, p. 37). Contrary to popular understanding, "'[d]ialect' does not mean a marginal, archaic, rustic, or degraded mode of speech" (Pullum, 1999, p. 44). Therefore, to avoid the popular stereotypes, linguists often refer instead to *language varieties* and to the way language varies, or *language variation*. In each case, the term is descriptive and neutral.

Registers, Formality, and Dialects

Within a given language variety—say, Southern English, Northern English, one of the regional Standards (see below), or a language variety associated with an occupational or social group—we can identify a range of levels of formality, from the most casual levels of speech to the most frozen, formal levels. This is called "stylistic variation" (Joos, 1967).

When schools talk about so-called Standard English, they usually mean formal written Standard English (what the *Columbia Guide* [Wilson, 1993] calls "Edited English"). When children come to school fluent in any of the many spoken Englishes, they all are confronted with the task of learning the conventions of this Edited American English, a language style that is quite different from conversational language. In written Standard, for example, we see sentence patterns that invert verbs and adverbials (e.g., *Never have I seen such tall mountains!*). Of course, the usual spoken word order is *I've never seen such tall mountains!* In written Standard, we see other highly formalized patterns, such as the subjunctive form of the verb (*were*)—*If I were to go now, I'd surely miss the traffic.* The more usual spoken language expresses this idea without the subjunctive verb—*If I was to go now. . . .* So, while we all vary our styles of language by formality, anyone who knows how to write in Standard Written English is showing skill they consciously learned in a formal educational setting. Unlike spoken language, which everyone learns naturally, written language comes only through explicit instruction and conscious study.

To explore why languages have dialects, we draw from a chapter in *American English: Dialects and Variation* by Wolfram and Schilling-Estes, who explain that distinct dialects emerged in American English, as in all languages, for sociohistoric and linguistic reasons (1998, pp. 25–55). We focus for a moment on the former, as it's more accessible and immediately relevant to our work in the classroom.

Wolfram and Schilling-Estes name a range of social and historical influences that lead people to speak differently: settlement patterns, migration routes, geographical factors, language contact, patterns of employment, social class considerations, and so forth (1998, pp. 24–32). We briefly explore settlement, migration, and geography patterns here. Regarding settlement patterns, Wolfram and Schilling-Estes explain:

> One of the most obvious explanations for why there are dialects is rooted in the settlement patterns of speakers in a given region. The history of American English does not begin with the initial arrival of English speakers in the "New World." . . . [S]ome of the dominant characteristics still found in varieties of American English can be traced to dialect differences that existed in the British Isles. (p. 25)

The distinctive language patterns of eastern New England and the Tidewater region in Virginia, for example, contain traces of the language of early settlers who came from southeastern England (Wolfram & Schilling-Estes, 1998, p. 25). Thus, when a person from the Tidewater region in Virginia (Williamsburg, Newport News, Hampton, Norfolk, etc.) pronounces the words *cart* or *work* as [caht] or [wohk], we hear the echoes of "proper" British English of the mid 1700s. In the eighteenth century, people living in southeastern Britain, including the areas around London, dropped the *-r* after vowels and before consonants. As these settlers immigrated to the colonies in the 1700s, they of course brought their particular patterns of British English with them, and in doing so planted the phonetic seed of the Tidewater dialect. Further, because these immigrants from southeastern England also landed in Massachusetts, we find that Bostonians often speak an *"r*-less" dialect (e.g., "Pahk the cah in Havahd yahd" for *Park the car in Harvard Yard*). So southern Virginians and Bostonians pronounce their *r*'s the same because their ancestors came from the same place in England, back when the colonies were being settled (pp. 92–95).

Migration routes and dialect boundaries also have a lot in common. The main dialect regions in the United States lie in an east-west direction, obviously correlating with the movement of early U.S. pioneers from east to west. And since "rivers, lakes, mountains, valleys and other features of the terrain determine the routes that people take and where they settle," it's not surprising that the great Mississippi River creates the border between the "Northern and Midland dialect areas which is still in place to some extent today" (Wolfram & Schilling-Estes, 1998, p. 27). As populations move and settle, they leave a lasting imprint of their language patterns in the enduring dialects of their descendants.

Standard English, Vernacular English, and So-Called "Nonstandard" English

While language structure itself always varies, we can see a different kind of variation in people's *attitudes* toward different types of language. "Standard" English is often called "good" English, whereas "nonstandard" English is considered "bad." Although these judgments feel like incontrovertible fact, the real fact is that judgments of "good" or "bad" reflect our beliefs about which groups are worthy of respect and admiration and which groups are not. To recap briefly from Chapter 1, what we call Standard is the language variety "associated with middle-class, educated, native speakers of the region" (Wolfram & Schilling-Estes, 1998, p. 284). People regard this variety as good because they regard its speakers as meritorious, but this judgment has nothing to do with an inherent structural superiority of so-called Standard English.

Vernaculars (i.e., nonstandard varieties) are those "varieties of a language which are not classified as standard dialects" (Wolfram & Schilling-Estes, 1998, p. 13). They contain socially stigmatized features such as the so-called English double negative (*I ain't got none*) or irregular verb forms (*I seen it*). Just as the public holds standard varieties in high regard because of its high regard for their speakers, so the public holds vernaculars in low regard and typically views its speakers with disdain. When people judge a language as poor or flawed, it's because they judge the speakers as poor or flawed in some way. This may sound harsh, but as we view a group of people, so we view their language.

African American English: *Not* Standard English with Mistakes

How do ideas from linguistics help the teacher of urban minority dialect students? The key linguistic ideas we've been describing—language variation, dialects, standards, vernaculars, the reasons for dialects, levels of formality, the structure of language, the nature of our attitudes toward language, etc.—all add up to transformational understandings in the classroom. With these tools from linguistics, the teacher can recognize that student language is not a mishmash of mistakes; it has its own grammar rules for pronunciation, word formation, and sentence structure.

Thus, when an African American student in urban America writes *Most day dat dog be scratchin'*, instead of throwing up their hands in dismay, teachers can recognize that everyday speech patterns have transferred into the student's expression. Knowing that dialects differ in sound patterns, teachers may recognize the regular correspondence between the first sounds in *dat* and *that*: the voiced [th] sound of formal English (a sound in which the vocal cords vibrate) corresponds to a [d] sound across many vernacular dialects in the nation (including African American English and southern and New York varieties). When students say *dat* or *dese* (or any other sound pattern characteristic of a given dialect), it is not a "sloppy" or "careless" version of [th]; it's a systematically different sound with different features of place, manner, and articulation. Truly astute teachers will also recognize that in *scratchin'* the student has not "left off" the written *-g*, but instead has used a wholly different sound: [n] as in *kin* or *pin*, rather than the sound as in *king* or *swing*. Teachers can do contrastive analysis with students' sound patterns too, just like the grammar contrasts we will be examining in this book. In that way, teachers can help students command the corresponding sounds of one of the regional Standard Englishes in the United States.

Likewise, knowing that language varieties differ in grammatical patterns, teachers will recognize the echoes of the everyday English plural and habitual *be* in the student's written expression.

Similarly, when linguistically savvy teachers living in Pennsylvania Dutch country read *The dog needs bathed*, instead of red-penning the sentence, they will hear the echo of historic settlement and migration patterns. They might envision a class project that blends social studies and language arts, allowing students to explore the unique cultural and linguistic heritage of their region. Of course, teachers will also want the students to learn that speakers in other regions of the country will likely express that meaning somewhat differently—*The dog needs to be bathed* or *The dog needs bathing*—and that when corresponding with others outside the region, students may want to use the more commonly recognized grammar patterns in order to communicate better with their audience.

Recognizing the integrity in student language creates a fundamental change in teacher attitude toward the student. In Chapter 1, we talked about how dialect prejudice against a student's home language affects student performance. When the teacher sees the student's language as "broken" and "poor" and the student as "lazy" and "ignorant," these perceptions spill over into what the teacher expects of the child in the classroom (Nieto, 2000, pp. 38–49). And when the teacher expects the child to do poorly, the child often does. Linguistically informed, a teacher can reverse her or his expectations and foster student success.

Now for the next step—how teachers can use this understanding about the structure of student language as a springboard to students' mastery of Standard English. The next chapter provides an overview of code-switching and contrastive analysis in the classroom and shares research results showing that contrastive analysis is the most effective tool in teaching Standard English.

4 Code-Switching Succeeds in Teaching Standard English

In this chapter, we show teachers how and why to begin the process of "flipping the switch" from correction to contrast in their classrooms. As broader context for our work with dialect minority students, we situate the conflict between prestige and nonprestige dialects in school within an international arena so that teachers can see that this is not just a U.S. phenomenon—the same issues occur throughout the world. As we respond to help minority dialect speakers learn Standard English, we share research demonstrating that code-switching works, and works better than traditional techniques of teaching Standard English. And you will see that in the United States, in spite of common practice, we've long known this to be the case.

Home Speech in the Classroom

Caribbean Students in Canada: Déjà Vu

When Caribbean students from Trinidad or Haiti go to school in Canada, they encounter a thicket of difficulty. The situation eerily parallels the plight of minority students in U.S. schools. A 1980 Toronto Board of Education survey of ninth-grade students, for example, found that Black students made up 7.0 percent of the student population but constituted 28.5 percent of the Basic Level (skills) group and that 31 percent of Black students were in the Learning Center, the Behavioural Program, and the Hearing and Physically Handicapped programs. In contrast, only 13 percent of Toronto's White children were placed in these programs (Coelho, 1988, p. 131). True to U.S. statistics, while Caribbean students overpopulated the skills and special education classes, only 5 percent of Black students were in the advanced programs (p. 132).

These lamentable statistics are paralleled more than two decades later in the United States. Ogbu, studying African American achievement in the affluent suburb of Shaker Heights, Ohio, found the very same types of numbers. Even though African American students came from comparably wealthy and educated families and attended the same school, having access to the same resources as the White students, they nonetheless filled the basic skills classes and were virtually absent from honors sections (Ogbu, 2003).

Not only do the statistics between Canada and the United States run hand in hand, but so do the teachers' responses to minority dialect students. In Canada, teachers see the Caribbean students as "careless with the language," as suffering "language problems," speaking "sub-Standard," "bad English" (Coelho, 1991, pp. 40–41). The response of Canadian linguists parallels that of linguists in the United States; the Caribbean Student Resource Committee has detailed a program that "will add Standard Canadian English to the language which the students bring to school. The program will not attempt to eradicate the students' first language; rather it will support and validate that language" as teachers build an ILA program around relevant culture, literature, and language (p. 90). Using the basics of contrastive analysis, Canadian educators describe a linguistically informed response to teaching minority dialect students. They recommend introducing one pattern at a time to show students the contrast between Creole and Standard English. With each pattern, Canadian linguists stress, the students need to practice translating from Creole to Canadian English (e.g., students should practice turning *paper make from wood* into the Standard equivalent *paper made from wood*). Only with practice translating from home to school speech will children really learn the school equivalents.

Trinidad and Tobago

We find the same kinds of concerns in West Indian schools. There, too, "language is the key to access to higher levels of education" (Kephart, 1992, p. 69). Kephart describes how minority dialect or language students fare in educational systems "dominated by ME [the English prescribed by the metropolitan power]" (p. 69). When students in Trinidad and Tobago took their standardized exams, they fared even worse than minority students in the United States. The exams used content

> set in England . . . [and having] absolutely nothing to do with West Indian language or culture. During the 1960s the pass rate was around 20 to 30 percent. . . . From 1974 through 1978, the pass rate for children in Trinidad and Tobago averaged 22 percent . . . [on] a test on what was supposed to be their native language. (p. 69)

Not only are students' scores familiar, but so are attitudes toward the language varieties of minority students. Yet again, teachers and the public scorn the community language, believing it to be "broken English," "corrupt," and "incapable of expressing complex ideas." In response, teachers "correct" the students' "errors" (Nidue, 1992, p. 13). Yet, clearly, given the test scores, correction didn't help. In response, Caribbean scholars are bringing a linguistically informed approach to the classroom, one that builds on students' home language as a springboard to mastering regional Standard English. Clearly, in nation after nation, it's time for a new approach to community language in the school classroom.

How to Talk the New Walk

But if we suggest that you do not use the usual descriptors in talking about student language, what words, terms, or images *do* we suggest you use? Reseeing what's going on in student language entails, in turn, talking about student language in new ways. Table 4.1 gives you a handhold on new ways of seeing, talking about, and responding to students and student writing.

Table 4.1. New ways for talking about language: from red pen to code-switching.

Correctionist Approach	Code-Switching/Contrastivist Approach
Language as ■ proper or improper ■ good or bad	**Language as** ■ appropriate or inappropriate ■ effective or ineffective in a setting (appropriate to the time, place, audience, and communicative purpose)
Language ■ is right or wrong ■ is correct or incorrect	**Language** ■ follows a pattern ■ ranges from formal to informal ■ varies by setting
The student ■ made mistakes, errors ■ is having a problem with plurals, possessives, tense, etc. ■ "left off" an *-s, -'s, -ed*	**The student** ■ is following the patterns of home speech/informal English ■ is using a grammatical pattern different from formal English
The student ■ should have, is supposed to, needs to correct . . .	**The student** ■ may *code-switch* (choose the language pattern to fit the setting)
Teachers ■ correct the language	**Teachers** ■ help students "translate, change, code-switch" from one variety to another

Instead of thinking of language as "good or bad," "right or wrong," for example, consider seeing it as effective or ineffective, a fit or not in the setting. That's actually an accurate characterization. Instead of talking about what students "should have" written or what they're "supposed to" write, ask students to choose the language variety that fits the setting. Or, as Mrs. Little, veteran eighth-grade teacher in downtown Newport News, says, "Flip the switch!"

Instead of "correcting" student language, help students code-switch or "translate" their writing into whatever language variety is appropriate. If you're conferencing with a student for an essay that's supposed to be written in Standard English, and if you find in the draft informal patterns you have already covered in class, here's how you might proceed: After talking about the content, organization, sentence structure, word choice, and so forth of the paper, when it comes time to talk about grammar, you might say, "Here [*Mama like to cook on the weekend*] you follow the pattern of informal subject-verb agreement [*Mama like*]. In this essay, we're trying to use formal English. Can you code-switch it? Check our charts. . . . Good! Now, let's check your paper for any other informal subject-verb patterns. . . ."

A teacher in one of Wheeler's workshops was impatient with all this change: "What's the big deal," she asked. "They're making errors! Correct 'em! I don't have time for all this. They've got to do it right and that's that!" She thought that moving from correction to contrast was just "political correctness."

Not at all. "Appropriate" language is not a politically correct codeword for Standard English. "Inappropriate" language is not a codeword for informal English, or everyday, community language. When we talk about appropriate and inappropriate, we truly mean "the variety that works (or doesn't) in the setting." This is a statement that is hard for teachers to hear. An activity that might help is one in which students and teachers think of a long list of settings where the most formal speech registers of Standard English would be wildly inappropriate. This will help allay people's suspicion that "appropriate" language really means Standard English.

How we talk about things in the world reflects how we think about and understand those things. Think about the evolution of racial language in our country. One author of this book remembers that during her childhood, chocolate-covered Brazil nuts were called "nigger toes," a label that would never fly today. Why? The "n" word reflects and embodies a worldview and a way of viewing Black people that is unacceptable to us. As our understanding of the world changes, so our language changes. Same thing with language about language.

Armed with the information provided in *Code-Switching*, teachers come to school knowing they will be working inside a different mindset, talking about language in different ways, seeing the students themselves as competent speakers of their own variety. Now, how do teachers integrate their new understandings into the language arts curriculum?

The Top Ten Patterns

You will find it useful to come to class equipped by knowing the top ten grammar patterns characteristic of your students' writing. Across the country, a very small set of home speech grammar patterns often transfer into minority students' school writing.

The Code-Switching Shopping List in Appendix A names the top nine grammar patterns Wheeler has found and works with in her consulting with K–16 schools. We show a few rows in Figure 4.1 (page 60), saving the full chart for Appendix A, where we collect various code-switching tools for you. The shopping list was originally developed for middle school students and as a teacher tool for tracking students' progress in commanding the forms. We leave it to your creativity to adapt this tool for elementary students.

These patterns are probably familiar to any teacher of urban or maybe southern students. At first, you can look for just the top few of these patterns in your students' work—especially subject-verb agreement and showing past time. Also look in your students' writing for patterns with nouns—plurals and possessives.

When Students Speak Informal English

Here's another tough one for teachers. When your students are participating in class discussion or generally talking in school, you're sure to hear them using patterns from their community language. Often, teachers correct students' speech. The problem is that correction derails the meaning of the conversation and aggravates and alienates the students. Further, correction does not teach the Standard English patterns.

Of course, the linguistically informed teacher does not sit idly by. We recommend that you make mental or actual notes of the home speech patterns that occur in student speech or writing. Keep a notepad on your desk and jot down the different grammar structures you hear, or use the Code-Switching Shopping List to tally the most common grammar patterns your students use. One of Wheeler's teacher education students said

Code-Switching Shopping List				
Name: _____ Do any of the top 10 or 12 informal English patterns appear in your paper? If so, put a check in the corresponding box and then code-switch to formal English! Put a smiley face, ☺, to show when you use formal patterns in your writing. "Flip the Switch!"				
Informal v. Formal English Patterns	Paper 1	Paper 2	Paper 3	Paper 4
1. Subject-verb agreement She walk_ v. She walk<u>s</u>				
2. Showing past time (1) I finish_ v. I finish<u>ed</u>				
5. Making negatives She <u>won't never</u> v. She won't <u>ever</u>				
7. Plurality: "Showing more than one" Three cat_ v. Three cat<u>s</u>				
8. Possessive (singular) The dog_ tail v. the dog<u>'s</u> tail				

Figure 4.1. Abbreviated Code-Switching Shopping List, by Rebecca S. Wheeler and the Huntington Middle School Writing Project.

she is planning to keep a running record on her desk of her students' language. This way, if visitors to her room witness her not correcting students when they speak with their community language variety, she will be able to point to her ledger, saying, "See, I am fully aware of the students' grammar. I record examples of specific home speech patterns they use. Then in my next daily oral language time, I'll do a minilesson on the most common grammar patterns and have students translate from informal to formal English. Researchers at CUNY (Fogel & Ehri, 2000) have shown that translating from home speech to school speech is the most effective way to teach Standard English." Likewise equipped with your list of students' home speech patterns, you can choose what pattern you will analyze using a contrastive analysis chart during your next daily oral language time. This way, in class discussion you attend to the subject at hand rather than derailing the meaning and focus of the content lesson, you keep the students' goodwill, and you don't waste time trying to put in place a grammar "correction" that never takes root. Instead, you are paying attention to and working with students' grammar in a way that research shows to be successful—with the technique of contrastive analysis, whereby students systematically translate between informal and formal English.

Contrastive Analysis

Let's look now at some research showing that contrastive analysis is successful in teaching Standard English to minority dialect speakers. We summarize a few studies here, but for a current, extensive treatment of contrastive analysis and dialectally aware programs, see Rickford, Sweetland, and Rickford (2004).

Research from Chicago

Hanni Taylor, director of the Learning Assistance Center at predominantly White Aurora University, got a call from the dean of students. The dean had referred a young man to the center because "he didn't talk right and didn't write right" (Taylor, 1991, p. 1). A great number of referrals soon followed—all African American, all writing differently from what the university expected. Taylor understood the basic insights from second language acquisition. She understood that the students' home dialect was transferring to their Standard English writing (pp. 6–7). She knew the usual response was to implement the traditional correctionist approach, but she wanted to try out ESL methods with her second dialect learners. What she found was stunning.

Taylor contrasted the performance of African American students across two first-year writing classes. With one group, she used the traditional English department techniques: correcting students and marking their "errors." In the other classroom, she led her students in contrastive analysis, so they discovered for themselves the systematic contrasts between the grammatical patterns of AAE and SE.

Her results were dramatic: after eleven weeks, the control group using the correctionist model showed an 8.5 percent *increase* in African American features in their writing, but the experimental group, using contrastive analysis, showed a remarkable 59.3 percent *decrease* in African American features. Taylor observed that students had been neither "aware of their dialect" nor of "grammatical black English features that interfere in their writing" (1991, pp. 149–50). Rickford comments on Taylor's study:

> The point Taylor made overall is that this process of comparing the two varieties seems to lead to much greater metalinguistic awareness of similarities and differences between the vernacular and the standard and allows kids to much more effectively negotiate the line between the two. (1999a, p. 340)

This is powerful affirmation for the success of code-switching and contrastive analysis as a way to teach Standard English mastery.

Research from New York

At the elementary level, we find similar research evidence that contrastive analysis is far more successful than traditional approaches in teaching Standard English. Educational psychologists Howard Fogel and Linnea Ehri (2000), from the Graduate Center of the City University of New York, studied different techniques for helping third- and fourth-grade African American students learn Standard English. Like Hanni Taylor, they contrasted traditional correctionist methods with a version of contrastive analysis. The testing cohort was divided into three groups. At the beginning of the experiment, all students were able to translate approximately 31 percent of the African American language patterns into Standard English. In the first test group, the students read Standard English and the experimenters urged them to look closely at the grammar. In the second group, the experimenters did the same and then added one step—they instructed the students in details of the Standard grammar. The third experimental group used a form of contrastive analysis. In this group, the teachers exposed students to Standard English forms, instructed them in Standard English patterns, and then went one step further—they guided the students as students *practiced* transforming sentences containing African American English features into the Standard English equivalents (Fogel & Ehri, 2000, p. 215).

Fogel and Ehri showed that contrastive analysis succeeds where traditional approaches fail. Indeed, they found that teaching Standard English grammar to children not only produced *no improvement* in their Standard English knowledge, but that some students produced even less Standard usage after receiving SE instruction. On the other hand, students in the contrastive analysis group nearly doubled their Standard English performance (2000, p. 222). Clearly, contrastive analysis holds great promise in fostering Standard English mastery.

Results from Georgia

Teachers in DeKalb County, Georgia, also implemented a contrastive approach. Thus, when a fifth grader answered a question with a double negative (*not no more*), the teacher prompted the student to code-switch, to which the student replied, "Not any more." The children learned to switch from their home speech to school speech at appropriate times and places, and learned that "the dialect they might use at home is valuable and 'effective' in that setting, but not for school, for work—or for American democracy" (Cumming, 1997, p. B1). This program has been designated a "center of excellence" by the National Council of Teachers of English.

Conclusion

Our schools have long served students who come to school from diverse communities speaking diverse dialects. We had our wake-up call when a northern school system was sued for educational malpractice. In 1979, "Michigan Legal services filed suit [*Martin Luther King Junior Elementary School Children v. Ann Arbor School District Board*] . . . on behalf of fifteen black, economically deprived children residing in a low-income housing project" (Smitherman, 2000, p. 133). The mothers of the Green Road housing project in Ann Arbor, Michigan, found that their children, perfectly intelligent, were at risk for becoming "functionally illiterate." These plaintiffs claimed that the school system had "failed to properly educate the children[;] . . . that school officials had improperly placed the children in learning disability and speech pathology classes; that they had suspended, disciplined, and repeatedly retained" the children at grade level; and that "they had failed to overcome language barriers preventing the children from learning standard English and learning to read" (p. 133).

The case resulted in a decision for the plaintiffs. The trial established that the "school district had failed to recognize the existence and legitimacy of the children's language, Black English" (Smitherman, 2000, p. 135), and that because teachers failed to recognize the regular structures of the language, continuing to see it as broken English, they held "negative attitudes toward the children's language [which] led to negative expectations of the children . . . [and in turn to] self-fulfilling prophecies" (p. 135). The court found that the suit had merit since federal law directed that "no child should be deprived of equal educational opportunity because of the failure of an educational agency to take appropriate action to overcome linguistic barriers" (Labov, 1995, p. 46). The judge found that Ann Arbor "had violated the children's rights to equal educational opportunity." The barrier, he stated, lay not in the child's language per se, but instead in the teachers' negative attitudes toward the children's language. This ruling

> affirmed the obligation of school districts to educate black children and [established] within a legal framework, what has been well documented in academic scholarship: Black English is a systematic, rule-governed language system developed by black Americans as they struggled to combine the cultures of Africa and the United States. (Smitherman, 2000, p. 135)

The court gave Ann Arbor thirty days to remedy the violation of students' educational rights.

That was over twenty-five years ago. Where are we now? Have we made any progress? Precious little. Will we finally take "appropriate action to overcome linguistic barriers" African American students face?

This book is about taking appropriate action. Through code-switching and contrastive analysis, we offer a way to unbind the negative stereotypes associated with African American English. We offer a research-proven way to teach Standard English. As Redd and Webb (2005) state, "code-switching is [the] goal, [and] contrastive analysis is the primary means . . . to achieve that end" (86). It's about time. Let's get to it!

II Classroom Practice

5 Diversity in Language

Now we're ready to begin the true how-to's of our book. How does the research-based approach of code-switching and contrastive analysis play out with real students in real classrooms? We'll talk you through it, from the very beginning. Although what we present here focuses on the K–5 classroom, everything we say is readily extendable into secondary school and even college. Indeed, Wheeler has consulted in schools using these materials from elementary through college levels.

In what follows, we describe how teachers can move away from a correctionist, red-pen classroom that assumes everyone lives in one culture and speaks always and only one dialect (Standard English) into a classroom that recognizes the true diversity of U.S. society—that we come from multiple cultures and many homes where we grow up speaking a rainbow of English—even as we help all children master Standard English, the language of wider communication.

Any teacher implementing this work will start at the beginning, anchoring in basic understandings of how variation is natural in our world, how variation is natural in language, and how language structures (grammar) vary by context (time, place, audience, and purpose).

Variation Is Natural

Let's get started! While terms such as *formal* and *informal* may seem rather lofty for a child in primary school, even very young children (K–2) readily understand these concepts. We begin our work with kids by anchoring our approach in what students already know. Students know that they engage in activities all along the spectrum of formality, from highly formal to highly informal. Simply ask a child what kind of clothes he or she should wear to play basketball. The child will most likely answer that a pair of shorts, a T-shirt or basketball jersey, and tennis shoes would all be good choices. You know the child is not going to suggest a suit and tie or a dress. This is because children understand that certain activities call for specific clothing.

Likewise, children understand that certain situations call for varying levels of behavioral formality. Running on the playground is completely acceptable. Running in the classroom or in a church, however, is not going to bring smiles from the teachers or church officials. So we see that children can often assess a situation and make immediate decisions about the level of formality it requires.

We can draw on children's understanding of levels of formality in clothing and behavior as a springboard to helping them learn about choosing language to fit the context. But first, before addressing language itself, we begin with students' grasp of how their clothing choices vary setting by setting. For a first class discussion, make a poster paper chart showing columns for places one might wear formal or informal clothing (see Figure 5.1). Ask students to name places for which they would dress nicely. Students will likely offer responses such as a nice restaurant, a wedding, or church. Write these responses under the formal heading. Reiterate to students that these are examples of places where they would wear formal clothing. Some students may observe that church is an informal place for them—that they wear jeans and sweatshirts to church. Don't worry; record the child's answer. The point here is for children to distinguish settings from one another and to become intentional about making choices to fit the setting.

Tell the students that the opposite of formal is informal. Next, try to elicit examples of informal clothing by saying something such as, "If formal means you have to dress up and might wear something like a suit and tie, what would you wear for something that is informal? Where might you be going in an informal outfit?" Students often respond with "the baseball field," "the beach," and "home on the weekend." For the outfits, they might respond with "jeans and sweatshirt" and "shorts and bathing suit" (see Figure 5.2).

In Swords's classroom, students got into an in-depth discussion of formal and informal clothing, activities, and localities. One child asserted that uniforms would be part of formal clothing and cited the school uniform as proof. Another student supported this statement by adding Girl Scout and Boy Scout uniforms to the list. "But I have to wear a uniform to play football, and it gets all dirty. So it would be informal," countered another child. The students were then able to find several examples of informal uniforms, including sports uniforms and prison uniforms. They also named additional examples of formal uniforms, including nursing and military uniforms. The students then offered several observations about the lists they had generated under the formal and informal headings. "If you get dirty, then you're probably not being formal," explained one student. "Yeah," another offered, "formal is like dress-up." Thus, by allowing students to rely on their own prior knowledge, Swords was able to facilitate a conversation that ultimately led to a set of student-created guidelines for determining the formality of an outfit or event.

Several activities, requiring increasingly difficult skill levels, can serve as extensions of this discussion.

Informal and Formal Places

Informal	*Formal*
baseball field	nice restaurant
the beach	wedding
home on the weekend	awards ceremony
church	church

Figure 5.1. Contrasting places by levels of formality.

Informal and Formal Clothing

Informal	*Formal*
jeans and sweatshirt	suit and tie
bathing suit	nursing uniforms
sports uniforms	military uniforms

Figure 5.2. Contrasting clothing by levels of formality.

The felt board. Give students examples to analyze. The simplest of these for the youngest students is a teacher-created activity involving a flannel board. To begin, you will need examples of formal and informal clothing. You can accomplish this either by drawing on felt or by cutting outfits out of a magazine, laminating the pictures, and then gluing them to felt. You will also need to type, laminate, and glue "Formal" and "Informal" headings on felt. Students can then manipulate the clothing on the flannel board by placing the clothing under the appropriate heading. Since the manipulatives are teacher-made, students are responsible only for categorizing the clothing. Therefore, this activity requires a rather low level of skill.

Construction paper. A similar but more challenging activity allows the students to both select the clothing examples and categorize their own examples. To do this, students will need a variety of magazines, scissors, and two different colors of construction paper. Before implementing this lesson, label the construction paper "Formal" and "Informal." For example, you might label yellow construction paper "Formal" and blue construction paper "Informal." Instruct the students to cut out different articles of clothing. The students can then paste the articles of clothing they have cut out onto the appropriate piece of paper. Encourage students to analyze and explore by having them discuss their decisions with at least two classmates. This social discourse forces students to defend their thinking, thus promoting metacognition. To help prompt students, you should circulate around the room asking questions such as "Why did you paste the Girl Scout uniform on the formal page?" This helps the students explain and justify their thinking. These collages can then be displayed around the classroom for future reference.

Personal picture and writing. Students need to recognize the importance of formality in their own lives. Therefore, for this next activity, begin by having each student draw a picture of himself or herself first in a formal outfit and then in an informal one. They should label these outfits appropriately. Then prompt the children to write a sentence telling where they are going in these outfits. When Swords used this activity with her second-grade students, she modeled the process for them. First she drew a picture of herself wearing a skirt and blouse and wrote above the picture the word *Formal.* Then she drew a picture of herself wearing overalls and a T-shirt, labeling this picture *Informal.* Under the drawings, she wrote, *I wear a skirt and a blouse when I go to school. I wear my favorite overalls and a T-shirt to clean my house on Saturdays.* The students then had a clear understanding of what was expected of them. This final step was meaningful to the students because they recognized themselves in *both* formal and informal pictures and explored when each way of presenting themselves was appropriate in their lives.

You might expand the discussion by leading the class in exploring how tone of voice, posture, and mannerisms vary depending on where we are and what kind of activity we're doing. Thus, students readily recognize that not only does their clothing vary by setting, but also how they stand or sit or gesture is quite different depending on whether they are in a house of worship or sitting around a campfire. Through these class discussions and activities, students become explicitly aware that we vary our self-presentation throughout the day, consistently, without a thought. They realize that variation is natural.

Language Variation Is Natural

The form of language we choose, like our clothing, varies by time, place, audience, and purpose. Students clearly already have some knowledge and understanding of this because they address adults and children in different ways (Adger, 1998). While Swords was teaching a third-grade science lesson, for example, one of her students excitedly commented, "Mrs. Swords, dis junk be tight!" Another student, in an appalled tone, countered, "McKenzie, you can't talk to Mrs. Swords like that!" McKenzie immediately apologized, explaining, "I mean dat stuff be cool." The interaction between the two students illustrates their ability to use different levels of formality within their language of nurture. The teacher can draw on this understanding to help students shift between the language of nurture and the language of wider communication as appropriate.

Some scholars note the limitations of the analogy between language and clothing. Richardson (2003) suggests that one can readily change clothing because clothing is not linked to a person's core identity. But, she reasons, since language is far more closely linked to a person's core identity, language is not so easy for a person to change.

We agree with Richardson that language is closely tied to identity. But the same can be true of some clothing. A woman raised in U.S. culture, for example, might well find it unfathomable to wear the full black Iranian robe and veil, the chador, so alien is it to her notion of self. Or it might be too bizarre for a construction worker to wear the full regalia of a British prince or the robes of a nomadic herder. In cases like these, we completely agree with Richardson. However, to the degree we experience ourselves as changing clothing within a culture or perhaps a proximal culture, the analogy between informal and formal language and clothing holds. And we have found the clothing analogy useful with students. Since we all have a range of different clothing styles we can choose from (e.g., clothing for relaxing on weekends versus clothing for occasions such as weddings or church), we'll stick with the clothing analogy as a way to illustrate how variation is natural throughout our lives.

Recognizing Formal and Informal Patterns

Since we have not yet discussed the particular patterns of formal and informal language with students, their initial experiences with language patterns will simply reflect their intuitions of what language is formal and what is informal.

Begin the process of distinguishing formal and informal language by first asking students to think about the different ways they talk to people. Then provide students with little bits of language and ask them where they think they might hear them. You might ask, for example, how they would greet the principal of the school. Which would be more appropriate to say: "Yo man! Waz' up?" or "Good morning, Mr. B."? Have the children explain why they selected the response they chose. To help the students recognize the differences between formal and informal language, use chart paper to create a two-column chart like the one in Figure 5.3.

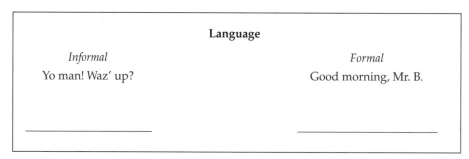

Figure 5.3. Contrasting formal and informal language.

Then elicit more examples of the two language styles from the children. After you give the initial example, students can draw on their personal experiences to provide more examples of both formal and informal language uses. As students share their ideas of different formal versus informal ways of speaking, invite the class as a whole to decide whether to list the phrase or sentence under the formal or informal heading. You might say, "If you were playing basketball, how would you ask someone to pass you the ball?" When Swords asked this question of her students, they responded with "Yo, man! Ain't you gonna pass the ball?" and "Dude, I'm open!"

To illustrate the contrast between formal and informal English, Swords asked the students whether they would ever say the following on a basketball court: "Excuse me, but I've noticed that you've retained possession of the ball for the majority of the game. Please relinquish custody of the ball so that I may take advantage of my current position to earn additional points for our team." The students tumbled into waves of laughter. They knew that such lofty language is not appropriate for the basketball court. So "proper English" is not always proper.

You may find that children report using what we've called informal language in church and at fancy family gatherings. True enough. The point is for children to choose the language to fit the setting. If the family uses informal English at church and fancy dinners, that language, of course, fits the setting. Swords points out that what students must remember is that formal school essays (like research reports) and statewide test essays tend to require formal Standard English.

Exploring Language Variation in Literature

After helping your students become comfortable distinguishing between informal and formal language, they are ready to begin exploring language in literature. Keep the chart of formal and informal language you have created as a class so that you can add sentences from the literature under each heading. Begin your examination of the literature by using read-alouds. A good book to start with is *Flossie and the Fox* (McKissack, 1986) because Flossie speaks informally, while the fox uses formal English. Ask your students to listen to the characters so that they can determine whether characters speak formal or informal English.

First, introduce the main characters. You might say, "This story is about a fox and a little girl named Flossie. I want you to listen to the way Flossie and the fox speak. At the end of the story, I am going to ask you if Flossie speaks informal or formal English. I am also going to ask you if the fox speaks informal or formal English, so listen carefully to what these characters have to say." Conclude this activity by having the students determine the formality of the language used by specific characters and add some choice sentences to the chart.

It is important to encourage the students to use what they already know about language. Swords was surprised at the number of informal speech patterns her students identified in *Flossie and the Fox*. Although the class had not discussed particular patterns, her students initiated a discussion about formality in speech that surpassed Swords's expectations. It began when she asked the students to listen for informal speech during a reading of the story. After reading the line *Shucks! You aine no fox. You a rabbit, all the time trying to fool me*, several students spoke up, saying that the line was informal. Swords asked Rennie to tell her why it was informal. "Because she said *ain't* and we don't say that," the child explained. The following class discussion showed Swords that children seven and eight years old are readily able to discuss formality in speech.

"I do. I say *ain't*," Juwan interjected.

"But we're not suppose to say it," Rennie said.

"Why not?" Juwan countered.

When Rennie did not offer a response, another student offered his thoughts: "Well, I think you can say it because I say it sometimes, but I think it might be informal."

"It's kinda like when you say *yeah* and change it to *yes* cuz you talkin' to a teacher or Mr. Bender," Ty'wuan added. "*Yes* is formal, but *yeah* is informal."

"So what you gonna say instead of *ain't*?" Juwan asked.

"You can say another word, like maybe *isn't*. I think it might change sometimes," Karishma explained.

The students seemed unclear about which formal word or words would mean the same thing as *ain't*, but they agreed that *ain't* was informal. Through their discussion, the students were able to make some astute observations about language.

As your students become more proficient in their ability to distinguish language styles, encourage them to find examples of formal and informal sentences in the stories they read on their own and in those read to them by others. The children can then add these sentences to the chart in a group setting. If your students find *Flossie and the Fox* too rural a story, build your lessons around a range of the other books listed in Appendix B or the works cited list for children's literature.

Some wonderful work in this arena is coming out of Stanford's Department of Linguistics. Julie Sweetland, a graduate student in linguistics, is developing a series of lessons for children grades 4–6 that help children discover and explore variation in language. She begins with vocabulary. In one of her first lesson plans, "The Words We Choose to Use: Special Vocabularies for Different Social Settings," children read one of the Frank and Ernest books by Alexandra Day (*Frank and Ernest* [1988]; *Frank and Ernest Play Ball* [1990]; *Frank and Ernest on the Road* [1994]). The purpose of the lesson is to help children become "curious and observant when it comes to language" and to "begin the process of demonstrating respect for students' language." As children explore how characters adapt to each setting, using different vocabulary in different settings, Sweetland is laying "the groundwork for altering discussions about social norms for use of 'Everyday Language' and 'Formal Language'" (Sweetland, 2004).

The Next Steps

We have begun describing the foundations for helping children learn that we use language differently in different settings. From here, we'll zoom in on the kinds of everyday language you are likely to see in your students' writing, and we'll explore a new way of responding.

6 Teaching Noun Patterns: Possessives

As a teacher sits down to respond to student writing, amid the usual spelling, punctuation, and capitalization errors she or he may discover that the student uses a range of grammar patterns not found in Standard English. This lesson deals with one of those structures—the possessive. We explored this pattern in general ways earlier. Here we detail the step-by-step process of how to approach teaching possessive patterns in the classroom. Students use contrastive analysis to learn the detailed differences between the language they currently use (the language of nurture) and the language patterns we're asking them to add (Standard English). Then, once students command the differences between the grammar patterns they're following from the home and the grammar patterns of the school, we show you how to ask them to code-switch as fits the setting, often into Standard English.

As teachers, we know that to show possession in written Standard English we (generally) add -'s to the noun. But our students often write in a different fashion (*My dog paws are muddy*). As noted earlier, our usual response is to think that the student has "left off the -s," or that the student is "having problems" with possession. We may mark the sentence "wrong," showing the student how she or he "should" show possession—by inserting the "missing" -s.

But if we step back and recall that all language is patterned, that language comes in different varieties, and that each variety is patterned, we have a new approach to a child's writing. With that insight in mind, the teacher can step outside the framework of "error" to look for the pattern in student writing. It's difficult, letting go of what feels certain, our sense that such examples are "missing an -s," or that the child has forgotten to use possession. And yet, another take on what's going on is far more effective and far more accurate, too.

The linguistically informed approach lets us confidently realize that the grammar patterns of the student's home language are transferring into school writing. The very fact that many students in the class use the same sentence pattern should tip us off to this possibility. When you see the same kind of sentence structure showing up in your students' writing, collect a range of examples. Of course, before you can help your students see the contrasts between the patterns of their home language and the patterns of school language, you need to understand the contrasts yourself.

Understanding Possessive Patterns

Here's where the basic tools of the scientific method first come into play.

Applying the Scientific Method

Perhaps surprisingly, the scientific method is the technique you will use to approach student language. Here's how it applies to analyzing student language:

> *Collect data*: First, collect a set of sentences from student writing showing a particular sentence pattern.
>
> *Examine data, seeking pattern*: Then examine your student data to see what particular arrangement of words happens again and again and what meaning accrues to the pattern.
>
> *Describe pattern*: Try to state what the pattern is in your own words.
>
> *Test and refine your description of the pattern*: Make sure the rule you write out captures other data you encounter.

Discovering the Pattern in Student Writing

Since you will guide your students through this scientific discovery, it is important to get a feeling for the process yourself. While we partially analyzed possession earlier, we skipped through it mighty quickly. Here we linger, walking you through the feeling of the actual reasoning process. In later sections, we'll pick up the pace as we describe how to lead your students in discovering formal and informal patterns. Let's begin by looking at some of the data we have collected from elementary students' writing.

1. a. Taylor cat is black.
    b. The boy coat is torn.
    c. A giraffe neck is long.
    d. Did you see the teacher pen?

We know from the context of the sentences that they somehow convey possession. To understand how the sentences show possession, we begin by translating each sentence into formal English, as follows:

	Informal	Formal
2. a.	<u>Taylor cat</u> is black.	<u>Taylor's cat</u> is black.
b.	The <u>boy coat</u> is torn.	The <u>boy's coat</u> is torn.
c.	A <u>giraffe neck</u> is long.	The <u>giraffe's neck</u> is long.
d.	Did you see the <u>teacher pen</u>?	Did you see the <u>teacher's pen</u>?

Let's begin by figuring out how we show possession in informal language. Look at the first sentence, *Taylor cat is black*. Ask yourself where the meaning of possession lies in the sentence. That is, what are the words that seem to have possessive meaning? Perhaps you realize that possession seems to happen in the phrase *Taylor cat*, as it does in the subsequent phrases *boy coat*, *giraffe neck*, and *teacher pen*. So let's underline those. You'll probably be tempted to think that these sentences would show possession if only the child hadn't left off the apostrophe -*s*, but that's where you catch yourself. Remind yourself that all language follows a pattern and that there is likely some rule, a grammar rule, going on here. So nobody has left anything out. These sentences *do* show possession—your job is to figure out how!

Formulating the Grammar Rule

Now you need to get specific and find the grammar rule. Focus on the underlined words in the informal column. What pattern do you see happening again and again in the informal examples? Continue seeking some pattern that might correspond to possessive meaning. Look for the patterns, beginning with *Taylor cat* and then *boy coat*. How does the arrangement of words in the sentence let us know that the cat belongs to Taylor or that the coat belongs to the boy? What arrangement of words happens in each sentence? In the first, the second, the third, etc.?

Perhaps you notice that there seems to be a pattern of noun + noun. Could this be how possession is signaled in informal English? Let's make it a hypothesis that we check:

> **Hypothesis**: "In informal English, we signal possession by noun + noun."

Testing Your Hypothesis

Let's test this theory. Look at each sentence systematically. Does each sentence contain a noun + noun combination? Checking the data, we see that yes, each does—we have *Taylor* + *cat*, *boy* + *coat*, *giraffe* + *neck*, and *teacher* + *pen*. In each of these examples, the relevant words sit side by side. That's a rule of grammar in Everyday English. If a person wants to use informal English and indicate possession, that's how she or he will do it—place the nouns side by side.

Now that you have identified the informal pattern, turn your focus back to the formal sentences. Look at the underlined words. How do they differ from the informal pattern we defined? Your immediate response to this question is probably that the formal sentences contain an apostrophe and then an *-s*. Let's get even more specific. Which word contains the "apostrophe *-s*"? You might say that, in the side-by-side noun pattern, the first noun ends with an *-'s* (or *-s'* in the case of plural possessive nouns). Again we must check this hypothesis against the data. You will find that each noun combination does indeed follow this pattern: *Taylor* + *-'s* + *cat*, *boy* + *-'s* + *coat*, *giraffe* + *-'s* + *neck*, etc. You might also have defined the pattern as owner + *-'s* + owned.

Patterns for possession with singular nouns
Informal English: owner + owned
Formal English: owner + *-'s* + owned

You have now defined the patterns that signal possession in both Everyday English and Standard English for singular nouns. These are the same steps you will use throughout your journey in helping students switch between informal and formal English as relevant to their needs.

The steps we've walked through here may seem long and drawn out and possibly daunting or unrealistic for everyday use in the classroom. Indeed, we've gone into considerable detail about how one reasons when applying the scientific method to student language. The process will become much shorter and quicker as you gain experience in the likely patterns of your students' language.

You will not need to go through this process fully with each new year's crop of students. As you become familiar with the kind of language your school's students tend to use, you'll know what patterns to expect. Once you've worked through (or looked up) and developed materials for the top ten or fifteen relevant grammar rules, you're set for future classes. While you will not need to figure out the patterns anew, you will consistently lead students in the scientific method so that each year's crop of students will discover and become conscious of and intentional about their grammar choices. We will help you with your journey. First, we will give you the analyses and graphic organizers for the dozen most frequent grammar patterns that have shown up in our urban students' writing (see Appendix A), and we will walk you through how to use these tools to teach code-switching in your classroom. Also, Chapter 13 explains how to handle patterns beyond those we treat in this book. So you're well on the way.

Refining Your Hypothesis

Before we turn to how to use contrastive analysis in the classroom, let's explore a fly in the ointment in student data and how you respond to it. What if the dataset you collected from student writing began with examples 3a–b and then continued with the sentences we just saw in 1a–d?

    3. a. My mom jeep is out of gas.

        b. My little brother dog is brown.

With examples such as 3a–b, you or your students might be tempted to conclude that the meaning of possession is signaled by the possessive pronoun *my*. That's a reasonable starting point. Indeed, it's a hypothesis (possession in informal English is signaled by *my*). As with any hypothesis, the next step is to check it, so you examine the rest of your data, 1a–d. These data tell you that your initial hypothesis can't be the whole story. While *my* surely signals something about possession in 3a–b, no possessive pronoun occurs in 1a–d, and yet these do convey a possessive meaning (*Taylor cat; boy coat; a giraffe neck; the teacher pen*). So you need to keep examining the data for a pattern, just as we did earlier. We'll round out the fuller picture of possession below.

What If You Don't Know the Answers to Students' Questions?

Checking data against your hypothesis will be an important skill to have as you lead your students in discovering the patterns of different language varieties. Students will undoubtedly come up with different possibilities for patterns that you won't have thought of. At first this can be daunting, and you might think, "Oh! I don't know the answer to that!" But don't worry. Just take their suggestion as a hypothesis about the language data and invite the whole class to examine whether it fits all the data. Indeed, you can simply say, "OK! Good, Shamika! You have described a hypothesis. Now let's all check the data to see if it works for each and every sentence." That way, everybody works through the hypothesis together and you all discover whether it holds. This way, as the teacher, you don't have to know the answer at the outset—you don't have to have a graduate degree in linguistics—you just need to follow the steps of the scientific method to check out the hypothesis in pursuit of one that fits the data at hand. Then you've got your grammar rule!

Teaching Possessive Patterns: Lesson 1

Now we explore how to teach Standard English possession to your students.

Anchor in Your Students' Writing

As always, anchor your teaching in your own students' writing. Listen to the way your students speak and look at various forms of their written work (e.g., journals, freewrites, formal essays). Jot down for yourself any examples you notice that don't fit Standard English patterns. For example, Swords often heard her students ask, "What time is we going to lunch?" and "Is we going to art today?" She noticed that the students used *is* where formal English would call for *are*. So she began keeping track of these examples. She did the same for other informal patterns she noticed, such as possessives, plurals, pronouns, and verb tenses (we'll be exploring these later). After she had obtained a collection of oral and written sentences containing informal patterns, Swords created a check sheet for herself (like the Code-Switching Shopping List in Appendix A). Whenever she found an informal pattern in her students' writing, she put a check in the box next to the pattern. This way, she was able to gauge which were the most frequent patterns in her students' writing. This let her focus her lessons on the most frequent ones. No need teaching about patterns that only one or two children used once or twice; truly frequent patterns such as possessives or subject-verb agreement—that's where a teacher should focus. Because Swords found many sentences with an informal possessive pattern, she chose to begin her exploration of grammar here. Note that whether or not your students use the informal possessive pattern, it is one of the easiest patterns to teach, and students recognize it even if they don't use it often themselves. For this reason, we always start our K–16 code-switching work with possession.

Start by Focusing on One Informal Pattern per Sentence

You might notice, as Swords did, that the sentences you are seeing in your students' work contain more than one informal pattern. Indeed, Swords's students might use two, three, four, or more informal patterns in one sentence. We'll demonstrate how to handle multiple patterns later, but for the moment, focus on one pattern at a time.

Here's how. Suppose you found the following sentence in one of your student's work: *My mama two friend be visitin'*. This sentence contains four specific informal grammatical patterns: possessive (*mama two friend*), plural (*two friend*), habitual *be* (*be*), and use of [*-in'*] instead of [*-ing*]. Since we're going to focus only on the possessive, shine a spotlight on that grammar pattern. In preparing your flip chart for students, translate the plural and the verb forms into the formal English patterns. Thus, the sentence you will use with the children will read, *My mama two friends are always visiting.* Tell your students that at the beginning, you will be changing parts of their sentences to help them focus on only one pattern at a time. That way, they're not surprised when a sentence from their work reads differently than the way they initially wrote it.

Create a Contrastive Analysis Chart

Once you have selected a range of sentences (data) from your students' work, create a chart that will help students compare and contrast the two language varieties. Begin by labeling the chart according to the grammatical pattern you're exploring; here, title your chart "Possessive Patterns." We find that it helps to put an example of the pattern right under the chart title, as in Figure 6.1. This helps capture the contrast in a visual nutshell. Then, create two columns, one labeled "Informal English" and the other "Formal English." Figure 6.1 provides an example from Swords's classroom, but each teacher should use sentences, both formal and informal, selected from his or her own students' writing. In Swords's case, she found *Taylor cat is black* in one of her student's papers. She used this as her first informal sentence and translated it to *Taylor's cat is black* to create the corresponding formal sentence. She used this same technique to add three more sentences to the chart. Underline the part of the sentence you will want the children to focus on. As you prepare for this lesson, you might want to make paper copies of the chart for each student.

Begin Your Lesson on Possessives

Begin your lesson by writing the term *possessive* on the board and asking students if they know what it means. If children are unable to answer, explain that the word *possessive* refers to ownership. You can also prompt discussion by using the word in a sentence. You might say, "My possessions include a car, a coffee mug, and the shoes I am wearing. What do you think the word *possession* might mean?" Once a student has defined the term *possession* as something a person owns, have the students give examples of some of their possessions. You will also want to provide examples using animals and inanimate objects as the owners, such as *The car's tire is flat* or *My dog fur is black.*

Directions: Write two more informal and two more formal sentences that include possessive patterns. Then answer the questions below.

Possessive Patterns

Taylor cat v. Taylor's cat

Informal English	**Formal English**
<u>Taylor cat</u> is black.	<u>Taylor's cat</u> is black.
The <u>boy coat</u> is torn.	The <u>boy's coat</u> is torn.
A <u>giraffe neck</u> is long.	A <u>giraffe's neck</u> is long.
Did you see the <u>teacher pen</u>?	Did you see the <u>teacher's pen</u>?

What is the pattern for showing possessive in Informal English?

_____

What is the pattern for showing possessive in Formal English?

_____

Figure 6.1. Chart for discovering possessive patterns.

Work with the Contrastive Analysis Charts

Now it's time to work with the language data. Show students the possessive patterns chart and ask them to pay close attention to the underlined words. Your goal will be to help students discover the rule for possessive patterns in informal and formal English. Later, you may want to have the students work in small groups to find ways to describe how each language variety expresses a given grammatical pattern, but for the moment, lead the discussion yourself. Ask the students if they know that the examples on the left-hand side (informal) have a meaning of possession. They will say yes. Then, just as you did in your own exploration of student data, ask them, "How do you know that *Taylor cat* and *The boy coat* show possessive meaning?"

Students will likely erupt with "This side did it wrong" or "This side left off the -*s*." Here is where you continue working to help your students understand that nobody left off anything and nobody did anything wrong. Instead, the students successfully followed a different pattern. Point your class back to their real job—to describe what the pattern is—and tell them they will learn how to switch patterns in a moment. Ask them to describe the pattern in a positive way, describing what they actually see, not what they *think* is missing. This is a good exercise in accurate observation and critical thinking for everyone.

Help Students Discover the Informal Pattern

Although you may need to help direct the discussion as students search for the possessive rule, it is important to use simple, straightforward language. If, for example, your students have difficulty with the term *noun*, don't include that term in the rule you help them to create. Let's say your students have figured out the pattern "owner + owned" as the possessive rule. Use those terms as you state the grammar rule.

Now is the time to help them check their hypothesis against the data. Tell your students that they've come up with a good guess—a hypothesis (this is a fertile place for language arts and science to cross-fertilize, as students apply the scientific method in language arts). The next step is to determine whether the hypothesis describes each and every sentence. You might say, "OK, we've got a pattern: owner + owned = possession. Let's look at the first sentence: *Taylor cat is black.* Does that sentence fit our pattern? How?" In Swords's class, Danielle responded that *Taylor*[1] is the owner, and he owns the cat, and the two words sit side by side. Therefore, this sentence fits the pattern the students suggested. The students carefully examined each sentence in the chart to determine whether the pattern really described all the data. In this way, students confirmed that they had successfully discovered and described the grammar rule for possession in informal English!

Help Students Discover the Formal Pattern

Now turn to the formal pattern for possession. You might think, "We don't need to look at that—everybody knows how to show possession, or the 'right' way to show possession." But clearly, that's not true. One reason that students' writing continues to show instances of informal English features is that they are unaware of the detailed contrasts between informal and formal English (Taylor, 1991, p. 150). The sort of careful contrastive analysis we're describing here is what gives our students explicit awareness and command of Standard English. So follow through by leading your students in a search for the formal English pattern of possession.

After a time, students will likely say that we show possession by "owner + -'s + owned." As with the hypothesis for informal possessive patterns, lead your students in checking whether their rule really accounts for each sentence in their data. Ask your class, "OK, our hypothesis says that inside formal English we show possession by 'owner + -'s + owned.'

Let's look at the first sentence—*Taylor's cat is black*. Does that follow the pattern?" Help the class track their way through the sentence. With one finger on "owner," point to *Taylor*, and then with your finger on the "-'s" of the rule, point to "-'s" in the example, and finally, with your finger on "owned" in the rule, point to *cat* in the example. In this way, you teach your students careful, systematic analysis while at the same time the whole class confirms that yes, the sentence follows the pattern described. Then ask students to follow your lead and track through each sentence in the formal column.

Now your class has discovered and confirmed the rules for possession in both informal and formal English.

Let Students Practice New Understanding

In your next lesson, before applying this understanding, you might give students a chance to practice the rules they've discovered. Create a list like the following that offers students a range of things owners might own. This will help younger students focus on the possessive pattern.

Owner	Owned
Dad	hat
dog	fur
car	tire
zookeeper	broom
Devante	book
tree	branches
pencil	eraser
bird	wing

You might have students practice making both formal and informal sentences with possession. This heightens their awareness and command of the pattern so they can better choose the pattern to fit the setting. Ask the students to think of an informal sentence about Dad and his hat. Then call on one or two students to share their sentences. One child might say, "My dad hat is blue and white." Help students isolate the pattern by asking a child to explain why the sentence is informal (*dad + hat* = informal possessive). After your class has explored an informal sentence, have students make up a formal sentence using *Dad* and his *hat*. An example could be *My dad's hat is in the closet*. Again, have a student describe why that sentence fits the formal possessive pattern. After students have offered several examples of both informal and formal sentences, have them independently create their own sentences from the chart. Circulate around the class giving the students feedback on whether they've used the informal pattern correctly and whether they've used the formal pattern correctly.

We initially had our students "flip the switch" and change the style of possession they used sentence by sentence. If a child's first sentence was *My dad hat is blue and white*, for example, their next job was to switch to the formal possessive pattern of *My dad's hat*. But if their next sentence was in formal English, *The tree's branches are broken*, their job was to translate it into informal—*The tree branches are broken*. We have found, however, that our local community sentiment required that we have students switch only from informal to formal. Since our goal is to foster Standard English mastery and since having students translate from informal to formal succeeds in teaching SE to minority dialect speakers, we reluctantly cede the broader multicultural point. Nonetheless, there are good reasons of equity why students should switch evenhandedly from informal to formal and from formal to informal. It also stands to reason that switching back and forth between the two would more deeply develop students' conscious grammar awareness and skills. Gauge your community sentiment and decide for yourself.

Such student work in code-switching and contrastive analysis will be most useful if the students can refer back to their analyses throughout the school year. To do this, you might have students build a section in their notebooks for their code-switching charts. The charts help students translate or code-switch from one form of English to another. You can create a code-switching notebook for each child simply by giving each a three-ring folder that they'll use for their charts. Then, whenever you teach a grammar pattern, you can either hand out a miniversion of the big flip chart you've created (just make one chart with the formal and informal patterns and photocopy it for the class), or hand out a formal–informal template to each student that they can then fill in.

The chart on the next page is an example of the formal–informal template you can hand out to each child as they learn to switch between language varieties during the school year. Before class discussion, they might copy the several examples on your big flip chart onto their desk copy. That way, they will have the examples right at their desk during class discussion and during the editing process.

Elementary students can decorate their folders at the beginning of the year and can use the templates during reading and writing to create specific patterns or to define patterns they read or hear.

INFORMAL |—————————————————| FORMAL

THE PATTERN

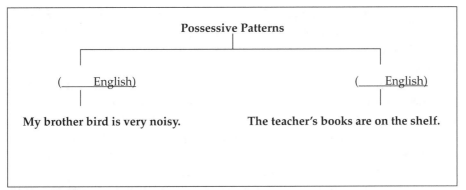

Figure 6.2. More practice in English possessives.

Teaching Possessive Patterns: Lesson 2

The purpose of this lesson is to reinforce lesson 1 (teaching possessive patterns) and to give students additional opportunities to demonstrate their understanding of both formal and informal possessive patterns.

For this activity, you will need to provide each student with a sentence strip. Each student will use his or her strip to write a sentence that illustrates a formal or informal possessive pattern. Draw the chart shown in Figure 6.2 on the chalkboard or, if space allows, use large sentence strips to create the chart on the wall. You can either use the examples shown in our chart or use sentences taken from your students' writings. Since you will want students to remain focused throughout the lesson, you should not provide the examples before the lesson begins. This chart looks a bit different from ones we've provided so far, because the formal and informal columns are not translations of each other. Instead, the children will first figure out whether the example is formal or informal, and then they will talk through how they know.

To begin review and work with this chart, have the students recall and share the purpose of possessive patterns. Ask the students what the term *possessive* means. Then remind them that different language varieties may show possession in different ways. Ask the students to remember the rules for showing possession in informal English and the rules for showing possession in formal English. Allow several students to provide the rules for each. Show the class the example of the possessive pattern in the left-hand column. Have the students isolate where the possessive meaning occurs. They should be able to identify who is the owner and what is owned: for example, *brother* is the owner and *bird* is the owned. Underline the possessive pattern (*brother bird*), and ask the students if the sentence shows a formal or an informal speech pattern. Students should say that the sentence uses the informal English pattern for possession.

After a student answers, ask the student(s) how he or she knows that the sentence is informal. The student should be able to state that, in informal English, "owner + owned = possession," so *brother* (owner) + *bird* (owned) follows the rule for informal possession. Repeat this process with the example of formal English. Reiterate the rule for formal English as "owner + -'s + owned = possession."

After you have reviewed the rules and examples of possession in both formal and informal English, give each student a sentence strip. If community sentiment permits, allow each student to decide which type of possessive sentence (formal or informal) he or she will write. Through a think-aloud, demonstrate the process of choosing a type of pattern and writing a sentence. You might say, for example, "I usually write formal sentences, so I'm going to challenge myself by writing an informal sentence. First, I have to decide what to write about. I need to think of an owner and something that can be owned. My mom just bought a new dress, so I think I'll use my mom as the owner and the dress as what she owns. Her dress is red with gold buttons, so I'm going to write, *My mom dress is red with gold buttons*." Write this sentence on a sentence strip and show the students the finished product. Give students ample time to complete their own sentences.

After the students have finished writing their sentences, let them assume the role of teacher and lead the class in practicing with sentence strips. Demonstrate the process for students; show them the sentence you wrote during the think-aloud and ask the class whether the pattern is formal or informal. Call on one student to respond, and have that student explain how the sentence fits the pattern (My *mom* is the owner and *dress* is what she owns, so owner + owned = informal possession). Using a highlighter, highlight the possessive structure *My mom dress*. Then tape the sentence under the heading "Informal English." Give each student a chance to read his or her sentence to the class and, using the process you have modeled, select a classmate to determine whether the sentence is informal or formal and explain why it fits that pattern. Then have the student who is assuming the role of teacher isolate the possessive pattern by highlighting the structure. The student will then tape the example under the correct heading on the wall.

It is important to note that both lessons 1 and 2 simply focus on helping students recognize differences in the two language varieties.

Since students are just learning that differences exist, we don't want to overwhelm them by having them apply this knowledge in reading and writing until they are comfortable in the knowledge itself. Later in this book, we address how to successfully integrate this knowledge into the reading and writing curriculum.

To extend the exercise in lesson 2, you might consider having students highlight examples of formal possessive patterns in their own writing or select examples of possessive patterns in literature. Leave on the wall the chart completed in either lesson 1 or lesson 2. You can then refer students to the chart when they are working with possessive patterns in their own writing. If you do not use a process method to teach writing, or you feel that your students could benefit from some additional practice, have the students complete the worksheet on the last page of this chapter.

Note

1. When we say that a specific word in a sentence (e.g., *Taylor*) is the owner (e.g., of *cat*), we are using nontechnical, lay terms. A more correct linguistic statement would be that the referent of the word *Taylor* owns the referent of the word *cat* (a referent is the thing to which a word refers). This degree of semantic precision, however, would introduce considerable convolution into the current text. Accordingly, we will treat our current wording—"*Taylor* is the owner, and he owns the *cat*"—as shorthand for the linguistically correct version.

Directions: Cut out the sentences below. Read each sentence carefully. Highlight the possessive pattern in each sentence, and paste the sentence under the correct heading. Use the blank boxes to write your own formal and informal sentences.

Possessive Patterns

Informal English   *Formal English*

The dog's fur is brown.	Is that girl coat blue?	The boy parents are late.
The book cover is torn.	That car's horn is loud.	Where is Nico's shoe?
My sister hair is long.	Taylor's desk is messy.	Have you seen David's car?
	Mary cat is very soft.	

Use these boxes to write one formal and one informal sentence.

7 Teaching Noun Patterns: Plurals

After students have gained an understanding of possessives, you can begin using contrastive analysis and code-switching to teach the pattern for plurals. Unlike the possessive pattern, in which we found a one-to-one correspondence, the plural pattern is more complex. In reviewing, you will recall that side-by-side nouns signaled the informal possessive pattern, whereas the pattern "owner + -'s + owned" gave us possession inside formal English. We could readily teach children to move between the two forms of language because the pattern was easily identified in both language varieties. You will find that teaching plural patterns is a bit more challenging.

Plural Patterns in Informal English

Let's begin by looking at some examples of student writing showing plurality that Swords found in her students' work:

1. a. I have two dog and two cat.
   b. The three ship sailed across the ocean.
   c. Taylor loves cat.
   d. All of the boy are here today.

Clearly, students are following a pattern for showing plurality that differs from that of Standard English. Our job now is to invite students to explore the data and discover the grammatical pattern at hand.

Using Contrastive Analysis to Teach Plurality

We introduce the concept of plurals to students using the same basic contrastive chart we used in teaching possessives. As you introduce each new pattern to your students, plan on creating the same basic layout in your charts. Doing so will give the students a familiar anchor point. To obtain data for the chart, collect examples of informal plurality from your students' writing. Then translate these to the formal pattern when you are making your flip charts. Although we have found that our local children (as well as community college students in New York and New Orleans) use informal English plural in their writing, if that's not true in your school, you of course wouldn't teach this pattern.

Start with One Informal Pattern per Sentence

Once again, as you put illustrative sentences from student writing into the chart, if you find a sentence that contains several informal grammar patterns, translate any other informal patterns into formal English, leaving only the plural in informal style. Tell the students what you're doing. Explain that while they are learning, you will make sure there's only one informal pattern per sentence so that they can better focus on that one pattern. Sentence 1d, for example, *All of the boy <u>are</u> here today*, originally read, *All of the boy <u>is</u> here today*. Since the focus for this lesson is the plural pattern, Swords changed the informal *is* to *are* so students wouldn't be distracted and confused by multiple patterns. Likewise, in the student's paper, sentence 1c initially read *Taylor love cat*. But since this shows two informal patterns (plurality and subject-verb agreement), Swords put the informal subject-verb pattern into the corresponding formal form—*Taylor loves cat*—in order to isolate the plural pattern. Although we do discuss verb patterns in later chapters, it is important that you introduce only one pattern at a time at this point.

Create Contrastive Analysis Chart for Plurals

Once you have collected some sample sentences and made sure only one informal pattern shows per sentence, create a chart like that in Figure 7.1 to compare and contrast the ways that formal and informal English show plurality. You will need to make a paper copy of the chart for each student to add to his or her code-switching notebook after this lesson is over.

Leading Students to Discover Plurality

Just as we did with possession, begin your lesson by talking about the meaning of the grammatical pattern. Before showing students the chart, write the term *plural* on the board and ask them what it means. If your students don't know, explain that the word *plural* means more than one. You will then need to provide some examples. You might say, "There are twenty-four students in this class. Twenty-four is more than one, so *students* must be plural. I have ten fingers, so I have a plural number of fingers." Instruct your students to think of something they have more than one of, and allow each student to say his or her sentence aloud. You might hear sentences such as *There was two bear at the circus* or *The bus has four tires*. You probably noticed that the first example, *There was two bear*, doesn't use formal English subject-verb agreement. Do not "correct" your student on this just now. Instead, at your desk, jot a note about it. Save

---

Directions: Write one more informal and one more formal sentence that include plural patterns. Then answer the questions below.

Plural Patterns

Informal English	*Formal English*
I have two dog_ and two cat_.	I have two dogs and two cats.
Three ship_ sailed across the ocean.	Three ships sailed across the ocean.
Taylor loves cat_.	Taylor loves cats.
All of the boy_ are here today.	All of the boys are here today.
_____	_____

How do we show "more than one" in informal English?

_____

How do we show "more than one" in formal English?

_____

Figure 7.1. Discovering plurality.

the note for when you teach subject-verb agreement later in the semester. For the moment, compliment your students on giving examples of plural patterns, in both formal and informal English.

The students are now ready to view the chart. Reveal one line at a time (the informal sentence and its translation) and read them aloud. So you'll read *I have two dog and two cat*, followed by *I have two dogs and two cats*. Remind students to pay close attention to how the sentences are alike and how they are different. This will help them recognize the existence of the *-s* on the end of the noun to show plurality inside formal English. (Note that we use the longer phrase *inside formal English* instead of *in formal English*. That's because *in formal English* sounds exactly like *informal English* and hence is confusing. The longer phrase—*inside formal English*—makes our meaning completely clear.) After reading each sentence, help the students focus on the formal pattern by noting how the formal is different from the informal. We start with the formal pattern in this case because it is defined by a single rule, whereas the informal has several rules and hence is more difficult.

Discover the Plural Pattern inside Formal English

Once your students have looked through all the examples, noting casually how formal and informal English seem to differ, focus on the formal English column. Ask the students to be specific about how formal English differs from informal English. Your students will most likely recognize the additional -*s* present in formal English. Children may say, "That one [the formal pattern] does it right, and the other one is wrong." Again, remind the students about what they learned about variation in life—that we wear different clothes for different occasions, and so on. A dress suit isn't always "right"—it's just a suit chosen for the occasion. Same thing here. Tell your students that now we're looking at how language can vary. Later we'll think about situations when we want to use one type of language and when we would want to use the other.

Once the children have identified the -*s*, you might think aloud, "Since formal English has an -*s* where informal English does not, I wonder how we would state the pattern for formal plurals." Allow your students to hypothesize about the rule as it makes sense to them and to discuss with one another the rule's validity before testing the hypothesis. For example, a student might say, "Words that end in -*s* are plural, so a word + -*s* = plural." Another student could insightfully counter that the name *Carlos* ends in an -*s*, but there is only one of him in the class. Yet another student might recall the lesson on possessives, in which the phrase *the teacher's desk* refers to the desk of one teacher, so *teacher's* ends with an -*s* but it's not plural. By allowing this type of student discourse, you are empowering your students to think through and refine responses themselves.

These are insightful comments students have made. You'll want to rely on the scientific method to help you reason through them. With *Carlos*, for example, you might note in class discussion that if the grammar pattern for plural inside formal English is "noun + -*s*," that suggests we can take off the –*s* to indicate one of something. That is, we can have *one dog, two dogs, three dogs*. So we can put the -*s* on and take it off, depending on whether the noun is singular or plural inside formal English. Then ask the students if they can take the -*s* off of *Carlos*. They will realize they cannot. That suggests that the -*s* on *Carlos* is not the plural -*s*. Similarly, for *the teacher's desk*, the ending of *teachers'* is not simply an -*s* but, in writing, an apostrophe -*s*, signaling possession (of course, matters get more complex with possession for plural nouns, but you don't need to handle those at the elementary level).

Once the students have agreed on a rule, such as "noun + -*s* = plural," you will need to help the children check their hypothesis against all of the given data. You might say, "Let's look at the first sentence. It says *I have two dogs and two cats*. Do you see any nouns that have an -*s* on the end? Which ones?" Your students will quickly find *dogs* and *cats*, both because these are the only words that end in -*s* and because you have identified these terms by underlining them. You then check the rule. *Dog* is a noun and it has an -*s* on the end. After establishing this fact, you might ask if the author of this sentence is talking about more than one dog. Students will most likely answer yes, at which point you can ask, "How do you know?" Students will probably respond that the number *two* in front of *dogs* indicates more than one. If this occurs, you might say, "Yes, the number does show us that it is more than one. But there's something else that shows us it is plural inside formal language. Do you remember what that is?" This should help students recall that the formal pattern is "noun + -*s* = plural." Repeat this entire dialogue with *cats* in the first sentence, *ships* in the second, *cats* in the third, and *boys* in the fourth. It is important that the students learn to check each sentence to see if the rule is valid. This will be especially pertinent when, as you will find with informal plurals, one rule will not suffice. Through this process, children become explicitly conscious of the grammar contrasts between informal and formal English.

Discover the Plural Pattern in Informal English

Now that you and the students have identified the pattern for plurals inside formal English, you can turn your attention to informal language. Here's how Swords approached it with her class.

"Let's look at the first sentence," Swords says, "*I have two dog and two cat*. How do we know there is more than one dog or cat?"

"It says *two*," Tiffany explains, "and that's more than one." Tiffany has identified one of the rules for showing plurality in informal language.

"Oh, so a number word tells us that *dog* and *cat* are plural," Swords affirms. "Let's see if that works for all of them." Swords reads the next sentence on the chart, *Three ship sailed across the ocean.* "Is there a number word that tells us there is more than one ship?"

"*Three!*" several students exclaim.

"Good, we know there is more than one ship because the number word *three* is in the sentence." Swords creates a heading at the bottom of her code-switching chart reading Plural Patterns. Under the informal column, she writes *number words* to show that number words are part of what signals plurality in informal English. "What about the next sentence, *Taylor likes cat*? I don't see a number word, so our rule doesn't work all of the time. How do we know if Taylor likes more than one cat?"

"If you only like one cat it would say *I like the cat* or *I like a cat*. There might be other words in the sentences before this one that tell you for sure," says Chelsea. Swords adds *other words in sentence* and *other words in paragraph*[1] to the bottom of the chart. Swords explains that we can think of the other words in the sentence or paragraph as clues or signal words that tell us that the noun's meaning is "more than one." She then reads the next sentence.

"What about this sentence, *All of the boy are here today*? How do you know the author means more than one boy?"

"Mrs. Swords!" Devante exclaims, "You can't have a fraction of a boy! If his arm comes to school, the rest has to come too, so you wouldn't say *all of the boy* except if you was talking about more than one boy!" So, she observes, "common knowledge" tells us it's plural. Swords adds "common knowledge" to the grammar rules for informal plural.

The discussion ended with the students determining four rules for showing plurality in informal language: number words, other words in the sentence, other words in the paragraph, or common knowledge. The finished code-switching chart is shown in Figure 7.2.

Showing Plurality

two dog v. two dogs

Informal English	*Formal English*
I have two dog_ and two cat_.	I have two dog<u>s</u> and two cat<u>s</u>.
Three ship_ sailed across the ocean.	Three ship<u>s</u> sailed across the ocean.
Taylor loves cat_.	Taylor loves cat<u>s</u>.
All of the boy_ are here today.	All of the boy<u>s</u> are here today.

Plural Patterns

number words	**noun + -*s***
other words in sentence	
other words in paragraph	
common knowledge	

Figure 7.2. Showing plurality.

Of course, some students may decide that words like *all* and *some* are number words, in which case only three rules would be needed. Or they may realize that number words are a special kind of signal word. In either case, it is important to emphasize the context in which the words are used. In the sentence *Devonne ate all of the sandwich*, for example, the word *all* does not necessarily signal plurality. The sentence is ambiguous and could mean "Devonne ate all of a single sandwich" or "all of a complete set of sandwiches." Therefore, as Chelsea pointed out, we must look at the sentence in the context of the entire paragraph to determine its meaning.

After students finish analyzing and discussing plurality inside formal and informal English, give them the worksheet from the previous section to complete in pairs or small groups. Again, you want the students to discuss their understanding of language patterns, because this leads to a greater understanding of the subject material. The students can add the completed sheet to their code-switching notebooks for future reference.

Reviewing Plural Patterns

This lesson is designed as a review of plural patterns. Before teaching this lesson, you will need to create a paragraph that includes many formal and informal plural patterns. You can use the following model or create your own paragraph. Write the paragraph on chart paper, but do not allow the students to see it before your lesson.

Jamestown

Last week all of the third-grade student took a trip to Jamestown. The student were divided into groups of two boys and two girl. All of the groups were given lists of thing to look for in Jamestown. There were twelve items on each list. My group only found some of the thing on the list. We saw two canoe and six longhouse that looked like the kind the Powhatan Indian used long ago. We were excited because both the canoes and the longhouses were on our list. However, we didn't see all three crop that the Powhatan Indians planted. Next time we have a task on a field trip, I hope my group is able to finish.

Begin the lesson by having the students recall the definition of plurality. They should be able to say that plural means more than one. Then have them explain the signals for showing plurality inside both informal and formal English. If you posted the Showing Plurality chart, you might remind children to refer to the chart if they have difficulty remembering the rules for the two patterns. After this brief review, call on different students to provide examples of each. For each example, have the students explain why their sentence is either formal or informal. For instance, Josh might give the sentence *I have three brother*. He should be able to explain that the sentence is informal because it has a number word and the noun is bare, or does not have an *-s* on the end. This quick review is important because it helps direct the students' attention for the actual lesson.

Following the examples and review, tell your students that you have a paragraph with both formal and informal plural patterns in it. Explain that this particular paragraph was written to put in the hallway for everyone to see. Ask students if they think we should use formal or informal language and why. Students should be able to respond that since school is a formal place, we need to make sure the paragraph uses formal school language. Now explain that, for this reason, you need their help in editing the paragraph.

Uncover the paragraph and read it slowly, pointing to each word as you say it. Ask the students if they see any formal language patterns in the paragraph. Since this is a formal assignment, and we intend to put the paragraph in a public location, we want to celebrate the formal patterns already present. Call on various children to locate the formal patterns. Make sure each child explains why the pattern is formal. For example, *boys* in the second sentence is formal because there is an *-s* on the end of *boy* and more than one boy was put in the group. Have the child use a highlighter or yellow marker to highlight the formal plural pattern. After students have found all of the formal patterns, ask them to look for informal patterns that they need to change to formal.

It is important to remind students that formal language is being applied because of the place (school) and audience (other teachers, parents, and students). As students locate the patterns, have them explain why it is informal. For example, *all of the third-grade student* (sentence 1) is informal because the word *all* shows more than one student and there is no *-s* on *student*—that is, *student* is a bare noun. Once a student has identified an informal structure, have him or her change the pattern to reflect formal language. A student might simply say, "I have to add an *-s* to *student* because inside formal language a noun + *-s* = plurality." Since we now have a formal pattern, have the student highlight the formal structure. After the students have located and discussed all of the plural patterns, be sure to reiterate the importance of selecting language based on place, time, audience, and purpose for communicating. We don't want students to think that the informal is incorrect—it's just not appropriate for this particular assignment. Remember that your students are just beginning to learn about code-switching between the formal and informal styles. For this reason, you need to focus on moving from what the students already know (the informal) to what they have not yet mastered (the formal). In future lessons, after students have gained an understanding of several formal and informal grammatical patterns, you can focus on using the informal patterns in creative writing.

To extend this lesson, have your students take out a piece of writing they are working on and highlight the formal plural patterns they see. Remind them that if they identify an informal pattern that they think needs to be formal, they can change it, and then highlight it. If you feel your students still need more practice with plurals, you might want to use the worksheet on page 101.

Reviewing Plural and Possessive Patterns

Children often have a difficult time distinguishing between plurals and possessives inside formal language. They tend to use the apostrophe to show plurality and forget to use it to indicate possession in written Standard English. As teachers, we know it is important to review these two patterns so that students use the two correctly. This lesson relies on students' understanding of the informal language patterns to correctly use the formal plural and possessive patterns. To begin, write the paragraph below (or create one of your own) on chart paper. Leave ample space between each word so children can decide whether a word is singular, plural, or singular possessive, etc., adding a letter as necessary. As with previous lessons, do not let the students see the paragraph ahead of time.

The Wall

One of the wall in our classroom looks like a farm . There is a big red barn , and there are many animal on the wall . The cow bell really rings , the sheep fur is made of cotton ball , and the haystack is made out of real piece of hay . There is even a mouse tail peeking out of the hay ! There are little flower all over the grass . There is also an apple tree with lots of red apple . I like to look at all of the colorful thing on our wall .

Review the meaning of the term *possessive* by asking a few students to explain what it means and to give examples. Your review sets the stage for the actual activity.

Let your students know that they are going to help you change a paragraph from informal to formal English. Reveal the paragraph and invite your students to read it aloud with you. Ask your students if they found any informal possessive or plural patterns. Have students read a portion that contains informal language and identify one of the patterns they found. A student might say that, in sentence 2, *there are many animal on the wall* is informal because the word *many* means more than one and *animal* is a bare noun. You can then underline *many animal* to help the students focus on the pattern. The student might then say, "More than one means it's plural, so we need to put an *-s* on the end of *animal* to make it formal." You want to make sure that your students are identifying the structure as plural or possessive so they can make an informed decision about how to make the pattern formal. You will need to discuss each structure in the paragraph in the same manner.

Once the students have located all of the informal patterns and changed them to formal, give them each a paper copy of the following paragraph (or create your own) to do on their own. Have them underline informal patterns before changing them to formal.

Directions: Underline the informal plural and possessive patterns. Change the informal patterns to formal patterns.

Kasey and Jake

Mrs. Swords has two dog named Kasey and Jake . Jake fur is red , and Kasey fur is black and brown . They have many toy . Kasey favorite toy is a pink pig . The pig fur is very soft . Jake likes to play with a stuffed rabbit . The rabbit fur is green and white . Mrs. Swords loves to buy toy for her dog .

Note

1. Although Swords agrees with the student that we know *cat* is plural because of other words in the paragraph, this is an oversimplification of what's really going on. Actually, *cats* is what's called a generic noun, referring to cats in general, not to specific multiple cats. But this level of detail is too much to go into with elementary students, and probably with middle school students too. So we allow this simplification in service of teaching the more basic point—that informal English shows plurality by other words in the sentence or paragraph, or even by common knowledge.

Directions: Cut out the sentences below. Read each sentence carefully. Highlight the possessive pattern in each sentence, and paste the sentence under the correct heading. Use the blank boxes to write your own formal and informal sentences.

Plural Patterns

Informal English

Formal English

Danielle has three sister.	Josh stacked all of the chair.	One of the girl went home.
My name has six letter.	One of the girls went home.	Danielle has three sisters.
Josh stacked all of the chairs.	My name has six letters.	

Use these boxes to write one formal and one informal sentence with the plural pattern.

8 Teaching Subject-Verb Agreement

In addition to the various informal noun patterns you might find in your students' work, you will likely notice a number of verbs following various informal patterns. In this section, we look at how subject-verb agreement is used in both formal and informal English. Suppose you came across the following sentences in your students' work:

1. a. My mom drive to work everyday.
    b. Devante play basketball with Josh.
    c. Somebody take you to a romantic place.
    d. He go to church on Sunday.

To help the students understand subject-verb agreement, we begin by teaching the pattern for regular verbs. Later, we will introduce *is/are* and *was/were* combinations since these are common but more difficult. Let's get started with subject-verb agreement.

Building Your Contrastive Analysis Chart

Once again we begin by collecting data to build a code-switching chart for class discussion. While examples 1a–d isolate the pattern for third-person singular, it is important to find subjects of all persons and numbers so that students can see the full verb paradigm. If we eliminate sentences with *I*, *you*, *we*, and *they* as subjects, we run the risk of having students draw incorrect conclusions about subject-verb combinations. That is, if we use only *he/she/it*-style subjects to define the rule, students might determine that a bare verb is always informal and formal verbs always have an *-s* on the end. But clearly that's not so.

Remember, if your students' sentences have multiple informal patterns, translate other patterns into formal English so that subject-verb agreement is the only informal pattern remaining. We also underline the subject and the verb to help students focus on the relationship between the two. Once again, you will create this chart (Figure 8.1) on chart paper and make copies for the students to put in their code-switching notebooks at the conclusion of the lesson.

Since we want to begin with a short review, keep the chart covered until you incorporate it into the lesson.

Directions: Write two more informal and two more formal sentences that include subject-verb agreement patterns. Then try to answer the questions below.

Subject-Verb Agreement

Informal English	*Formal English*
I run quickly.	I run quickly.
You sing well.	You sing well.
He play ball after school.	He plays ball after school.
She walk to school.	She walks to school.
My dad clean the car.	My dad cleans the car.
Cassidy color neatly.	Cassidy colors neatly.
We paint in art.	We paint in art.
They sit on the carpet.	They sit on the carpet.

_____   _____

_____   _____

What is the rule for subject-verb agreement in informal English?

_____

_____

What is the rule for subject-verb agreement in formal English?

_____

_____

Figure 8.1. Preliminary Subject-Verb Agreement chart.

Reviewing Subjects and Action Verbs

Ask your students to recall what an action verb is. Most students learn that a verb shows action but are unaware that verbs can also indicate a state of being. Since this lesson focuses on verbs that show action, we label them action verbs. This will help to cut down on the confusion students often have over the *be* verbs (*am, are, is; was, were*). Once your students have determined that action verbs show action, explain that the subject of the sentence is who or what the sentence is about. If this is the first time your students have discussed subjects as they pertain to sentences, you will need to provide an example. You might write *Chelsea carries her books* on the board and explain, "This sentence is about Chelsea. It tells what Chelsea does, so Chelsea is the subject. The word *carries* tells what she does. It shows action, so *carries* is the verb." Underline *Chelsea carries* and say, "Let's look at some other sentences with subjects and verbs to see if we can find a pattern that holds between the subject and the endings on a verb."

Teaching Subject-Verb Agreement: Lesson 1

Uncover one line of the chart at a time and read the two corresponding sentences. For example, you will read *He play ball after school* and then *He plays ball after school*. After you have read all of the sentences, have your students compare and contrast formal and informal agreement. Your students will most likely say that some of the verbs in formal English have an *-s* on the end. If your students say that the right-hand column is "right" and the left-hand column is "wrong," by now you know how to respond. Since the verb form changes inside formal language, concentrate on formal English first.

Discovering the Pattern in Formal Language

To help students understand subject-verb agreement inside formal English, tell them to look closely at the underlined words for a clue as to what the rule might be. If your students still do not see a correlation, you might try a think-aloud by saying, "I wonder what the rule is for using an *-s* on the end of a verb. In the sentence *He plays ball after school*, *he* is the subject. In *My dad cleans the car*, *my dad* (a phrase you can replace with *he*) is the subject. In *Cassidy colors neatly*, *Cassidy*, or *she*, is the subject. What is the subject in the sentence *She walks to school*?" By now your students should be able to determine that the subject is *she*. Ask your students what the subject is in the sentence *The bell rings loudly*. Once students have determined that *the bell* is the subject, you can say, "The word *it* can take the place of *bell* without changing the meaning of the sentence, so we can say that *bell* is an *it*-styled word." Ask your students what they think the rule might be for using an *-s* on the end of a verb. You might need to help them determine that *he/she/it* + verb + *-s* is the rule. Remember to check your rule against the data to make sure it's accurate. You might ask, "In *Cassidy colors neatly*, do we have a *he-*, *she-*, or *it*-type word or phrase?" Then ask, "Do we have a verb + *-s*?" Since we do, that sentence fits the rule. Go through each of the *he/she/it* sentences in this way to make sure each sentence fits the given rule.

Once your students have created a rule for subject-verb agreement with *he/she/it*, guide their attention to the remaining sentences in the contrastive analysis chart. Swords noted that once her students had figured out the *-s* rule for *he/she/it* subjects, they quickly asserted that *-s* was missing with *they*, *we*, *I*, and *you*. Given that the first part of our subject-verb agreement rule specifies that *he/she/it*-styled words take *-s*, we can continue the rule as follows: "otherwise, subject + bare verb." The students then checked each of the remaining sentences to see if the rule (otherwise, subject [*I/you/we/they*] + bare verb) was accurate. Again, invite your students to take the next step: describing what the pattern *is*, not what it is not. Swords's students realized that the verb looked bare, the way it appears when you look up the word in a dictionary. We call this the bare verb or the dictionary form of the verb. So, after determining that the pattern was correct, we wrote the rule—"otherwise, subject + bare verb = agreement." Now that the students have identified the patterns for formal language, direct their attention to the informal language.

What Subject-Verb Agreement Really Means

We are accustomed to thinking that subject-verb agreement is what happens in Standard English. When students say or write *My mom deserve a good job*, we may be tempted to say that the student doesn't know subject-verb agreement or is struggling with it, or that the subject and verb don't agree. Linguistics has a different story to tell. While it is true that this sentence and others like it do not show the Standard English subject-verb agreement, that's quite different from saying that the subject doesn't agree with the verb. It does.

All "agreement" means is that verbs show a particular ending or shape corresponding to a particular person and number of the subject. Thus, formal English shows a particular pattern of verb shape and endings. Informal English shows nearly the same pattern, differing in only one element—third-person singular. They are both predictable, and so both formal and informal English show subject-verb agreement.

Interestingly, the agreement pattern for African American English is the same as that in the languages spoken in many Asian countries (e.g., The People's Republic of China, Taiwan, Hong Kong, Macao, Malaysia, Singapore). According to Ann Raimes in *Keys for Writers*, Chinese does not use word endings to show plurality or tense or verb agreement. Instead,

> [m]ost words in Chinese have just one form, often just one syllable, so changes reflecting number, tense, part of speech, or agree-

ment cause difficulty [when Chinese students are learning to speak and write Standard English]: *"The singer have a big band." (1996, pp. 42–43)

Discovering Subject-Verb Agreement in Informal Language

Your students are now ready to look for the informal subject-verb agreement pattern. Have them read each of the informal sentences in the Subject-Verb Agreement chart (Figure 8.1) aloud with you and ask them what they think the rule might be. Their initial response will most likely be that none of the verbs has an -s on the end.

To help students focus on the pattern, simply say, "Inside formal English, we decided that *he/she/it*-type words take -s, and otherwise, in any other case (*I-, you-, we-*, and *they*-type words), we use a bare verb. What happens when we see a *he/she/it*-type word inside informal English?" At this point, your students should not need any further prompting to see that these subjects in informal English call for a bare verb. Next, we move to the other types of subjects. You can say, "Inside formal English, we saw that all the rest of the types of subject (*I, you, we, they*) took a bare verb. What happens inside informal English?" Swords's students quickly responded to the prompt with, "It's the same!" Since the children had been focusing on the differences between the two language varieties in previous lessons, they were surprised to find that some of the same grammar rules worked in both formal and informal language.

Swords then asked the students to state the rule. You can simply prompt your students by asking what the rule might be for the *he, she,* or *it* subjects. Swords's students exclaimed that the *he/she/it*-type subjects use a bare verb. After checking each single-subject sentence, Swords wrote the rule, "*he/she/it* + bare verb = agreement," on the board. Next, you can direct students to look for the rule for the rest of the subjects. Swords's students were clear that the verb-agreement rule for these subjects in informal English was "*I/you/we/they* + bare verb = agreement," just as it was in formal English. Again, students checked every sentence that contained one of these subjects and a bare verb to verify their claim. Swords wrote this rule on the board.

Then, students noticed that the two rules were the same for informal English—in informal English, all types of subjects use a bare verb. We can capture that generalization in this way: in informal English, agreement = subject + bare verb. Figure 8.2 shows what the final Subject-Verb Agreement chart looks like.

Subject-Verb Agreement

He play ball v. *He plays ball*

Informal English	*Formal English*
I <u>run</u> quickly.	I <u>run</u> quickly.
<u>He play</u> ball after school.	<u>He plays</u> ball after school.
<u>She walk</u> to school.	<u>She walks</u> to school.
<u>My dad clean</u> the car.	<u>My dad cleans</u> the car.
<u>Cassidy color</u> neatly.	<u>Cassidy colors</u> neatly.
<u>We paint</u> in art.	<u>We paint</u> in art.
<u>You sing</u> well.	<u>You sing</u> well.
<u>They sit</u> on the carpet.	<u>They sit</u> on the carpet.

The Patterns

Subject + bare verb	*he/she/it* + **verb + -*s*** **Otherwise:** **Subject (***I/we/you/they***)** **+ bare verb**

Figure 8.2. Regular subject-verb agreement (present tense).

Teaching Subject-Verb Agreement: Lesson 2

The purpose of this lesson is to reemphasize the similarities and differences in formal and informal English subject-verb agreement. You will need to reproduce worksheets like those in Figures 8.3 and 8.4 for each student in the class. We include two versions of the same worksheet for reasons discussed earlier. The first version (Figure 8.3) has students translating from informal to formal and also formal to informal. The second version (Figure 8.4) has students translating only from informal to formal. If your community will follow your lead in translating evenhandedly from informal to formal and formal to informal, we recommend this approach. Please use or amend any remaining worksheets in this fashion to suit your own student population and community needs.

Before you give students their worksheets, take some time to review subject-verb relationships. Using the chart created in lesson 1, cover the rules you created as a class. Read the sentence *He play ball after school* and ask students to identify the subject. Once a child has responded that *he* is the subject, ask the children how they know this. Students should be able to say that the sentence is about what *he* does. Then ask students to find and name the verb.

Directions: Complete the chart below by code-switching the sentences. The first one has been done for you.

Subject-Verb Agreement

Informal English   *Formal English*

Karishma eat pizza for lunch.   Karishma eats pizza for lunch.

The dog wag his tail.   _____

_____   They sing in the choir.

My mom drive to work.   _____

_____   The cat drinks milk.

The school day end at 3:45.   _____

_____   Nico and Taylor sit at that table.

The baby need his mom.   _____

_____   We love to draw in art.

Figure 8.3. Subject-verb translation from both formal to informal and informal to formal English.

Directions: Complete the chart below by code-switching the sentences. The first one has been done for you.

Subject-Verb Agreement

Informal   *Formal*

Karishma eat pizza for lunch.   Karishma eats pizza for lunch.

The dog wag his tail.   _____

They sing in the choir.   _____

My mom drive to work.   _____

The cat drink milk.   _____

The school day end at 3:45.   _____

Nico and Taylor sit at that table.   _____

The baby need his mom.   _____

We love to draw in art.   _____

Figure 8.4. Subject-verb agreement from informal to formal English.

After someone has called out *play*, remind the students that in a previous lesson they came up with one rule for subject-verb agreement inside informal English. Ask a child if he or she remembers the rule. Once someone answers "Subject + bare verb," ask students to check that this example follows the informal English rule for subject-verb agreement. Students can easily verify that it does.

Then ask the children to define the formal English rule for *he/she/it*-type words. A student will surely remember the rule: "*he/she/it* + verb + *-s*." Again, have students check that this rule is correct. Next, ask students if they remember the formal subject-verb agreement rule that holds in all other cases. Someone should recall that the rule is "otherwise, subject (*I/you/we/they*-type words) + bare verb." Explain that students are going to be completing a chart on their own today. Give each student a copy of the worksheet to complete in pairs or small groups.

Teaching *Was/Were* Patterns for Subject-Verb Agreement

Although subject-verb agreement may seem relatively simple to teach, it can become tricky once the *be* verbs are introduced. In the rules for agreement laid out in the previous two lessons, there was significant overlap between informal English rules and those for formal English: all subjects in informal English and the majority of subjects inside formal English (*I, we, you, they*) all call for the same verb form—the bare verb. Not so for *was/were*. This can be confusing for children and adults alike, because the rules seem to have changed. As you might recall, however, we defined the verbs in the previous lesson as action verbs. We did not introduce the *be* verbs at that time. We did that intentionally to keep matters simple initially.

Lesson 1: *Was/Were*

Once again, we begin by creating a chart comparing and contrasting formal and informal language (see Figure 8.5). We label this chart *Was/Were* Patterns. We do not want to call it Subject-Verb Agreement, because we have already created a chart with that title. Don't forget to make copies of the chart for each student. We will hand out these charts at the end of the lesson so that students will have a copy in their code-switching notebooks.

Following the steps we have established, read each line of the chart to your students. Ask them what patterns they see for *was* and *were* in the sentences you read. Your students will probably respond by saying that the informal uses only *was* and the formal uses *was* and *were*. Of course, we want the students to get more specific than that in describing the rules. To do so, begin with formal language because there the verb differs according to the different persons and numbers of the subject.

Directions: Write one more informal and one more formal sentence that include *was/were* patterns. Then answer the questions below.

Was/Were Patterns

Informal English	*Formal English*
<u>I was</u> sleeping.	<u>I was</u> sleeping.
<u>The dog was</u> sleeping.	<u>The dog was</u> sleeping.
<u>She was</u> sleeping.	<u>She was</u> sleeping.
<u>Nico was</u> sleeping.	<u>Nico was</u> sleeping.
<u>We was</u> sleeping.	<u>We were</u> sleeping.
<u>You was</u> sleeping.	<u>You were</u> sleeping.
<u>The girls was</u> sleeping.	<u>The girls were</u> sleeping.
<u>They was</u> sleeping.	<u>They were</u> sleeping.

_____.   _____.

What is the rule for using *was* or *were* in informal English?
_____

What is the rule for using *was* or *were* in formal English?
_____

Figure 8.5. Initial *Was/Were* Patterns chart.

Discovering the *Was/Were* Pattern in Formal Language

Tell your students that you will be focusing on the rule for using *was* inside formal language. Remind them that the last language lesson was about how subjects and verbs work together. You might say, "I wonder if the subject has anything to do with the *was/were* patterns. On our Subject-Verb Agreement chart, we noticed that certain subjects used the same type of verb. Let's look at the underlined parts of the sentences that use *was*." Read the sentences that include *was* aloud to your students and then ask, "Do you notice anything about the subjects in these sentences?" Since your students recently discussed the topic of subjects in a sentence, they will most likely be able to answer that the subjects included *I*, *he*, *she*, and *it*. Once you've gotten this far, ask your students if they can create a rule about when to use *was*. Swords found that her students were quick to establish the rule as "*I/he/she/it* + *was*." Don't forget to have the students check each sentence to make sure the rule is accurate.

After your class has tested their hypothesis and found that it correctly describes the data, have your students look at sentences with *were*.

Swords's students did not need additional prompting to determine that all the rest of the subjects occurred with *were*. Therefore, the rule was "otherwise, *we/you/they + were*."

Discovering the *Was/Were* Pattern in Informal Language

Now that you have created rules for formal language, turn your attention to the informal sentences. Begin by asking the students if they can come up with some rules for using *was* or *were* in informal language. It is important that students do not simply conclude that the rule for informal English is "always use *was*." While *were* is not used in informal language, you still want students to recognize the existence of a relationship between *was* and the subject. You might say, "You're right, *was* is used in every sentence. However, we made rules about the different subjects in formal language, so we need to check sentences in informal language in the same way. Inside formal language, we saw that *was* goes with *I*, *he*, *she*, and *it*. What happens when we have one of these subjects in informal language?" Now that you have directed the students' attention to the subject, they will quickly determine the pattern to be "*I/he/she/it + was*," just as in formal language. Again, have students check the rule, sentence by sentence.

Then ask students what happens in the other cases. By this time, students, quite accustomed to the process, will probably be able to state that the rule is "*we/you/they + was*." Then ask your students if they see anything the two informal grammar rules have in common (*I/he/she/it + was*; *we/you/they + was*). Perhaps they will find that all subjects occur with *was*. Just as we can reduce fractions to the lowest common denominator ($2/6 = 1/3$), we can reduce our grammar rules. We reduce our grammar rules to show this generalization: any subject + *was*. After checking the rule for accuracy, you might then affirm the students' initial response that, yes, the pattern is *was* for all types of subjects. You can then give each student his or her individual copy of the chart. Have the students complete the chart in pairs or small groups while you circulate throughout the room to check for understanding.

The final *was/were* chart looks like the one in Figure 8.6.

Reviewing *Was/Were*

This lesson reviews the *was/were* pattern. You will need to make copies of the worksheet on page 113 before teaching this lesson. Begin by asking the students to recall the rules for using *was* and *were* inside formal language. They should be able to state that *was* is used with *I/he/she/it*,

---

Was/Were Patterns

We was late v. We were late

Informal English	*Formal English*
<u>I was</u> sleeping.	<u>I was</u> sleeping.
<u>The dog was</u> sleeping.	<u>The dog was</u> sleeping.
<u>She was</u> sleeping.	<u>She was</u> sleeping.
<u>Nico was</u> sleeping.	<u>Nico was</u> sleeping.
<u>We was</u> sleeping.	<u>We were</u> sleeping.
<u>You was</u> sleeping.	<u>You were</u> sleeping.
<u>The girls was</u> sleeping.	<u>The girls were</u> sleeping.
<u>They was</u> sleeping.	<u>They were</u> sleeping.

The Patterns

Any subject + *was*   ***I/he/she/it* + *was***
                                                    Otherwise: *we/you/they* + *were*

Figure 8.6. The *was/were* patterns.

and *were* is used with all other types of subjects (*we/you/they*). Have several students provide examples of sentences that use *was* and *were*. As before, once a child has given an example, ask the student how it follows the rule. Some students might note that some examples look the same in both formal and informal English. Affirm these observations, because your students are absolutely right. Informal English has its own paradigm for how verbs agree with subjects, and formal English has its own paradigm for how verbs agree with subjects. There's just some overlap between the two.

After students have given several examples for formal language, have them define the rules for informal language. Remember to help them address the relationship between *was* and the subject by having them state that any subject (*I/he/she/it/we/you/they*) occurs with *was*. Have your students provide sample sentences, and then have them talk about the rule they're following. Allow students to give a few examples before showing them the worksheet on page 113. Tell your students that they will be using the sentences in the boxes to create a chart much like the one they used in the previous lesson. Have the students complete the worksheet on their own or in small groups.

Was/Were

Directions: Cut out the sentences below. Read each sentence carefully. Highlight the subject and *was* or *were* in each sentence, and paste the sentence under the correct heading. Use the blank boxes to write your own formal and informal sentences.

Informal English   *Formal English*

What time was you leaving?	I was the first person in line.	They were running in the hall.
The children was washing their hands.	The children were washing their hands.	What time were you leaving?
Was Rennie reading that book?	They was running in the hall.	Was Rennie reading that book?
	I was the first person in line.	

Use these boxes to write one formal and one informal sentence.

Teaching *Is* and *Are* Patterns

You will probably find that *is/are* patterns are fairly simple to teach. This is because, with the exception of *I*, the patterns are quite similar to those found with *was/were*. We need to add one cautionary note about *is/are* in informal English. As a quick glance at various African American English grammar resources will show (Green, 2002; Pullum, 1999; Rickford, 1999a, 1999b), the verb system in this language variety is complex. In particular, regarding the verb *be*, we find a range of nuanced uses. Thus, in the example in Chapter 2 in which the teacher asked a student, "What does your mother do every day?" the student answered, "She be at home," drawing a clear distinction between that and "She is at home." The two utterances carry a different grammatical meaning: *be at home* means that she is routinely at home, whereas *is at home* carries the grammatical meaning of being at home at that very moment. The former is called "habitual *be*," a construction we will explore in detail later. One of the many other uses of *be* in AAE is its selective absence from a sentence (*He fine*). Thus, according to Pullum, when "the copula [the verb *be*] is present tense, not first person, not accented, not negative, and not expressing the habitual or the remote present perfect . . . [it can] be omitted in AAVE speech" (1999, p. 46).

So AAE grammar has very specific rules about when *be* is present and when it's absent. As you explore *is/are* patterns with your students, you'll want to look at the patterns when *be* is present—in emphatic, present-tense sentences (Green, 2002, p. 37). In what follows, we draw on Green's verb paradigm for emphatic, affirmed uses of *be* (*I am tall*; *he, she, it, we, you, they is tall*). She indicates the emphatic intonation in these sentences by all capitals in the verb, but since we are working with elementary students, leave the verbs lowercase so as not to confuse them about capitalization.

Lesson 1: *Is/Are*

In this lesson, you will explore *is* and *are* (instances of the verb *be*) followed by an adjective. If you find examples like those in Figure 8.7 in your students' writing, use them, but if not, use the constructed data set we've provided here. We use simple or constructed data at this point because the grammar of the AAE verb string is so intricate that if you choose your own sentences with *be* you may make a mistake inside AAE or inadvertently stumble into a different verb pattern (see Green, 2002, pp. 36–38). Remember to make copies of the chart in Figure 8.7 for each student to add to his or her code-switching notebook. Don't forget to recreate the chart on chart paper to use during the lesson.

Directions: Write one more informal and one more formal sentence that include formal and informal *be*. Then answer the questions below.

Is/Are Patterns

Informal English	*Formal English*
<u>I am</u> tall.	<u>I am</u> tall.
<u>You is</u> tall.	<u>You are</u> tall.
<u>Jaden is</u> tall.	<u>Jaden is</u> tall.
<u>We is</u> tall.	<u>We are</u> tall.
<u>You is</u> tall.	<u>You are</u> tall.
<u>They is</u> tall.	<u>They are</u> tall.

What are the patterns for using *is* or *are* in informal English?

_____

What are the patterns for using *is* or *are* in formal English?

_____

_____

When do we use *am* in formal and informal English?

_____

Figure 8.7. Initial *Is/Are* Patterns chart.

Since this is our third lesson on subject-verb agreement, begin with a short review and then allow the students to work in small groups to define the *is/are* patterns.

Discovering *Is/Are* Patterns in Informal and Formal Language

Explain to the students that today they are going to be discovering the rules for using *is* and *are* in both formal and informal language. Since they have spent so much time working with subject-verb relationships, you are going to shift the responsibility for defining these patterns from the teacher to the students. Rather than prompting students to discover rules, you are going to allow the students to discover the rules in small groups on their own. Give each student a copy of the worksheet and divide the class into pairs or groups of three. Explain that instead of discussing the rules as a class and then filling out the worksheets, they will do the op-

Is/Are Patterns

You is v. You are

Informal English	*Formal English*
<u>I am</u> tall.	<u>I am</u> tall.
<u>Jaden is</u> tall.	<u>Jaden is</u> tall.
<u>We is</u> tall.	<u>We are</u> tall.
<u>You is</u> tall.	<u>You are</u> tall.
<u>They is</u> tall.	<u>They are</u> tall.

The Patterns

I + am **Otherwise, any subject + *is***	*I + am* *he/she/it + is* **Otherwise, any subject + *are***

Figure 8.8. The *is/are* patterns.

posite. The students will be doing the worksheets first and then the class will discuss the rules.

Remind the students that the subject of the sentence is very important and that they will need to use the subject as part of their rule. You might say, "Remember when we discovered that only certain subjects use *was* in formal language? Today we will need to look for which subjects occur with *is*, *are*, or *am*." As the children work in their groups to define the rules, you will need to circulate throughout the classroom, prompting those students who are having difficulty. Make sure your students are checking for the relationship between subject and verb in both formal and informal patterns. If one rule for formal language is "*he/she/it + is*," for example, students should check to see what particular form of verb occurs with these third-person singular subjects (*he/she/it*) in informal English. Students will find that while *he/she/it* words occur with their own verb type, informal English shows different patterning. Students will discover the grammar rules as they systematically seek patterns in what kind of verb goes with what kind of subject.

Give the students ample time to complete the worksheet. When most of the groups have finished the activity, have the entire class reconvene to discuss the rules they created in their groups. Once a student gives a rule, help the rest of the students check the rule against the data. Be sure to have your students watch for exceptions to the rules. See Figure 8.8 for the final *is/are* chart for emphatic *be*.

Lesson 2: *Is/Are*

As with all new concepts, it is important to give students the opportunity to apply their new knowledge. This lesson is used as a review of the *is/are* pattern. Before beginning this lesson, make copies of the worksheet on the next page.

Review the *is/are* pattern by asking students to recall one of the rules they created for formal language and having them check it against sample sentences, using the earlier chart as an anchor for their discussion. Since they have used worksheets similar to the one on page 120 in several lessons, your students will likely feel comfortable completing it with relatively few directions. They can complete the worksheet independently or in small groups.

Reviewing Subject-Verb Agreement

By now, you have spent a substantial amount of time teaching various patterns of subject-verb agreement, and it is important to take time to review all of the rules you have created. We don't recommend going over specific examples of each of the rules, as that would take too much time, and you want students to be alert and interested in the activity you are going to do. First, make several copies of the following set of sentences.

Adam and Karishma is reading a story.

Those three dogs bark every night.

We are going to the circus on Friday.

I listen to the radio on my way to school.

Rena was the tallest girl in the school last year.

The caterpillar turn into a butterfly.

Tiaunna and Bianca was in a parade on Saturday.

The frog's legs are very long.

Joshua's eyes is brown.

We is learning about spiders in science.

Is Cassidy going on the field trip tomorrow?

What time are we going to lunch?

The parking lot is full of cars.

Chris sweep the floor at the end of the day.

Juwan kicks the ball over the fence.

We eat our lunch in the cafeteria.

Rennie practice the piano every night.

I am going to my grandmother's house this summer.

The sun is shining in my eyes.

Sometimes it snow in the winter.

Tyler leads the class to the gym.

My mom drives me to school every morning.

Then, using chart paper, make several copies of charts with headers like these:

Formal Language	Informal Language	Both

Before revealing any of the charts, remind the students that some of the rules they described for both formal and informal language were the same. Have several students recall these rules. When we use action verbs, for example, the rule "*I + am*" is true for both formal and informal language.

Once you have reviewed the similarities between the two language varieties, show the students the empty chart and the page of sentences. Explain that they will be working in groups to fill in the chart. Tell the students that they will need to cut out the sentence strips and, as a team, decide which category each sentence best fits in. You will need to circulate throughout the room while the children work and ask about their reasons for putting particular sentences in certain categories. Except for *was/were*, assume all these examples are in present tense.

Directions: Cut out the sentences below. Read each sentence carefully. Highlight the subject and *is* or *are* in each sentence, and paste the sentence under the correct heading. Use the blank boxes to write your own formal and informal sentences.

Is/Are Patterns

Informal English   *Formal English*

All the crayons are broken.	Tyler is my best friend.	My dog is black and brown.
The birds are sitting in the tree.	The birds is sitting in the tree.	Tyler is my best friend.
All the crayons is broken.	My dog is black and brown.	

Use these boxes to write one formal and one informal sentence.

9 Teaching Past Time

After spending several weeks working with subject-verb agreement patterns, we now focus on showing past time. As usual, we begin by collecting and analyzing data that show students expressing past time in their writing. Let's look at the following set of data from two different students:

Student A

1. a. Yesterday my mom walk to the store.

   b. Last Christmas I wrap all my own present.

   c. I paint two picture when we was at art.

   d. I learn all about spiders in first grade.

Student B

2. a. My dad worked at the shipyard last year.

   b. The baby cried all night.

   c. I played basketball every day this summer.

   d. Mr. Steve cleaned all the classrooms.

Discovering Patterns for Past Time

Our job, as always, is to figure out the grammar in student language. In this case, how do sentences 1a–d show that an action happened in the past? A glance at these examples reveals that the student uses words or phrases to locate the action in the past: *yesterday*, *last Christmas*, and *was*. Sentence 1d indicates past time in a slightly different fashion—through common knowledge. Because Swords's students are second or third graders, it's clear that first grade was in the past. In this way, we say that example 1d shows past time through background knowledge or common knowledge.

As teachers, we now turn our attention to the sentences in example 2 to see how that student signals past time. We see that sometimes the student uses words or phrases conveying an adverbial meaning (*last year*), and other times the only indication of the event being past is the shape of the verb (*was*) or its ending (*-ed*). In other words, on analyzing all of the examples, we discover that both students have a clear understanding of how to express past actions. Now that we can see the patterns used in both informal (Student A) and formal (Student B) English, we need to help our students embrace and define these patterns.

Teaching Time/Tense Contrasts

As always, begin by collecting student data, with one focal pattern per sentence—the verb. In addition to creating your chart on chart paper, make paper copies of the chart in Figure 9.1 for the students to add to their personal code-switching notebooks.

Begin this lesson by reviewing the definition of *action verbs*. Your students will likely respond that action verbs show action. Since we want students to go beyond simple recall, have several students give examples (e.g., *run*, *play*, and *laugh*). Explain to the students that they will be learning about how to show past actions in both informal and formal language. Write the word *past* on the board and ask the students what it means. Your students will probably say that *past* means something that has already happened. Verify this by saying, "Yes, when we talk about something happening in the past, we mean that it has already happened. Today we are going to look at how we can show actions that have already happened in both formal and informal language."

Reveal the chart and read each sentence aloud. This is important because, as we discussed in previous lessons, people tend to read what they would speak rather than what is written. While a sentence might read *We walked to the store*, an informal speaker might well read *We walk to the store*. We want students to become aware of the *-ed* that often signals past time inside formal English.

Discovering the Informal Pattern for Showing Past Time

After reading each sentence, have students focus on the informal sentences, and ask how they know the action has already happened. You might say, "The title of the chart is Showing Past Time. Let's look at the first sentence, *Yesterday they play in the park*. How do we know that the action is in the past? How do we know they're not playing in the park right now?" The students, who by now are accustomed to carefully examining sentence structures, should be able to explain that the word *yesterday* defines a time that is past. Once students have identified the importance of the word *yesterday*, circle it on the chart. Discuss each sentence with your students in this way, circling the words that the students say indicate past time. After the students have discussed each sentence, read the words they determined show time (*yesterday*, *this morning*, *last Saturday*, and *two days ago*).

You might then say, "Look at each of these sentences again, focusing on the words we circled. What rule can we write about showing past time in informal language?" Rather than responding with a single rule,

---

Directions: Write one more informal and one more formal sentence that include the pattern below. Then answer the questions below.

Showing Past Time

Informal English

Yesterday they <u>play</u> in the park.

She <u>mail</u> the letter this morning.

Last Saturday we <u>watch</u> that movie.

I <u>call</u> my grandma two days ago.

Martin Luther King <u>talk</u> to his people.

Formal English

Yesterday they <u>played</u> in the park.

She <u>mailed</u> the letter this morning.

Last Saturday we <u>watched</u> that movie.

I <u>called</u> my grandma two days ago.

Martin Luther King <u>talked</u> to his people.

_____   _____

_____   _____

What is the rule or rules for showing past time in informal English?

_____

_____

What is the rule or rules for showing past time in formal English?

_____

_____

Figure 9.1. Initial Showing Past Time chart.

your students will probably repeat each of the words that are circled on the chart. You can then say, "Oh, so you're saying that there are *other words in the sentence* that tell us something happened in the past. This reminds me of the pattern we use with informal plurals. We always have to look for clues or signal words in the sentence. It's a good thing we're such careful readers."

Perhaps you have talked to your students about adverbs and phrases that do an adverb-like job—in these examples, we have noun phrases (*yesterday, this morning, last Saturday*, etc.) that are doing adverb-like jobs of telling us about time.

Now that your students have orally identified the main rule for showing past time inside informal English, you will need to write the rule on the chart paper under informal English. There's one more step—bringing in how we can recognize past time through common knowledge.

Notice that the last sentence under the informal column, *Martin Luther King talk to his people*, does not use any adverbials to show past time, and yet we know the sentence refers to past time. How does that work? Ask your students. They will likely say that everybody knows Dr. King lived in the past. Praise their clear understanding! "Yes, you're exactly right. We know this sentence refers to past time because of our common knowledge. We all know that Dr. King lived in a past time, so it's our common knowledge that signals past time." In this way, you have two rules for showing past time inside informal English: other words (clue words) in the sentence and common knowledge show past time.

Discovering the Formal Pattern for Showing Past Time

Next, turn your attention to the formal pattern. Read the first sentence, *Yesterday they played in the park*, and ask the students how the sentence differs from its informal counterpart. Your students will probably notice the addition of the *-ed* on the end of *play*. Once they've noted the *-ed*, you can lead your students in an exploration of the additional sentences to see if they all contain a verb with that ending. Then have the students determine the rule for formal language: "verb + *-ed* = past actions." Once your students have identified the patterns for both formal and informal past time, have them work individually or in small groups to complete the worksheet.

Reviewing Past Time in Informal and Formal English

In this lesson, students have an opportunity to review the rules for past actions and apply these rules in their translations of various sentences. Before the lesson, make copies of the sheet on page 125 for students to complete on their own. As before, you may choose to have students translate back and forth between formal and informal or you may choose to have them go only in the direction of informal → formal.

Begin the lesson by asking students to recall the rules for showing past time in informal English. Since you want to treat both language varieties equally, now turn your attention to formal English. Ask the students to recall the rule for showing formal past time. After several students give examples and the class identifies the pattern in each sentence, give the students the worksheets. They should be familiar with this activity. Have the students work individually or in groups to finish the assignment.

Directions: Complete the chart below by code-switching the given sentences. The first one has been done for you.

Past Actions

Informal English

Formal English

My mom walk me to school this morning.

My mom walked me to school this morning.

I finish all my work yesterday.

_____

_____

We watched that movie last Saturday.

My mom shop there before.

_____

_____

We listened to a good story on Monday.

_____

Remember that day we raced home?

Last year our hamster escape from the cage.

_____

_____

I picked a flower on my way to school.

10 Teaching *Gonna/Going to*

So far we have introduced our students to grammatical patterns involving verbs and nouns. And so far, the grammar patterns we've treated have been patterns in African American English. But as we said in Chapter 1, the principles and techniques we explore apply equally when any student, from any walk of life, speaks (and writes) something other than the school's target language variety—formal Standard English. The pattern we talk about in this short chapter—*gonna* versus *going to*—is a contrast found across many dialects. Indeed, it's found in the fast speech versus slow speech of most speakers. As a teacher, you might have noticed that the words *gonna* and *wanna* crop up quite often in your students' writing. This is because students write the way the words sound when they talk. We explore *gonna* in this chapter and then leave it to the reader to extend our treatment to *wanna*.

Finding the Pattern: *Gonna*

Since many students use *gonna* when speaking, this usage transfers into their writing—until they learn the conventions of formal written English. Swords found that many of her students did not make a connection between *gonna* and *going to* before she taught it. But before we can teach the patterns, we must have a clear understanding ourselves about how this pattern works. Let's suppose you had collected the following sample sentences:

1. a. She was gonna call me last night.
   b. I'm gonna write a story.
   c. They gonna move to Miami.
   d. That cat gonna have babies.

In examples 1a–d, the informal *gonna* translates to *going to* in formal English. (Note that there are some complexities about the presence or absence of the verb *be* in 1c and 1d that we treat in a later chapter. For now, we focus only on *gonna*.) This might lead one to believe that *gonna* equals *going to*. Let's suppose, however, the data also included these sentences:

2. a. My dad is going to North Carolina.
   b. Are we going to the zoo?
   c. I am going to my grandma's house.

In sentences 2a–c, *going to* is not the formal equivalent of *gonna*. There-fore, while *gonna* is always translated to *going to*, the reverse does not hold true. We would not say "My dad is gonna North Carolina," because that does not follow any grammar pattern in any variety of English. Why would we say "I'm gonna write a story" but not *"I'm gonna North Caro-lina"?[1] Here's where linguistics helps us out. We can say "I'm gonna" when the *to* is part of a verb—for example, *to write*—but we cannot say *gonna* when the *to* is part of a prepositional phrase, as in "I'm going to North Carolina." It's an example of how we all command the grammar of our language at an unconscious level. Nobody ever taught us "Now, don't say *gonna* when *to* is part of a prepositional phrase." Nobody taught us because neither our teachers nor our parents were likely to have ever consciously noticed it. But we somehow know it anyway—that's part of what linguists mean when they say that our knowledge of language is largely unconscious.

At any rate, the only data we need to be concerned about in our classroom is what the students actually say or write, since we're helping them springboard from the informal language they do use to the formal language often required by the schools and the business world. So our descriptive job is rather simple.

Lesson 1: *Gonna/Going to*

In keeping with our trend of requiring students to be more responsible for identifying and defining the patterns of both formal and informal language, this time we allow the students to determine which informa-tion is important enough to be underlined. We also ask the students to name the chart at the end of the lesson. As usual, begin by collecting stu-dent writing data. Be sure to isolate the *gonna/going to* pattern by trans-lating any other informal patterns into formal English. Then use the data to create a wall chart on chart paper (see Figure 10.1). As with all of the previous lessons, students should keep a copy of the chart in their code-switching notebooks.

Discovering and Naming the Patterns: *Gonna* v. *Going to*

Begin by explaining to the students that they are going to decide which information is important enough to be underlined. Also tell them that they will choose the title after they have defined the patterns. Since you want students to pay close attention to each word in each sentence, slowly read each pair of corresponding sentences in the chart. After you have read all the sentences aloud, reread the first two sentences and then ask

Directions: Write two more informal and two more formal sentences that include the pattern below. Then answer the questions below.

_____

Informal English	*Formal English*
I'm gonna play basketball.	I'm going to play basketball.
Are you gonna drink that milk?	Are you going to drink that milk?
Palermo was gonna use that pencil.	Palermo was going to use that pencil.
What time are we gonna leave?	What time are we going to leave?
They were gonna walk to school.	They were going to walk to school.

_____   _____

_____   _____

What is the rule used in informal English?

_____

What is the rule used in formal English?

_____

Figure 10.1. Initial *Gonna/Going to* chart.

the children to identify any differences. It is important to help the students realize that *gonna* is the informal equivalent of *going to*, not just *going*. For example, the sentences *Are you gonna go away this summer?* and *Are you going to go away this summer?* are comparable. However, *Are you going away this summer?* does not translate to *Are you gonna away this summer?* Students who are just learning formal language will easily make this mistake as they begin to consciously analyze the patterns. For this reason, take them through a word-by-word comparison of the sentences in the chart.

Once you have read each sentence, ask the students where they see differences between the formal and informal sentences. Begin by looking at the first two sentences. Reread each sentence, *I'm gonna play basketball* and *I'm going to play basketball*. Ask the children how the sentences differ. They will most likely respond that the informal sentence uses *gonna* and the formal sentence uses *going*. Since students tend to look for a one-to-one correspondence, they probably will not see that *gonna* translates as *going to*. This is easy to deal with. Simply say, "Let's check to make sure that's the only difference. The informal sentence starts with *I'm*. Does the formal sentence start with *I'm*?" Your students will nod, and you can proceed to the next word: "The informal sentence continues with *gonna*. What is in the formal sentence?" The answer is *going*. Continue by noting that the informal next says *play*. Ask what the next word in the formal sentence is. Children will see that the next word is *to*. In this way, you can lead students to discover that *gonna* translates as *going to*. By comparing each word, one at a time, you can lead the students to discover the patterns for themselves. This is much more powerful than simply telling the students about the patterns, because they are able to take ownership of their own learning. Having your students check each sentence word by word emphasizes the consistency involved in patterns.

After the class has examined each sentence and you have underlined the differences, it is time to have the students create the rules that define these differences. In this case, the patterns are simply "informal = *gonna*" and "formal = *going to*." Write these rules under the corresponding section of the chart, and then have several different children give examples of sentences using the defined patterns. After each example, have another child translate the sentence using the corresponding pattern. Devonne might say, "When are you gonna finish that work?" Ask the students what pattern Devonne used, formal or informal. Once the students have determined that the sentence is informal, have another student give the formal translation. Thus, Chelsea might say, "When are you going to finish that work?" Now that they have an understanding of the pattern, have the students create a name for the chart, such as Using *Going to* and *Gonna* or *Gonna/Going to*. After the children have given several examples, have them work independently or in small groups to complete the worksheet.

Lesson 2: Reviewing *Gonna/Going to*

The purpose of this lesson is simply to reinforce what was taught in lesson 1. You will need to make copies of the worksheet on page 131 before the lesson. Begin with a brief review of the rules for *gonna* and *going to*.

Ask students to volunteer sample sentences using either *gonna* or *going to*. After each sentence, have the other students signal whether the sentence is formal or informal. This can be done in the whole group by having the students hold their hands palm up for informal and palm down for formal. You can also use thumbs up and thumbs to the side. We do not recommend using thumbs down because this gesture is generally negative, and we do not want the children to feel that one language variety is less preferred. Thus, if Chelsea gives the example *I'm gonna be a cheerleader*, the other students would silently use palms up or thumbs up to show that they understand *gonna* is informal. This is also a quick way to check the status of the class to determine whether your students are having difficulty understanding *gonna* and *going to*. After students have given several formal and informal sentences, give them the worksheet on page 131 to complete individually or in small groups.

Note

1. Linguists use an asterisk to signal that a sentence is ungrammatical or otherwise structurally ill-formed. Thus, "I'm gonna North Carolina" is not an English sentence; it does not follow the rules of grammar for any variety of English.

Directions: Complete the chart below by code-switching the given sentences. The first one has been done for you.

Gonna/Going to

Informal

Are we gonna eat breakfast?

Are you gonna finish that book?

_____

My uncle is gonna pick me up.

_____

Is the school gonna close early tomorrow?

_____

I'm gonna sing in the concert.

_____

Formal

Are we going to eat breakfast?

_____

We were going to visit the zoo.

_____

Is the baby going to cry all night?

_____

The boys are going to eat lunch now.

_____

Josh is going to be a great artist.

11 Code-Switching with More Complex Patterns

We have now spent a significant amount of time teaching students individual formal and informal grammatical patterns. In order to teach these language differences, we have selected patterns that have a simple, direct, one-to-one correspondence between formal and informal language. In a simple connection, one meaning (e.g., possession) is signaled by one syntactic pattern in each language variety (e.g., for formal language, "possession = owner + apostrophe + -s + owned," and in informal language, "possession = owner + owned"). Thus, translation between formal and informal is fairly straightforward. Additionally, so far we have methodically simplified students' everyday sentences to show only one grammatical pattern at a time.

But actual sentences are not so simple in student speech or writing. If we take a close look at informal expression, we find that multiple informal grammatical patterns often exist within a single sentence. Some of these informal patterns are easily translated into formal language, while others are more complex. In this chapter, we discuss these more complex patterns as well as how to help children translate sentences that contain multiple patterns.

Multiple Patterns in a Single Sentence

Before you begin looking at multiple patterns within a single sentence, you will need to quickly scan the major patterns already covered. Without referring to the charts you have made, ask your students to name the patterns they have learned about (i.e., possession, plural, subject-verb agreement, showing past time, *is/are*, *was/were*, and *gonna/going to*). If your students are unable to name all of the patterns, have them look at the charts to find which ones they missed.

Once the students have reviewed the patterns explored so far, you are ready to help your students discover and translate multiple patterns in sentences. Write a sentence like the one below on a piece of chart paper.

Informal Sentence: All of my dad friend was at the party.

Ask your students if they see in this sentence any of the informal patterns they have studied. Some of the children may be confused because they are looking for a single pattern but instead see several patterns (possessive, plural, and *was/were*). Tell your students the sentence has more than one informal pattern. One student might say that he sees the informal possessive pattern, while another will find the informal plural pattern in the sentence. You can prompt your students if they do not find all of the patterns by saying something like, "There's one more. Does anybody see it?" A student might then recognize that the *was/were* pattern is also used. When students have identified all the patterns, you can make an observation about the sentence such as, "Wow, this sentence has three patterns. All of the other sentences we have talked about only had one. Since this sentence has more patterns, it's going to be a little more difficult to translate to formal English. Let's see if we can change this sentence from informal to formal."

Have the students focus on one pattern at a time as they change the sentence from informal to formal. Begin by rereading the sentence and having the students determine which pattern to address first. You might refer to the students who named the patterns initially: "Bobby mentioned that he saw the informal possessive pattern. Who can tell us where that pattern is?" Select a student to explain that the pattern is found in the words *my dad friend*. Have the students translate this portion of the sentence to formal language (*my dad's friend*). Continue discussing and translating each pattern until the class has rewritten the entire sentence in formal language.

Formal Translation: All of my dad's friends were at the party.

Explain to the students that many sentences contain more than one pattern; then translate several more sentences as a class. Let's use the following sentence:

Informal Sentence: David and Devante was best friend last year.

To translate this sentence to formal English, the students must be able to identify two patterns (*was/were* and plural). Once they have determined the informal patterns, the students can translate the sentence into the following formal sentence:

Formal Translation: David and Devante were best friends last year.

You might also use the following sentence:

Informal Sentence: My sister dog like to walk in the park.

In this example, the students would need to identify two patterns (possessive and subject-verb agreement). Thus, the translation of the sentence would be:

Formal Translation: My sister's dog likes to walk in the park.

After the students have practiced translating sentences as a class, they can work in pairs or individually to complete a worksheet like the one in Figure 11.1 to demonstrate their understanding of multiple patterns. This concept should not be difficult, because the students are combining knowledge they already have rather than learning something new. You will note that we have used a new pattern in this worksheet—*got* versus *have*. Although we have not covered this in previous chapters, the pattern is simple enough (and frequent enough) that you could challenge your students to create code-switching materials (wall charts and charts for their code-switching notebooks) for the *got/have* pattern. The answer key is provided in Figure 11.2.

One-Many Relation between Form and Meaning

Habitual *Be*

Let's examine a more complex pattern from African American English—"habitual *be*." We treated this in Chapter 2. Now we'll see how to help children learn to springboard between habitual *be* and formal English equivalents.

Directions: Change each informal sentence to formal. Write your answer on the line under each informal sentence.

1. When is we gonna finish our art project?

   Answer: _____

2. I got two dog whose name is Kasey and Jake.

   Answer: _____

3. My friend dad like to play basketball.

   Answer: _____

4. Is Shannon and Heather gonna go play today?

   Answer: _____

Figure 11.1. A multiple-pattern worksheet.

Informal Sentence: She be teachin' math in the afternoon.

Look at the meaning associated with this grammatical pattern. When speakers say, "I be playing" (or "I be singing," "be watching," etc.), they indicate—through their grammar—that they are usually, frequently, or habitually doing that action. Linguists call this form "habitual *be*."

Teaching Habitual *Be*

Make your contrastive analysis chart using examples from your students' writing. After Figure 11.2, you'll find some samples to help you.

Answer Key and Explanation of Steps to Translation

1. When is we gonna finish our art project?
Answer: When **are we going to** finish our art project?

Patterns	Informal Structure	Formal Translation
is/are	is we	are we
gonna/going to	gonna	going to

2. I got two dog whose name is Kasey and Jake.
Answer: I **have two dogs whose names are** Kasey and Jake.

Patterns	Informal Structure	Formal Translation
got/have	got	have
Plural	two dog whose name	two dogs whose names
is/are	names is	names are

3. My friend dad like to play basketball.
Answer: My **friend's dad likes** to play basketball.

Patterns	Informal Structure	Formal Translation
Possessive	friend dad	friend's dad
Subject/Verb Agreement	dad like	dad likes

4. Is Shannon and Heather gonna go play today?
Answer: **Are Shannon and Heather going to** go play today?

Patterns	Informal Structure	Formal Translation
is/are	Is Shannon and Heather	Are Shannon and Heather
gonna/going to	gonna	going to

Figure 11.2. Answer key and translation explanation of multiple patterns.

Habitual *Be*
He be walking to school in the morning.
She be at work.
They be best friends.
Y'all be playing.

Begin by showing this list to students and explaining that they will be exploring a new pattern. After reading each of the sentences, have students hypothesize about the rules at work in them. Your students will likely say that *be* can be translated into formal English as *is* or *are*, but we will see this is not accurate. To help students better understand the pattern, present the following chart:

Habitual *Be*	
Informal	*Formal*
Kim <u>be talking</u> during math, but today she was very quiet.	Kim <u>is usually/always</u> talking during math, but today she was very quiet.

Lead the students in discovering that *be* in informal English says more than just *is/am/are*—it signals that the activity or state is usually going on. Now return to the first list of *be* examples and ask students to translate the sentences into formal English. Ask the students if the *is/are* translation works in the last sentence. Your students should realize that their original hypothesis is not correct—*Y'all are playing* is not a translation of *Y'all be playing*. To translate *Y'all be playing* into formal English, we need to add a word that shows habitual action, as in the following alternatives:

Informal Language	*Formal Language*
Y'all <u>be playing</u>.	You are <u>usually</u> playing. You are <u>always</u> playing. You are <u>typically</u> playing.

We want our students to understand why we call the pattern habitual *be*. To help students understand this concept, you might do a think-aloud: "A habit is something that you do frequently. For example, if you are in the habit of eating a snack when you get home from school, then you usually or frequently eat a snack after school. *Habitual* means frequently, consistently, or usually. So *habitual* is the label we use for the things that are or happen on a regular basis." You can then have your students share things they do on a regular basis in the form of an informal sentence. Begin by giving an example of your own, such as *I be getting to work at 7:30 in the morning*. Explain that you would use the habitual *be* in this informal sentence since you usually get to work at 7:30. Now that the students have had the opportunity to discuss the translations and uses of habitual *be* as a whole class, have them work on the worksheet on page 139 individually. The answer key is on page 140.

"*Be* Understood"

African American English contains instances in which the *is* and *are* forms of the verb *to be* do not appear in specific sentence structures. Let's take a look at the following sentences:

1. a. You smart.
   b. We the best team.
   c. They going to school.
   d. He eating in the classroom.

In certain instances, *be* can be "understood," rather than present, when it is the main verb (as in examples 1a and b) or when it is a helping verb (as in examples 1c and d). But it's most important to note that this particular pattern only occurs "where contracted forms of *is* or *are* may occur in Standard English" (Wolfram, Adger, & Christian, 1999, p. 213). *She my best friend* exemplifies the "*be* understood" pattern. Translated, the sentence would read *She's my best friend* or *She is my best friend*. The key to translating here is that *be* can be contracted. In contrast, the sentence *Do you know where she is?* would not permit "*be* understood" because *she is* cannot be contracted here (*Do you know where she __?*) (Pullum, 1999).

Teaching "*Be* Understood"

Begin by having the children read all of the sentences in the following chart and look for differences between formal and informal English. The students have had a lot of practice in identifying and defining patterns, so a few students should recognize that the formal sentences have a form of the verb *to be* while the informal ones do not. Your students may explain that the formal sentences include the pattern "subject + *'s, 're,* or *are.*" Once you've come this far, you might want to elaborate on the appropriate situations in which *is* and *are* are used in the sentences. You can simply tell the students that each of the formal subject + *be* verb combinations in the sample sentences are either contractions or words that can be made into contractions (see Chapter 2 for a more complete statement of the constraints).

Be Understood

Informal	*Formal*
We __ walking to school.	<u>We are</u> walking to school.
She __ my best friend.	<u>She is</u> my best friend.
I'll play when you __ finished.	I'll play when <u>you're</u> finished.
He __ playing basketball.	<u>He's</u> playing basketball.
They __ brothers.	<u>They are</u> brothers.

Just as the students described and defined the formal pattern, you will need to have them determine the rule for informal language. Most of your students will probably describe the informal pattern as "missing a form of the *be* verb." You might talk to them about how Standard English adds in a form of *be* where other languages—like Russian—do not (see Chapter 1). Informal English is like Russian in this regard. Then reveal the title of the chart (*Be* Understood). Once students have defined both patterns, tell them that they will each be completing a worksheet (see page 141). Part of the worksheet will require students to integrate the "*be* understood" pattern they have just learned with patterns they already know. See page 142 for the worksheet answer key.

Directions: Write two formal translations for each informal sentence and then answer the question at the bottom of the page.

1. My mom be at work, but today she is at home.

    Answer A. _____

    Answer B. _____

2. We be going to football games at night, but today we are going right after lunch.

    Answer A. _____

    Answer B. _____

3. We be going to math after lunch, but today we have an assembly instead.

    Answer A. _____

    Answer B. _____

Question: Explain why the informal *be* cannot be translated to formal language using *is* or *are*.

_____

_____

_____

_____

_____

Answer Key: Any combinations of the following translations may be used. Additional translations may be accepted.

1. My mom be at work, but today she is at home.

   A. <u>My mom is usually at work, but today she is at home.</u>

   B. <u>My mom is constantly at work, but today she is at home.</u>

   C. <u>My mom is always at work, but today she is at home.</u>

2. We be going to football games at night, but today we are going right after lunch.

   A. <u>We typically go to football games at night, but today we are going right after lunch.</u>

   B. <u>We always go to football games at night, but today we are going right after lunch.</u>

3. We be going to math after lunch, but today we have an assembly instead.

   A. <u>We usually go to math after lunch, but today we have an assembly instead.</u>

   B. <u>We habitually go to math after lunch, but today we have an assembly instead.</u>

   C. <u>We often go to math after lunch, but today we have an assembly instead.</u>

Question: Explain why the informal *be* cannot be translated to formal language using *is* or *are*.

Responses should include some variation on the following: Habitual *be* cannot be translated to *is* or *are* because these translations would not make sense in the sample sentences and would not capture the meaning of the original. *Be* in informal English means more than that.

Let's look at the first example, *My mom be at work, but today she is at home*. If we translate the sentences as *My mom is at work, but today she is at home*, the sentence does not make sense. In this case, *my mom* would have to be in two places at once (work and home) if we replaced the informal *be* with *is*. Clearly, *is* does not translate to *be* in this example.

In the second example, replacing *be* with *is/are* would make the sentence *We are going to football games at night, but today we are going right after lunch*. Since *after lunch* refers to the afternoon, not at night, the two parts of the sentence are similarly contradictory. So we cannot translate *be* as *are*.

As in example 2, the words *but* and *instead* in example 3 mark an event that varies from the norm. We cannot go to math after lunch if we have an assembly instead.

Using the three examples provided, it is clear that *is* and *are* are not by themselves good translations for the informal habitual *be* pattern.

Code-Switching: Teaching Standard English in Urban Classrooms by Rebecca S. Wheeler and Rachel Swords © 2006 NCTE.

Directions: Rewrite each sentence using the formal *be* pattern.

1. He going to his grandparent's house this weekend.

Answer: _____

2. Tomorrow we playing ball at the park.

Answer: _____

3. Do you know if they going to the game?

Answer: _____

4. Shannon the smartest girl in class.

Answer: _____

Directions: Rewrite each sentence using formal English.

5. You gonna win the game.

Answer: _____

6. They my best friend.

Answer: _____

7. She taking six class this year.

Answer: _____

8. Jason dad is gonna drive us home when we finished with our game.

Answer: _____

Answer Key

1. He going to his grandparent's house this weekend.

Answer: He is (or he's) going to his grandparent's house this weekend.

2. Tomorrow we playing ball at the park.

Answer: Tomorrow **we are (or we're)** playing ball at the park.

3. Do you know if they going to the game?

Answer: Do you know if **they are (or they're)** going to the game?

4. Shannon the smartest girl in class.

Answer: **Shannon is (or Shannon's)** the smartest girl in class.

5. You gonna win the game.
Answer: **You are (or you're) going to** win the game.

Pattern	Informal Structure	Formal Translation
be understood	You ___	You are or You're
gonna/going to	gonna	going to

6. They my best friend.

Answer: **They are (or They're)** my best **friends.**

Pattern	Informal Structure	Formal Translation
be understood	They ___	They are or They're
Plural	They . . . friend	They . . . friends

7. She taking six class this year.

Answer: **She is (or she's)** taking **six classes** this year.

Pattern	Informal Structure	Formal Translation
be understood	She ___	She is or She's
Plural	six class	six classes

8. Jason dad is gonna drive us home when we finished with our game.

Answer: **Jason's dad** is **going to** drive us home when **we are** finished with our game.

Pattern	Informal Structure	Formal Translation
Possessive	Jason dad	Jason's dad
gonna/going to	gonna	going to
be understood	we ___	we are or we're

Code-Switching: Teaching Standard English in Urban Classrooms by Rebecca S. Wheeler and Rachel Swords © 2006 NCTE.

12 Code-Switching in the Reading and Writing Classroom

So far we have focused on how to introduce various grammatical patterns in the classroom. Although we have introduced a range of grammar lessons, we have not yet explored how our contrastive model serves students in their reading and writing. This chapter discusses how our approach plays a role as the students read literature and write their own essays. We will explain how to use literature to enhance the children's appreciation of language, as well as explore how to enable students to move beyond the grammar minilessons to implement their understanding of language varieties in their own writing.

Language Diversity and Reading

Before you introduce linguistically informed reading and writing in the classroom, assemble various examples of writing that reflect both formal and informal grammar. Many teachers make the mistake of believing that this simply means they must acquire a diverse collection of literature to keep in their classroom libraries. But in order for students to embrace differences in ethnicity, language, culture, purpose, and setting, we must do more than have a collection available. Rather, we must present these texts to the students in a way that allows them to experience and discuss the differences in language choice. We can accomplish this by providing and presenting a broad range of literature, including fiction and nonfiction books, newspapers, magazines, and personal journals. As children read and are exposed to a diversity of sentence structures, they are increasingly able to bring a similar kind of sentence variety to their own writing.

Perceiving Language Differences in Literature

We begin the school year by having students read literature that contains examples of both formal and informal language (e.g., Carolivia Herron's *Nappy Hair* [1998], Patricia McKissack's *Flossie and the Fox* [1986], Patricia McKissack's *A Million Fish . . . More or Less* [1992], Alan Schroeder's *Caro-*

lina Shout! [1995], John Steptoe's *Daddy Is a Monster . . . Sometimes* [1980], and Sherley Anne William's *Working Cotton* [1992]). Then we invite students to imitate the various styles in their own writing. We start with linguistically diverse literature as a bridge, since students generally enter the classroom with a certain amount of proficiency in informal language. But because students may not make a concentrated effort to distinguish informal language from formal language, the first step in teaching Standard English to speakers with a different language of nurture is to ensure that the children see the grammatical differences between the two varieties. Further, beginning the year with examples of renowned writers who utilize both formal and informal English also boosts the children's confidence. Students need to view themselves as good writers. When they see published authors who use both formal and informal language, the students realize that both forms of language are valid and important.

Since our first goal at the beginning of the year is to have the children hear the linguistic differences in the stories we select, we simply tell the students to listen for formal and informal language in the story. Later we address additional goals, such as having the children analyze linguistic differences, practice translating from one language variety to another, and integrate traits they observe in literature into their own writing. During the first few informal stories Swords read, students would excitedly interrupt to point out informal language. Repeatedly, the children would say, "That's informal!" In order to allow the students to interact with the story without interrupting, Swords had them hold up one finger every time they heard informal language and two fingers when they heard formal language. Some students may choose to simply listen, while others will enjoy indicating formal and informal language patterns using these signals. When Swords read *Working Cotton* by Sherley Anne Williams (1992), her students quickly recognized that the phrase *we gets to the fields early* contained informal language. They were not sophisticated enough in their understanding of language to explain that the pattern related to subject-verb agreement, but they knew that the language was informal. They also recognized the pattern again in the phrase *after we moves to a new field*. Although the students were unaware of the specific patterns of the language, they were able to differentiate between formal and informal language.

While hand signals can be used with all books, some stories lend themselves to additional types of interaction. *Nappy Hair* by Carolivia Herron (1998) is one such book. The story is written in a "call and response" format. This style, created by slaves in the 1800s, is an interac-

Well.

Yep.

Don't cha know.

No, it ain't.

That's what it is.

Figure 12.1. Students' speaking parts from Herron's *Nappy Hair*.

tive way of storytelling in which both the teller and the listeners participate in spinning the tale. Since the children will have a speaking role, you will need to write their part on chart paper, as shown in the example in Figure 12.1. Make sure you mimic the size and boldness of the print in the book, as this identifies the volume at which the children should speak the words

Herron (1998) provides an explanation of the call-and-response style in the front of the book. Read this aloud to the children. After reading the first few lines about the style being created by slaves as a means of storytelling, take this opportunity to explain that the book uses informal English. You can then lead a discussion about why Herron might have decided to use informal language for this particular story. If the children do not suggest that the author is rendering language in a style similar to what the slaves might have used, you can emphasize this. Additionally, just as the students would most likely use informal language when telling a story to their friends or family, the narrator in this story is considering audience by using informal language.

After taking a moment to discuss the time and place of the story, read aloud the remainder of Herron's introduction to the book. Herron suggests that the caller (the teacher) read Uncle Mordecai's lines and that the audience (the students) read the responses. She also explains that the large, bold words are to be read loudly, while the other lines are read in a softer voice. You will need to model the volume changes before reading the book. Once you have read through some of the students' lines (see Figure 12.1 for an example), have the children read the lines with you. Now that the students have spent a few minutes practicing their roles, you are ready to read the book together. Your students can then rely on the chart or look at the book pages to stay on track. By making the students active participants in reading the story, you are allowing them to practice oral reading while demonstrating the importance of using informal language when it is appropriate.

Selecting and Teaching Grammar Patterns through Literature

Much of *Code-Switching* has been dedicated to exploring how to use various informal language structures to teach Standard English. We have discussed how to find common informal structures in student writing samples, as well as how to teach the formal counterparts of these informal structures. We have not yet talked about how to use literature to foster students' abilities to produce Standard English.

Begin, as always, with the language of your students. Once you have identified a home speech grammatical pattern that is prevalent among the students in your classroom, you will need to find literature that reflects these same patterns. To make this task less daunting, we have included a concordance of AAE resources showing informal patterns found in each of the texts listed (see Appendix B).

Using Literature to Enhance Contrastive Analysis Lessons

Once you have located stories that contain the grammatical patterns most often used by your students, you can use the literature to enhance your lessons in contrastive analysis. When you are using a work of literature to emphasize a specific pattern, highlight this pattern by writing examples from the book on chart paper and discussing them before reading the story aloud. You might, for example, create the chart in Figure 12.2 if you were using *Working Cotton* to aid in your teaching of subject-verb agreement patterns. Remember that you are using the literature to supplement your language lessons. Therefore, the students should have studied the pattern before you use the book as part of doing contrastive analysis to teach a structure. Of course, you may have students read the story before you teach a specific pattern if you used this book to help children hear the differences in language.

Subject-Verb Agreement	
Informal Language	*Formal Language*
Everyone speak	
Daddy say	
Daddy pick	
Mamma keep	
Mamma sing; Daddy hum	
Cotton smell	
It smell	
Mamma bring	
The bus come	

Figure 12.2. From *Working Cotton* by Sherley Ann Williams (1992).

Before inviting your students to read the story, reveal the chart. You might say, "Sherley Anne Williams uses many informal patterns in the book *Working Cotton*. Since we have been learning about subject-verb agreement, we are going to look at how Ms. Williams uses the informal pattern. Here are some examples from the book." You can then read through the chart. After you remind the students to listen for examples of informal subject-verb agreement patterns, read the story aloud.

Class Discussion

Once you have read the story, take a few minutes to lead a discussion about why the author chose to use informal language or, in many cases, both formal and informal language. Sherley Anne Williams (1992) and Carolivia Herron (1998), for example, may have used informal language to capture the language of the slaves in their respective books *Working Cotton* and *Nappy Hair*. Just as Patricia C. McKissack (1992) used informal language for the characters in *A Million Fish . . . More or Less*, so she chose informal language for Flossie and formal language for the fox to help develop distinct characters.

Indeed, Patricia McKissack's (1986) *Flossie and the Fox* is a good place to start because language is a defining feature of the title characters. The story vividly describes how one little girl is able to protect a basket of eggs from a sly fox. In the story, Flossie speaks informally while the fox uses formal language. The book avoids linguistic stereotypes, as the informal Flossie is able to outwit the fox.

After reading the book, you can ask your students how Flossie and the fox are different. Even students who have not spent a considerable amount of time studying language should quickly explain that the two characters speak differently. To aid students in their understanding of character, you might even consider creating a Venn diagram comparing and contrasting the two characters. Swords found that her students initially believed that the fox was more intelligent based on his language skills. The students found it ironic that Flossie outsmarts the fox. "He talk smart, but Flossie trick him anyway," explained one third grader. Although there is no indication of the fox's age in the story, the children also believed that the fox was an adult, because his language was so formal.

Practice: Switching from Informal to Formal Language

Once students have made these observations about the characters, ask the class if they think the story would be as fun to read if both of the characters spoke like the fox or both spoke like Flossie. Your students will likely respond that the story would not be as much fun to read, although they may have trouble articulating why.

Return to *Working Cotton*. Since you have already discussed possible reasons why Williams used informal language, ask the students how the story might differ if she had used formal language instead. Juwan, one of Swords's students, responded, "It wouldn't sound right. She talkin' about slavery, and that ain't formal." Clearly, your students are capable of determining the appropriateness of language given a specific time, place, and communicative purpose. We want children to recognize when authors utilize formal and informal language so that their own writing can reflect this careful selection of language.

Language Diversity and Writing

Using Language to Build Characters

Now that the students have had an opportunity to experiment with the effect of language on character development, they are ready to create their own stories. Before having your students write their own stories, you will need to model the thinking process involved in determining what to write about and how to create the characters. You can accomplish this by doing a think-aloud in combination with a shared writing, or a story that the students are invited to help write. You might say, "We are going to write a story of our own, and we are going to use dialogue. Of course, if we use dialogue, we will need to decide if our characters are going to speak formally or informally. Since I speak formally most of the time, I'm going to challenge myself to create one informal character. I think I will make the other character speak formally because I like how Patricia McKissack did that in *Flossie and the Fox*." At this point, you can introduce an idea for a story or ask the students for ideas. We recommend asking the students for ideas first, because you want this writing to be shared by all of the class. Swords found that her students were quick to come up with ideas; they ultimately decided to write a fictional story about a student who saves the class from a giant bug. Since this is your class's first attempt at using dialogue, you may want to limit the number of characters to two. Swords's class decided to have a dialogue between the teacher and the student. Students then had to determine which character should speak formally and which should speak informally. The students voted to have the teacher use informal language, while the student used formal language.

Give the students several minutes to think about the type of stories they would like to write. Then ask them to raise their hands if they know what they will be writing about. Allow children who raise their hands to share what their story will be about and whether their characters will speak formally or informally. The students should feel empowered to determine the language used by their own characters. As the children listen to one another, you will find that many who did not initially raise their hands will decide on a topic and want to share their ideas with the class.

Reflecting on Language Differences in Personal Journals

Another way we can encourage children's writing throughout the year is by allowing them to write in either formal or informal language in a personal journal. These journals allow children to write in any form with which they are comfortable. These writings can be prompted or unprompted. Swords uses classroom journals as a means for students to record personal stories and thoughts. While these writings are unprompted, Swords has noticed that many students write about the use of informal language in the books she reads to them. They also tend to explain new language patterns in their journals. One student wrote, "Mrs. Swords teach us to write formal and informal. I want to write formal so I can get a good job." Another student, in response to *Flossie and the Fox*, wrote, "I like Flossie the best because she talk just like me." These unprompted writings reveal the importance of language in children's lives. As the children become more proficient in recognizing the differences between formal and informal language, and in practicing translating from informal to formal and back again, they will select a language variety based on the purpose of their writing and the intended audience.

Editing and Conferencing

Once the students have had an opportunity to work on their writings, you will want to hold individual conferences with each student to discuss editing and revising. Remember that editing refers both to making changes in the mechanical aspects of the paper (such as punctuation and spelling) and to word and language choice (such as formal or informal language, the use of details, and descriptive language). One way to approach editing is to discuss only one or two specific aspects of the paper during the one-on-one conference.

Although the task of meeting with each child may seem overwhelming, you will find that these conferences are easily accomplished during your regular writing time. The conference should be limited to three to five minutes, and you should meet with each child at least once during the course of a week. During this conference, it will often be impossible to read and comment on an entire piece of work. Instead, skim through the paper and select one or two areas on which to focus. As students are practicing making appropriate language choices in their writing, many will struggle with maintaining a language variety in which they are not yet proficient. A conference is the perfect time to discuss these specific language issues. During one particular conference in Swords's classroom, Lorenzo focused on a biography he was working on about Frederick Douglass. Although the first few sentences were written in formal English, most of the paper was written informally. Swords asked Lorenzo if he thought the biography should use formal or informal English. Lorenzo responded that he wanted to write using formal English. Rather than show Lorenzo areas where he failed to use Standard English, Swords reviewed the formal patterns they had learned in class. Then she had Lorenzo reread a section of the paper and highlight the places he succeeded in using these formal patterns. When Lorenzo read a sentence that contained an informal pattern, he immediately realized he needed to change it to formal. Once he changed the structure to formal English, he could then highlight the pattern. By having a child focus on one aspect of his or her writing, you can keep the student from becoming overwhelmed with the task of editing.

Swords found that the children love to highlight their work in an effort to celebrate their understanding of a particular feature in writing. In order to highlight more of the text, the students carefully read their work and make appropriate changes. Eventually, the students will become proficient in a particular aspect of writing and they will no longer need to highlight that specific feature. At that point, the teacher and student will focus on a new area of editing in subsequent conferences.

While teacher-student conferences are an integral part of the writing process, it is equally important to promote student-to-student conferences within the classroom. You will not have time to meet with every child each time someone has a question. Therefore, students need to learn to discuss concerns with one another. These conferences should mimic the teacher-student conferences in several ways. First, the children should not simply exchange papers in an attempt to correct each other's "mistakes." Rather, the students should engage in a dialogue concerning a specific issue in one piece of writing. You can facilitate this in two ways. If one student has a question about a particular aspect of his or her writing, that should be the basis of the conference. For example, Karishma, a third grader in Swords's class, had written a ghost story that included detailed characters, a setting, and a basic problem the characters needed to solve. The characters went through a series of events to solve the problem. Once Karishma had completed the story, however, she was not sure all of the events were necessary in solving the initial problem. She asked her classmates Adam and Josh to listen to her story and help her decide which events made sense and which she needed to eliminate. By the time Karishma brought the story to the teacher-student conference, she no longer needed help with this particular aspect of her work.

The second way in which you can work to facilitate a meaningful dialogue about writing strategies among students is to give the students a list of possible areas to focus on during their conferences. You can simply write these suggested focal points on a piece of chart paper to remind the students of their editing options. The chart can include various aspects you have been working on throughout the year. You will need to change the chart periodically to reflect your current focal areas. Try to keep a maximum of five or six items on the list so the students are not overwhelmed. Your list might include, for example, punctuation, capitalization, using formal possessive patterns, using informal possessive patterns in dialogue, and using descriptive words. Students can then select an item from the list to discuss in a conference. It is very important for students to discuss their writing with both the teacher and their classmates because we want students to see writing as a process rather than just a product. The Code-Switching Shopping List (see Appendix A), which focuses uniquely on formal/informal patterns, is also useful in this regard. This list helps students to focus on which informal grammar patterns they tend to use and then to code-switch these to formal English. Although it's designed for middle school students, you could adapt the Code-Switching Shopping List to meet the particular needs of your own class.

Publishing

The final step in encouraging students' reading and writing of both formal and informal language is publishing. Many teachers have their students work for several days on a single piece of writing. Once the writing is complete, the teacher grades the work and returns the writing to the student. This practice, however, sends the message that the purpose of writing is to receive a grade. We want the students to recognize their abilities as writers and to be able to write (for a variety of purposes) for audiences who will actually read their work. This section addresses how to celebrate writing by allowing children to publish their work in the classroom.

One simple way to publish work is to create a venue in which children can orally share their writings. This can be built into your daily writing time by using the last five or ten minutes of your writing schedule to allow children to voluntarily read a piece of writing. This writing does not have to be complete, nor does a child necessarily need to share an entire piece of work. A student might read the best portion of the story or a portion for which he or she wants feedback. You will also find that the children often try to incorporate features of one another's stories in their own work. Swords found this most apparent with a particular group of third graders. Before one oral publishing session, Adam had written a story full of unformatted dialogue. Since the class had not covered how to use dialogue in a story, she conferenced one-on-one with him about format. After the students heard Adam's story, Swords had so many of her students using dialogue in their stories that she spent several days teaching the whole class how to effectively and appropriately show their characters talking. This was enormously meaningful to the students because it pertained to their own interests and applied immediately to their work.

Since we have spent a significant amount of time focusing on the reasons authors select a particular style of language, we want to approach our student authors' works in the same way. Therefore, after the student has read his or her work to the class, have the class decide whether the writer used formal, informal, or both formal and informal language in the piece of writing. Then have the author justify his or her reasons for selecting the type of language used. Timesha, a third grader in Swords's class, wrote a story in which chickens, rather than children, attended school. In the story, the teacher asks a variety of questions. Some of the chickens respond formally and others respond informally. After Timesha read the first chapter of her story aloud, Swords asked the class how Timesha had used formal and informal language in the story. "The teacher speak formal, but the chickens is all messed up," Juwan responded. When Swords asked him to explain, Juwan replied that the chickens should speak informally, but some of them were speaking formally. Timesha defended her language choices by explaining that all of the students in a real classroom speak differently, so the chickens in her classroom wouldn't all speak in the same manner. Juwan and the rest of the class ultimately agreed with Timesha. During this discussion, the class was able to determine how an author makes appropriate decisions regarding the language for a story. In this way, oral publishing benefits an entire class.

In addition to having students share their stories orally, you should have a place in the classroom where students can publish hard copies of their stories for other children to read. To accomplish this, you can simply staple paper together to form a book and have students write and illustrate their final copies in the book. You can use an empty shoebox decorated with wrapping paper to showcase these books. By having students put completed copies of their work on display, you are letting them know that they are real authors. You will find that both the authors of the featured selections and other children will read these books on a regular basis. You might be surprised, as was Swords, by the quality of work your students can produce when given the appropriate tools.

13 Encountering New Patterns

We have talked in great detail about a range of informal patterns. We have explored patterns in the noun phrase (possession and plurality) and patterns in the verb phrase (subject-verb agreement—present tense, regular verbs, *is/are*, *was/were*; showing past time; habitual *be* and *be* understood). Of course, this doesn't even scratch the surface of the patterns you see and hear in your students' written and spoken expression. What are you to do with the rest of the language patterns you come across during your school day? We offer you a three-tiered response.

Drawing on the Top-Ten Patterns

First, while the sound, word, and grammatical contrasts between AAE and Standard English are extensive (Green, 2002; Rickford, 1999a, 1999b), students don't transfer all the possible AAE grammar into their schooltime expression, and the patterns that do transfer, don't transfer all the time (Wolfram, 1969). Instead, only a handful of patterns regularly turn up in student writing. Over several years of working with her local school system, for example, Wheeler has consistently found that two or three dozen AAE grammar patterns occur in student writing. Of those, we can identify a fairly consistent top ten or twelve patterns, patterns that scholars have examined repeatedly in different studies (Smitherman, 2000; Fogel & Ehri, 2000). The top patterns we have found in students' work are these:

Informal v. Formal English Patterns

1. Subject-verb agreement   She walk_ v. She walk<u>s</u>
2. Showing past time (1)   I finish_ v. I finish<u>ed</u>
3. Showing past time (2)   I <u>seen</u> my aunt v. I <u>saw</u> my aunt
4. *be* understood   He __ cool with me v. He <u>is</u> cool with me
5. Making negatives   She <u>won't never</u> v. She won't <u>ever</u>
6. *be/have* + action word   He was name_ Tarik v. He was nam<u>ed</u> Tarik

	. . . have turn_ in my paper v. have turn<u>ed</u> in
	. . . a boy name_Tarik v. a boy nam<u>ed</u> Tarik
7. Plurality: "Showing more than one"	Three cat_ v. Three cat<u>s</u>
8. Possessive	The dog_ tail v. The dog<u>'s</u> tail
9. *a* v. *an*	An rapper v. A rapper

The relative frequency of these patterns may vary in your students' writing, and the order in which you teach them will vary, because some are easier to teach than others. For example, although the possessive is not the top, or most frequent, pattern, it's the first one we teach because it's so straightforward and it so clearly illustrates the principles underlying code-switching. At any rate, just handling these top ten will take you a long way in helping your students produce more Standard English when they need to.

To help you with the most frequent patterns, we include full-page contrastive analysis charts in Appendix A for each of these patterns, as well as for a few others.

Working through a New Pattern on Your Own

Whenever you find a new pattern beyond those discussed in this book, you have a variety of resources available to you. Sometimes you will readily figure out the grammar rule on your own. For example, perhaps many of your students write sentences like *Mom ask could I go; I wonder could the bird fly*, etc. To figure out what dialect pattern is transferring into student writing, follow the scientific method we've been using throughout this book (reproduced here for your convenience):

- Collect data.
- Examine the data, seeking the pattern.
- Describe the pattern.
- Test your description of the pattern.
- Refine your description of the pattern.

If you can find a pattern, you likely have found a grammatical rule. So the first thing to do is collect a number of examples of sentences with a similar grammar issue from your students' writing. Then begin searching for a pattern. The best way to do this is to make your own contrastive analysis chart. Translate each sentence into formal English (*Mom asked whether I could go; I wonder if the bird could fly*).

Here's a sample chart with just those two sentences:

Informal English	**Formal English**
Mom ask could I go.	Mom asked whether I could go.
I wonder could the bird fly.	I wonder if the bird could fly.

Now you're in a position to systematically probe the differences between the two varieties. Perhaps you notice first that "there's no *if* or *whether*" in the informal sentences. Again, recast that perception. Stick with describing each dialect's pattern in and of itself. Don't be surprised if you don't know the answer right away. You're not supposed to—this is a bit of language research, and in research one doesn't know the outcome at the outset (or shouldn't).

Look for where the two sentences differ: it's after the verb. So, inside informal English, we see subject + verb + question clause (*Mom + ask + could I go*). Inside formal English, we see subject + verb + *if/whether* + statement clause (*Mom + asked + whether I could go*). That's the difference!

Notice that the words after *ask* inside informal English could stand alone as their own sentence—(*Could I go?*)—whereas the words after *asked* inside formal English could not; they would be a fragment (*whether I could go*). Where have we seen the pattern *Could I go* before? Of course, we have seen it when the main clause forms a question (*Mama, could I go?*). So African American English uses the same rule for forming questions both for the main clause and after the verb.

That's the pattern, or at least that's our hypothesis of the pattern. Let's see if we can write it down.

Informal English	**Formal English**
Mom asked <u>could I go</u>	*Mom asked <u>whether I could go</u>*
Subject + verb + [question clause]	Subject + verb + *if/whether* + [statement clause]

You would then check your hypothesis against all the data you find, and you would find that you are right. You have discovered and identified how AAE and SE do "indirect questions" (questions that occur after the main verb inside a sentence).

The next step is to create your own contrastive analysis chart to help students discover the explicit contrasts between their everyday English and formal English. In doing this, you are extending the work we have practiced in this book. Grammar patterns such as this one are, of course, more appropriate for work in the upper school years.

Once you have worked through a pattern and made your contrastive analysis chart, you won't have to do it again. Just add it to your code-switching book for future reference.

Drawing on Existing Dialect Resources

Finally, perhaps you see a pattern and you're really not sure what's going on, or you don't have time for your own inquiry. Or perhaps you've just worked through a new pattern and want to check your conclusions. You don't have to reinvent the wheel, defining patterns on your own. Instead, when you have the sense that an informal pattern is afoot in your students' writing, existing AAE resources (or books characteristic of the dialect of your local region) will surely detail the pattern for you. The following resources constitute a good short shelf to have in your own library to support your work in code-switching:

Green, Lisa. (2002). *African American English: A Linguistic Introduction*. Cambridge, UK: Cambridge University Press.

Redd, Teresa M., & Webb, Karen Schuster. (2005). *A Teacher's Introduction to African American English: What a Writing Teacher Should Know*. Urbana, IL: National Council of Teachers of English.

Rickford, John. (1999). *African American Vernacular English*. Malden, MA: Blackwell.

Wolfram, Walt, Adger, Carolyn Temple, & Christian, Donna. (Eds.). (1999). *Dialects in Schools and Communities*. Mahwah, NJ: Lawrence Erlbaum.

Wolfram, Walt, & Schilling-Estes, Natalie. (1998). *American English: Dialects and Variation*. Malden, MA: Blackwell.

Each of these books either has an inventory of AAE structures or individual chapters devoted to a given structure (like habitual *be*, emphatic *been*, etc.) or, as in the case of Green, is more like a grammar of the language. Once you find the pattern you're addressing in one of your reference books, return to the method we've shared—contrastive analysis charts and code-switching—integrating it into your students' daily oral language and the writing process.

14 Conclusion: How to Talk about Code-Switching with Others

Thank you for sharing this journey with us, for the path of code-switching and contrastive analysis in the classroom is indeed a journey, requiring courage, openness, compassion, and commitment to our students. Perhaps you have a sense of excitement, of new possibilities for your classroom. Perhaps you have a sense of concern as you wonder what your principal, other teachers, and parents will think when you propose changing aspects of your English teaching methods.

We certainly understand. In this short chapter, we list some of the questions you might encounter and offer tips on how you might present your code-switching work to parents, teachers, and principals.

First, in the classroom, *start small*. Get your feet wet. Try out the beginning lessons that focus on how naturally we all vary our self-presentation from setting to setting. Get your students involved and let them run with the idea as they give examples, draw cartoons, and act out scenarios in which they vary clothing, behavior, posture, and tone of voice, or in which they vary table settings, house decorations, and so on. You will feel bolstered by how quickly and naturally students grasp the concept of *formal* versus *informal*.

Then, *talk in general ways about how language varies*. Find age-appropriate literature for your class that contains characters speaking with the cadences of different regions of the country. Have your students talk about the language. Is it formal? Informal? What do they know about the character based on his or her language? How does the language contribute to the setting, the story? Questions such as these help atune students to how language varies setting by setting, character by character.

Work with code-switching charts to identify a simple pattern relevant to your students' language use. To begin, collect a sample of student writing. As you read your students' work, think about whether it reveals a pattern that crops up again and again. If you are an urban teacher, you will almost certainly find the informal third-person subject-verb agreement pattern (*She walk to the store*). Don't start with this pattern, because it's too complex for beginning work. Instead, see if your students write using informal possessive (*My goldfish name is Scaley*) or plural (*I have three dog and three cat*) patterns. If so, these are good places to start the code-switching process with the whole class.

Pull out the possessive or plural chart from the back of this book. Either replicate it on a wall chart, or build a parallel chart using examples from your students' writing. Reread the portion of our book that talks about how to teach possessives or plurals.

At this point, you are just gaining experience and confidence in the new approach, doing a pilot study in your own classroom, so to speak. Our experience is that students love code-switching. Indeed, with code-switching, the dynamics of the whole classroom change, from teacher as grammar police, to teacher as co-participant in the enterprise of crafting writing that fits the setting.

Next, we suggest that you build a set of resources supporting your work in code-switching to explain and justify why you are changing or augmenting your language arts approach. Here are some basic questions you may encounter in one form or another, followed by answers:

Question 1: *Why should you use a new approach?*
Answer 1: We need a new approach in English language arts because *existing methods fail to teach African American students Standard English.*

Data showing the achievement gap between White and Black students:

- Collect data for the achievement gap in your district. You can find this data by going on the district Web site and looking at the test scores broken down by demographic group (age, gender, race) school by school. Compile evidence on the extent of the achievement gap in your school and your district. Get the test data for your own previous year's classes.

- See published resources on the achievement gap and the failure of existing language arts methods to succeed in reaching African American students.

  ♦ Jencks, Christopher, and Meredith Phillips (Eds.). (1998). *The Black-White Test Score Gap*. Washington, DC: Brookings Institution Press.

  ♦ Data from the U.S. Department of Education, National Institute for Educational Statistics (http://nces.ed.gov/nations reportcard/naepdata/get data.asp).

National Writing Tests: The Gap between White and Black Students

	1998	2002
Grade 4	26%	21%
Grade 8	26%	25.4%
Grade 12	21.4%	23.8%

These are just a few of the possible data sources. Track the achievement gap on Google. You will find many sources on the achievement gap between Black and White students.

Why does this achievement gap matter? Aside from the obvious moral and ethical reasons, it matters because the No Child Left Behind Act (NCLB) requires schools to ensure that all students succeed. Previously, schools gained accreditation based on the strength of the White students' performance. No longer can school officials depend on White scores "pulling up" the scores of minority students; NCLB requires that all subgroups of a school pass the statewide tests, or the school will lose its accreditation.

Clearly, given African American student failure in writing, our current English language arts methods do not succeed with minority students. Ability to produce and understand Standard English is one piece of that writing puzzle, so helping all students succeed means we need to do a better job of teaching Standard English.

Question 2: *Why use contrastive analysis and code-switching?*
Answer 2: Research shows that contrastive analysis and code-switching work. With contrastive analysis, teachers accurately diagnose student writing needs and find a successful technique for teaching Standard English. Then code-switching allows students to choose the language to fit the setting. We owe it to our students to use approaches that foster student success.

Sources: Print out the following articles or chapters for your resource notebook. Highlight the useful quotes and write out a short (four- or five-sentence) summary of each article or chapter.

- John Rickford's (n.d.) "Using the Vernacular to Teach the Standard" (http://www.stanford.edu/~rickford/papers/Vernacular ToTeachStandard.html).

- Howard Fogel and Linnea Ehri's (2000) "Teaching Elementary Students Who Speak Black English Vernacular to Write in Standard English: Effects of Dialect Transformation Practice." *Contemporary Educational Psychology*, *25*, 212–35 (available through library services online PDF format or through interlibrary loan).

- Rebecca S. Wheeler and Rachel Swords's (2004) "Codeswitching: Tools of Language and Culture Transform the Dialectally Diverse Classroom." *Language Arts, 81*(6), 470–80 (also available at http://www.ncte.org/profdev/onsite/consultants/wheeler).

- Rebecca S. Wheeler's (2005) "Code-Switch to Teach Standard English," an invited column of Teaching in the World, *English Journal, 94*(5), 108–112 (also available at http://www.ncte.org/profdev/onsite/consultants/wheeler).

- Teresa M. Redd and Karen Schuster Webb's (2005) *A Teacher's Introduction to African American English: What a Writing Teacher Should Know* [esp. Chapter 3, "Does AAE Affect Students' Ability to Write SWE?" and Chapter 4, "How Can AAE Speakers Become Effective SWE Writers?"]. Urbana, IL: National Council of Teachers of English.

Teaching Standard English isn't the only reason to use code-switching, of course. We have talked about how it changes the classroom climate, promotes a positive self-fulfilling prophecy, and so forth. While these are important issues, we don't recommend that you include them in your initial justification for why you're using code-switching. These benefits are too intangible at this point. *After* you demonstrate that students are able to improve their writing and their writing scores, *then* you can discuss the truths of transforming classroom culture and promoting a sense of student pride, etc.

Question 3: *This doesn't have anything to do with that Ebonics, does it?*
Answer 3: No, this has nothing to do with Ebonics. When people ask if code-switching has to do with Ebonics, they are usually referring to one of the prevalent misconceptions that developed around the Oakland Ebonics controversy of 1996. Some may wonder, "Are you teaching students Ebonics, street slang?" The answer to that is simple. No, we are not teaching children the language of the home—they already know it. We are teaching Standard English.

One more point. As discussed in the introduction, we suggest that you refrain from referring to race when describing code-switching. It's not about race. While we have occasionally used the term *African American English* to refer to the language spoken by some urban minority children, our purpose has been to enable you to find and read the linguistic literature on this language variety. As we noted, however, race-based terms don't fly well with students, parents, or administrators. So we urge you to not name groups of speakers. Instead, talk about effective approaches for responding to grammar patterns you find cropping up in student writing. That's what's important.

Next, *begin pulling together specific code-switching lesson plans*. This book provides plenty of material you can use to get started. You can work straight from the book, or you might develop a range of specific lesson plans extracted from our discussions. This may seem like a lot of material. But remember, the top ten patterns take you a long way in addressing students' needs (see Appendix A). If you find other patterns characteristic of your students' writing, you can slowly augment those charts as necessary. Your work is cumulative, so the resources you build now will be the foundation of your future work. You won't be reinventing the wheel.

Finally, *look closely at how you talk about language*. Pay attention to the terms you use. Wheeler has found that her teacher education students struggle to become conscious of their language as they continue to see "students making errors," feel a "need to correct," and try to "fix students' problems," etc. Remember to think about how you characterize student language *before* you voice your opinions or give students directions to "correct errors." How we talk about a thing reflects our analysis and understanding of that thing. Code-switching is nothing if not transformational.

Expect that the insights underlying code-switching will permeate and transform your language arts life. Under the code-switching approach, you will consider student language as data. You will make notes on prevalent grammar patterns you hear or read, and you will build those into contrastive analysis lessons in upcoming days. Plan on keeping a log of the patterns you hear or read in student work. That way, if a visitor comes into your class and sees you not correcting a student for speaking in the language of nurture, you can point to your running record and tell the visitor that interrupting the student is not an effective approach. Instead, you will be teaching the Standard English equivalents during regularly scheduled language work.

Finally, as you build your library of code-switching resource materials, plan on having a section for writing and one for literature. Perhaps you will duplicate our top ten code-switching patterns and the Code-Switching Shopping List, or alter the list so it reflects the patterns your students use. Perhaps you will begin collecting examples of dialectally diverse literature to use with your students, making note of your sources and how you use them in your code-switching resource book.

And so, welcome to the journey. Come with us as we reach out to the students of urban America. We look forward to seeing you along the way.

Appendix A

Selected African American English Structures

Here we summarize the structures we've treated in this book, and we offer some teaching tools for use in your classroom—the contrastive analysis charts for highly frequent patterns in AAE. Use these charts in your work with your students.

Structures discussed in this book

I.   Noun patterns

    a. Possessive

    b. Plural

II. Verb patterns

    a. Subject-verb agreement (regular verbs)

    b. Agreement—*was/were*

    c. Agreement—*is/are*

    d. Past time

III. More complex patterns

    a. Habitual *be*

    b. *be* understood

Code-Switching Shopping List

Name: _____

Do any of the top 10 or so informal English patterns appear in your paper? If so, put a check in the corresponding box and then code-switch to formal English! Add a smiley face, ☺, to show when you use formal patterns in your writing. "Flip the Switch!"

Informal v. Formal English Patterns	Paper 1	Paper 2	Paper 3	Paper 4
1. Subject-verb agreement She walk_ v. She walk<u>s</u>				
2. Showing past time (1) I finish_ v. I finish<u>ed</u>				
3. Showing past time (2) She <u>seen</u> the dog v. She <u>saw/had seen</u> . . .				
4. *be* understood He __ cool with me v. He <u>is</u> cool with me				
5. Making negatives She <u>won't never</u> v. She won't <u>ever</u>				
6. *be/have* + action word He was name_ Tarik v. He was nam<u>ed</u> Tarik A boy name_ Tarik v. A boy nam<u>ed</u> Tarik				
7. Plurality: "Showing more than one" Three cat_ v. Three cat<u>s</u>				
8. Possessive (singular) The dog_ tail v. the dog<u>'s</u> tail				
9. *a* v. *an* An rapper v. a rapper A elephant v. an elephant				
10. Other pattern _____				

By Rebecca S. Wheeler and the Huntington Middle School Writing Project.

SUBJECT-VERB AGREEMENT (1)

She walk_ v. She walks

INFORMAL ———————————————— **FORMAL**

INFORMAL	FORMAL
I run quickly.	I run quickly.
You sing well.	You sing well.
He respect_ me.	He respects me.
Respect smell_ like . . .	Respect smells like . . .
It just feel_ good.	It just feels good.
We paint in art.	We paint in art.
They sit on the carpet.	They sit on the carpet.

THE PATTERN

Subject + bare verb

he / she / it-type subjects
Usually take *-s* ending

Otherwise,
subject (*I / you / we / they*) + bare verb

Code-Switching: Teaching Standard English in Urban Classrooms by Rebecca S. Wheeler and Rachel Swords © 2006 NCTE.

SUBJECT-VERB AGREEMENT (2)

*They looks v. They look_*

INFORMAL ——————————————— **FORMAL**

INFORMAL

They probably looks up to you . . .

The judges says, "We have a winner!"

We gets to the fields early.

FORMAL

They probably look_ up to you . . .

The judges say_, "We have a winner!"

We get to the fields early.

THE PATTERN

Plural subjects + bare verbs + -s

Plural subjects + bare verb

SHOWING PAST TIME (1)

I finish_ v. I finished

INFORMAL |——————————————|—————————————| FORMAL

INFORMAL	FORMAL
I already finish_ my paper.	I already finished my paper.
Nat Turner change_ the world.	Nat Turner changed the world.
Yesterday, I went home and turn_ on the TV.	Yesterday, I went home and turned on the TV.
The sign say Whites only.	The sign said Whites only.
When he said, "I have a dream," everything change_.	When he said, "I have a dream," everything changed.

THE PATTERN

Verb + -*ed*

(or other change in shape: "said, meant," etc.)

Signal words in sentence

Common knowledge

SHOWING PAST TIME (2)

I seen my aunt v. I saw my aunt
I seen my aunt v. I had seen my aunt

INFORMAL ———————————— **FORMAL**

INFORMAL	FORMAL
I looked up and <u>seen</u> my aunt.	I looked up and <u>saw</u> my aunt.
He <u>thrown</u> a reception to the other team.	He <u>threw</u> a reception to the other team.
I could not believe who I <u>seen</u>.	I could not believe who I <u>had seen</u>.
She deserves a lot more for what she <u>done</u>.	She deserves a lot more for what she <u>has done</u>.

THE PATTERN

Past participle form (*seen, thrown,* etc.)	Verb + *-ed* (or change in shape)
	"have" + past participle (*seen / done . . .*)

Code-Switching: Teaching Standard English in Urban Classrooms by Rebecca S. Wheeler and Rachel Swords © 2006 NCTE.

Be UNDERSTOOD

He ___ cool with me v. He's cool with me

INFORMAL	FORMAL
That_ why I chose Martin Luther King.	That's why I chose Martin Luther King.
He_ cool with me and that_ why . . .	He's cool with me and that is why . . .
This_ who I want to go on a coin.	This's who I want to go on a coin.
She_ the kind of person who would . . .	She's the kind of person who would . . .

THE PATTERN

INFORMAL	FORMAL
Subject + ___	Subject + *be* contracted

Code-Switching: Teaching Standard English in Urban Classrooms by Rebecca S. Wheeler and Rachel Swords © 2006 NCTE.

MAKING NEGATIVES

She won't never v. She won't ever

INFORMAL		FORMAL

INFORMAL

<u>No</u> judgments should be made about <u>nobody</u>.

He <u>didn't</u> let <u>nobody</u> put him down.

He <u>doesn't</u> want <u>no</u> trouble.

I <u>don't</u> like <u>no</u> other star but him.

She <u>won't</u> never say . . .

THE PATTERN

Negative (*no, didn't, doesn't, won't,* etc.)

+

no/nobody/never, etc.

FORMAL

<u>No</u> judgments should be made about <u>anybody</u>.

He <u>didn't</u> let <u>anybody</u> put him down.

He <u>doesn't</u> want <u>any</u> trouble.

I <u>don't</u> like <u>any</u> other star but him.

She <u>won't</u> ever say . . .

Negative (*no, didn't, doesn't, won't,* etc.)

+

any/anybody/ever, etc.

Code-Switching: Teaching Standard English in Urban Classrooms by Rebecca S. Wheeler and Rachel Swords © 2006 NCTE.

Be/Have + ACTION WORD

was name_ v. was named
had turn_ v. had turned

INFORMAL ———————|——————— **FORMAL**

INFORMAL	FORMAL
A boy was name_ Tarik.	A boy was named Tarik.
I will be delight_ . . .	I will be delighted . . .
I was surprise_ . . .	I was surprised . . .
I had turn_ on the TV . . .	I had turned on the TV . . . .

THE PATTERN

have/be + bare form of verb	*have/be* + verb + *-ed/en*

Code-Switching: Teaching Standard English in Urban Classrooms by Rebecca S. Wheeler and Rachel Swords © 2006 NCTE.

PLURALITY

"Showing more than one"
I have two cat_ v. I have two cats

INFORMAL

FORMAL

INFORMAL	FORMAL
They call people name_.	They call people names.
I could answer some more question_.	I could answer some more questions.
Respect looks like those flower_.	Respect looks like those flowers.
Respect is many different thing_.	Respect is many different things.
If you respect other_, they will respect you.	If you respect others, they will respect you.
She has three cat_ and one dog.	She has three cats and one dog.

THE PATTERN

Other signal words in the sentence in the paragraph Common knowledge	Noun + -s

Code-Switching: Teaching Standard English in Urban Classrooms by Rebecca S. Wheeler and Rachel Swords © 2006 NCTE.

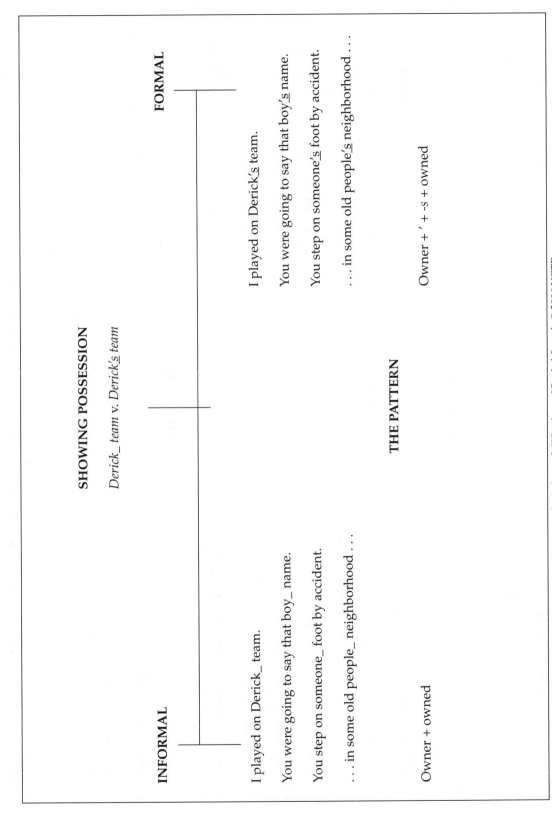

SHOWING POSSESSION

Derick_ team v. Derick's team

INFORMAL	FORMAL
I played on Derick_ team.	I played on Derick's team.
You were going to say that boy_ name.	You were going to say that boy's name.
You step on someone_ foot by accident.	You step on someone's foot by accident.
. . in some old people_ neighborhood . . .	. . . in some old people's neighborhood . . .

THE PATTERN

Owner + owned	Owner + ' + -s + owned

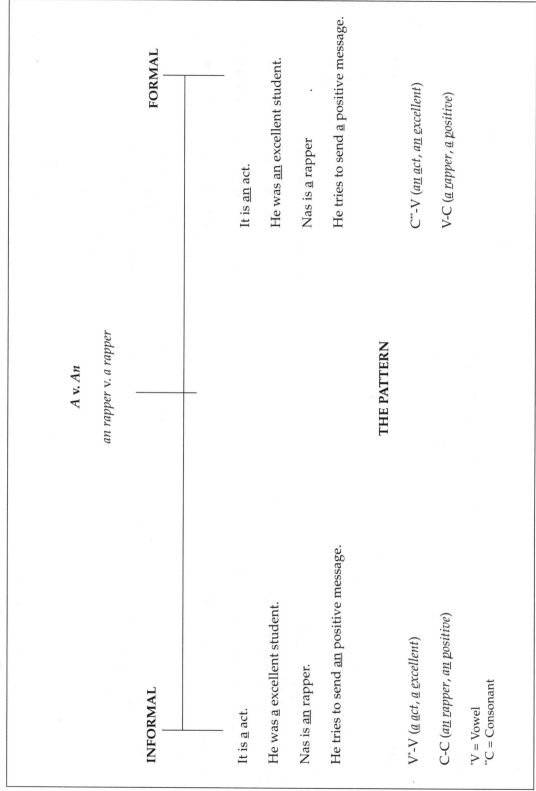

INFORMAL

FORMAL

A v. An

an rapper v. a rapper

It is a act.

He was a excellent student.

Nas is an rapper.

He tries to send an positive message.

It is an act.

He was an excellent student.

Nas is a rapper   .

He tries to send a positive message.

THE PATTERN

V*-V (*a act, a excellent*)

C-C (*an rapper, an positive*)

*V = Vowel
**C = Consonant

C**-V (*an act, an excellent*)

V-C (*a rapper, a positive*)

Code-Switching: Teaching Standard English in Urban Classrooms by Rebecca S. Wheeler and Rachel Swords © 2006 NCTE.

ENDINGS FOR SINGULAR NOUNS

*If a presidents v. If a president_*

INFORMAL

FORMAL

The men that were going to be presidents . . .

If a presidents was to . . .

She wants me to pass every grades.

They deserve to be on a U.S. coins.

The men that were going to be president_ . . .

If a president_ was to . . .

She wants me to pass every grade_.

They deserve to be on a U.S. coin_.

THE PATTERN

Singular noun + -s

Singular noun_

Code-Switching: Teaching Standard English in Urban Classrooms by Rebecca S. Wheeler and Rachel Swords © 2006 NCTE.

Is/Are

You is v. *You are*

INFORMAL	FORMAL
I am tall.	I am tall.
She is tall.	She is tall.
Jaden is tall.	Jaden is tall.
We is tall.	We are tall.
You is tall.	You are tall.
They is tall.	They are tall.

PATTERNS

I + am	*I + am*
	he/she/it + is
Otherwise,	Otherwise,
subject (*he/she/it/we/you/they*)+ *is*	subject (*we/you/they*) + *are*

Was/Were

You <u>was</u> v. *You <u>were</u>*

INFORMAL

<u>I was</u> sleeping.

<u>The dog was</u> sleeping.

<u>She was</u> sleeping.

<u>We was</u> sleeping.

<u>You was</u> sleeping.

The <u>girls was</u> sleeping.

<u>They was</u> sleeping.

FORMAL

<u>I was</u> sleeping.

<u>The dog was</u> sleeping.

<u>She was</u> sleeping.

<u>We were</u> sleeping.

<u>You were</u> sleeping.

The <u>girls were</u> sleeping.

<u>They were</u> sleeping.

PATTERNS

Subject + *was*

I/he/she/it + *was*

Otherwise,
subject (*we/you/they*) + *were*

Appendix B

A Literary Grammatical Concordance

This section provides literary resources to accompany your work in contrastive analysis. Here's how to use this appendix: If you're preparing to teach a lesson on subject-verb agreement, look under the heading Verb Patterns and find the subheading Subject-Verb Agreement. Under that heading, you will find a list of books that use the informal subject-verb agreement pattern—*Daddy Is a Monster . . . Sometimes*; *Flossie and the Fox*; *A Million Fish . . . More or Less*; *Working Cotton*; *Kinda Blue*; and *Mirandy and Brother Wind*. You can then use any or all of these resources to supplement your lessons on subject-verb agreement. These resources are all picture books and rarely contain page numbers. For this reason, our page count begins on the first page that contains text in the story. Further, many of the examples we offer include more than one informal English pattern. When we convert to formal English, we convert *only* the target boldface structure, leaving any other informal structures intact.

1. Noun Patterns

1.1. Plurals
Kinda Blue (page 12—seed/seeds)
Working Cotton
      (Informal) Cotton **flower** this late in the year bound to bring us luck (25).
      (Formal) Cotton **flowers** this late in the year bound to bring us luck.

1.2. Pronouns
Back Home (page 5—*them/those*; page 10—*me/I*; page 28—*them/those*)
      (Informal) I think you'd best wait, and change out of **them** fancy clothes first (5).
      (Formal) I think you'd best wait, and change out of **those** fancy clothes first.
Grandmama's Joy (page 12)
      (Informal) **Me and Tippy** was just watching the ball game (12).
      (Formal) **Tippy and I** was just watching the ball game.
Kinda Blue (page 1—*me/I*)
A Million Fish . . . More or Less (pages 1 and 2—*me/I*; page 21—*me/my*)
      (Informal) Now I'll be takin' **me** fish (21).
      (Formal) Now I'll be takin' **my** fish.
Mirandy and Brother Wind (page 29—*them/those*)
Nappy Hair (pages 6, 10, and 21— *them/those*)
Pink and Say (page 2—*them/those*; pages 13 and 27—*they/there*)
Working Cotton (pages 17 and 19—*it's/there's*; page 26—*us/we, me/I*)
      (Informal) Sometime **it's** a little piece of meat in your bowl (17).
      (Formal) Sometime **there's** a little piece of meat in your bowl.

2. Verb Patterns

2.1. Tense
Daddy Is a Monster . . . Sometimes (page 6—*come/came*)
Flossie and the Fox (page 8—*come/came*; page 17—*say/said*; page 19—*say/said*)
> (Informal) Flossie commenced to skip along, when she **come** upon a critter she couldn't recollect ever seeing (8).
> (Formal) Flossie commenced to skip along, when she **came** upon a critter she couldn't recollect ever seeing.

Kinda Blue (pages 5, 15, and 16—*knowed/knew*)
A Million Fish . . . More or Less (page 5—*run/ran*)
> (Informal) The hounds broke and **run** (5).
> (Formal) The hounds broke and **ran**.

Mirandy and Brother Wind (page 1—*come/came*; page 4—*say/said*; page 5—*come/came*; page 8—*say/said*; page 12—*say/said*; page 13—*come/came, say/said*; page 17—*come/came*; page 21—*say/said*; page 26—*say/said*)
Nappy Hair (page 9—*comb/combs*; page 16—*say/said*; page 21—*come/comes*; page 22—*come/came*; page 26—*shout/shouted, jump/jumped, say/said*; page 28—*say/said*)
Nettie Jo's Friends (pages 1, 4, 8, 9, and 19—*say/said*)
> (Informal) "Hold still while I size this dress," Mama **say** (1).
> (Formal) "Hold still while I size this dress," Mama **said**.

Pink and Say (page 10—*took/taken, brung/brought*; page 13—*runned/ran*; page 27—*run/ran*)

2.2. Subject-Verb Agreement
Daddy Is a Monster . . . Sometimes (page 15—*read/reads, kiss/kisses, cut/cuts, start/starts, come/comes*)
Flossie and the Fox (page 4—*seem/seems*; page 17—*use/uses*)
> (Informal) **Seem** like they been troubled by a fox (4).
> (Formal) **Seems** like they been troubled by a fox.

Kinda Blue (page 11—*talks/talk*; page 12—*knows/know*; page 13—*thinks/think*; page 23—*talks/talk*; page 24—*shows/show, needs/need, gives/give*; page 26—*knows/know, looks/look, thinks/think, wishes/wish*; page 29—*loves/love*)
A Million Fish . . . More or Less (pages 16 and 21—*take/takes*)
> (Informal) You win, **we takes** half the catch (16).
> (Formal) You win, **we take** half the catch.

Mirandy and Brother Wind (pages 4 and 8—*catch/catches*)
Working Cotton (page 1—*get/gets*; page 3—*send/sends, speak/speaks*; page 5—*say/says*; page 6—*pick/pick*; page 7—*keep/keeps, sing/sings, hum/hums*; page 11—*smell/smells*; page 14—*take/takes*; page 17—*bring/brings*; page 19—*move/moves*; page 25—*say/says*; page 26—*come/comes*)

2.3. *Is/are*
Back Home (page 28)
> (Informal) Don't you know **them's** Avery bugs out at your old house (28).
> (Formal) Don't you know **those are** Avery bugs out at your old house.

Mirandy and Brother Wind (page 29)

2.4. *Was/were*
Carolina Shout! (page 13)
> (Informal) Squeezing the tomatoes like they **was** squeezin' the cheeks of some little baby.
> (Formal) Squeezing the tomatoes like they **were** squeezin' the cheeks of some little baby.

Daddy Is a Monster . . . Sometimes (pages 1, 5, and 10)
Flossie and the Fox (page 23)
> (Informal) Come tellin' me you **was** a fox, then can't prove it (23).
> (Formal) Come tellin' me you **were** a fox, then can't prove it.

Grandmama's Joy (page 12)
> (Informal) Me and Tippy **was** just watching the ball game (12).
> (Formal) Me and Tippy **were** just watching the ball game.

Kinda Blue (pages 2 and 20)
A Million Fish . . . More or Less (pages 1 and 3)
> (Informal) As we **was** marchin' that gobbler home, I spied a lantern (3).
> (Formal) As we **were** marchin' that gobbler home, I spied a lantern.

Pink and Say (pages 16, 21, and 23)

2.5. *Do/does*
Carolina Shout! (page 21)
> (Informal) Sweep it out, and do it fine—or lady o' the house **don't** pay a dime!
> (Formal) Sweep it out, and do it fine—or lady o' the house **doesn't** pay a dime!

Flossie and the Fox (pages 5, 15, and 25)
> (Informal) How **do** a fox look (5)?
> (Formal) How **does** a fox look?

Grandmama's Joy (page 12)
> (Informal) I guess she **don't** feel like talking right now (12).
> (Formal) I guess she **doesn't** feel like talking right now.

Kinda Blue (pages 23 and 24)
Mirandy and Brother Wind (page 12)
Pink and Say (pages 5, 10, and 27)
Working Cotton
> (Informal) Sometime cotton **don't** know when it be spring (25).
> (Formal) Sometime cotton **doesn't** know when it be spring.

2.6. *Got/have*
Carolina Shout! (page 11)
> (Informal) Every muscle I **got's** in pain (11)!
> (Formal) Every muscle I **have is** in pain!

Daddy Is a Monster . . . Sometimes (page 15)
Flossie and the Fox (pages 15, 19, and 22)
> (Informal) Rats **got** long pointed noses (15).
> (Formal) Rats **have** long pointed noses.

Goin' Someplace Special (page 27)
> (Informal) They **got** to go 'round back and sit up in the Buzzard's Roost (27).

(Formal) They **have** to go 'round back and sit up in the Buzzard's Roost.
Grandmama's Joy (pages 4, 15, and 23)
>   (Informal) I **got** a surprise for you (4).
>   (Formal) I **have** a surprise for you.
Nappy Hair (pages 3, 12, 14, 28, and 29)
Nettie Jo's Friends (page 2)
>   (Informal) This'n is the only one I **got** (2).
>   (Formal) This'n is the only one I **have**.
Pink and Say (pages 13 and 19)
Ragtime Tumpie (page 19)
>   (Informal) I **got** a shiny silver dollar for the winner (19).
>   (Formal) I **have** a shiny silver dollar for the winner.

2.7. Gonna

Back Home (page 8)
>   (Informal) I was **gonna** show you my new kid (8).
>   (Formal) I was **going to** show you my new kid.
Daddy Is a Monster . . . Sometimes (pages 5, 10, 17, 19, and 26)
Kinda Blue (pages 5 and 6)
Nappy Hair (page 12)
The Patchwork Quilt (pages 1, 2, 7, and 11)
>   (Informal) I'm **gonna** talk to Grandma (1).
>   (Formal) I'm **going to** talk to Grandma.
Ragtime Tumpie (pages 11,15, 17, and 25)
>   (Informal) I'm **gonna** be a honky-tonk dancer (11).
>   (Formal) I'm **going to** be a honky-tonk dancer.

2.8. Wanna

Carolina Shout! (page 1)
>   (Informal) There's plenty of music, if you **wanna** hear it (1).
>   (Formal) There's plenty of music, if you **want to** hear it.
Flossie and the Fox (page16)
>   (Informal) You can beg all you **wanna** (16).
>   (Formal) You can beg all you **want to**.

2.9. Ain't

Daddy Is a Monster . . . Sometimes (page 10)
Grandmama's Joy (page 12)
>   (Informal) Melissa **ain't** sick, is she (12)?
>   (Formal) Melissa **isn't** sick, is she?
Kinda Blue (page 24)
Pink and Say (pages 19, 23, 24, 26, 28, and 32)
Ragtime Tumpie (page 21)
>   (Informal) I **ain't** too little (21)!
>   (Formal) I **am not** too little!
William and the Good Old Days (page 22)
>   (Informal) This **ain't** William (22)?
>   (Formal) This **isn't** William?

2.10. *Be* **Understood**
Back Home (page 28)
      (Informal) What __ you searching for (28)?
      (Formal) What **are** you searching for?
Daddy Is a Monster . . . Sometimes (pages 1 and 26)
Flossie and the Fox (pages 4, 9, 11, 14, 15, and 23)
      (Informal) I don't believe you __ a fox (9).
      (Formal) I don't believe you **are** a fox.
Goin' Someplace Special (pages 24 and 27)
      (Informal) __ You lost, Child (24)?
      (Formal) **Are** you lost, Child?
Kinda Blue (pages 9, 12, and 17)
Mirandy and Brother Wind (page 8, 20, 21, 24, and 26)
Nappy Hair (pages 6, 9, 12, 14, 19, and 25)
Nettie Jo's Friends (pages 1 and 10)
      (Informal) Annie Mae, we__ goin' to a wedding (1).
      (Formal) Annie Mae, we **are** goin' to a wedding.
The Patchwork Quilt (page 7)
      (Informal) Makin' this quilt __ gonna be a joy (7).
      (Formal) Makin' this quilt **is** gonna be a joy.
Pink and Say (pages 5, 6, 13, and 27)
William and the Good Old Days (page 8)
      (Informal) I know you __ not talking to Mama like that (8).
      (Formal) I know you **are** not talking to Mama like that.
Working Cotton (pages 6 and 14)

2.11. Habitual *be*
Daddy Is a Monster . . . Sometimes (page 15)
Flossie and the Fox (pages 4, 5, 6, 8, and 19)
      (Informal) Oh well, a fox **be** just a fox (6).
      (Formal) Oh well, a fox **is** just a fox.
Kinda Blue (pages 4, 13, 14, 15, 16, 20, 24, 26, and 27)
Mirandy and Brother Wind (page 5)
Working Cotton (pages 1, 3, 7, 19, 20, 25, and 26)
      (Informal) It **be** cold, cold, cold (3).
      (Formal) It **is** always cold, cold, cold.

2.12. Multiple Negation
Back Home (pages 8 and 19)
Daddy Is a Monster . . . Sometimes (page 9)
Flossie and the Fox (pages 14, 16, and 19)
      (Informal) I'll not accord you **nothing** (14)!
      (Formal) I'll not accord you **anything**!
Goin' Someplace Special (page 27)
      (Informal) **Don't** you know **nothing** (27)?
      (Formal) **Don't** you know **anything**?
Kinda Blue (page 11)
Mirandy and Brother Wind (pages 5, 13, and 26)
Nappy Hair (pages 19, 22, and 24)

Nettie Jo's Friends (page 10)
    (Informal) I **can't** see **nothing** (10).
    (Formal) I **can't** see **anything**.
Pink and Say (pages 13, 16, 27, and 29)

Bibliography

Children's Literature

Day, A. (1988). *Frank and Ernest*. New York: Scholastic.

Day, A. (1990). *Frank and Ernest play ball*. New York: Scholastic.

Day, A. (1994). *Frank and Ernest on the road*. New York: Scholastic.

Flournoy, V. (1985). *The patchwork quilt* (J. Pinkney, Illus.). New York: Dial.

Greenfield, E. (1980). *Grandmama's joy* (C. Byard, Illus.). New York: Philomel.

Greenfield, E. (1993). *William and the good old days* (J. Spivey Gilchrist, Illus.). New York: HarperCollins.

Grifalconi, A. (1993). *Kinda blue*. Boston: Little, Brown.

Herron, C. (1998). *Nappy hair* (J. Cepeda, Illus.). New York: Dragonfly Books.

McKissack, P. C. (1986). *Flossie and the fox* (R. Isadora, Illus.). New York: Scholastic.

McKissack, P. C. (1988). *Mirandy and Brother Wind* (J. Pinkney, Illus.). New York: Knopf.

McKissack, P. C. (1989). *Nettie Jo's friends* (S. Cook, Illus.). New York: Knopf.

McKissack, P. C. (1992). *A million fish . . . more or less* (D. Schutzer, Illus.). New York: Knopf, 1992.

McKissack, P. C. (2001). *Goin' someplace special* (J. Pinkney, Illus.). New York: Scholastic.

Pinkney, G. J. (1992). *Back home* (J. Pinkney, Illus.). New York: Puffin.

Polacco, P. (1994). *Pink and Say*. New York: Philomel.

Schroeder, A. (1989). *Ragtime Tumpie* (B. Fuchs, Illus.). Boston: Little, Brown.

Schroeder, A. (1995). *Carolina shout!* (B. Fuchs, Illus.). New York: Dial.

Steptoe, J. (1980). *Daddy is a monster . . . sometimes*. New York: HarperCollins.

Williams, S. A. (1992). *Working cotton* (C. Byard, Illus.). San Diego: Harcourt.

Academic

Adger, C. T. (1998). Register shifting with dialect resources in instructional discourse. In S. M. Hoyle & C. T. Adger (Eds.), *Kids talk: Strategic language use in later childhood* (pp. 151–69). New York: Oxford UP.

Adger, C. T., Christian, D., & Taylor, O. L. (Eds.). (1999). *Making the connection: Language and academic achievement among African American students*. Washington, DC: Center for Applied Linguistics.

Barth, R. S. (2002). The culture builder. *Educational Leadership, 59*(8), 6–11.

Baugh, J. (1981). Design and implementation of writing instruction for speakers of non-Standard English: Perspectives for a national neighborhood literacy program. In B. Cronnell (Ed.), *The writing needs of linguistically different students*. Los Alamitos, CA: SWRL Educational Research and Development.

Baugh, J. (1999). *Out of the mouths of slaves: African American language and educational malpractice*. Austin: University of Texas Press.

Baugh, J. (2000a). *Beyond Ebonics: Linguistic pride and racial prejudice*. New York: Oxford University Press.

Baugh, J. (2000b). Racial identification by speech. *American Speech, 75*(4), 362–64.

Birch, B. (2001). Grammar standards: It's all in your attitude. *Language Arts, 78*(6), 535–42.

Bowie, D. (2003). Early development of the Card-Cord merger in Utah. *American Speech, 78*, 31–51.

Canagarajah, S. (2003). Foreword. In G. Smitherman & V. Villanueva (Eds.), *Language diversity in the classroom: From intention to practice* (pp. ix–xiv). Carbondale: Southern Illinois University Press.

Cassidy, F. G. (Ed.). (1985). *Dictionary of American regional English*. Vol. 1: Introduction and A–C. Cambridge, MA: Belknap Press.

Chesebro, J., Berko, R., Hopson, C., Cooper, P., & Hodges, H. (1995). Effective strategies for increasing achievement in oral communication. In Robert W. Cole (Ed.), *Educating everybody's children: Diverse teaching strategies for diverse learners* (pp. 139–66). Alexandria, VA: Association for Supervision and Curriculum Development.

Christenbury, L. (2000). *Making the journey: Being and becoming a teacher of English language arts* (2nd ed.). Portsmouth, NH: Boynton/Cook.

Coelho, E. (1988). *Caribbean students in Canadian schools*. Toronto: Carib-Can.

Coelho, E. (1991). *Caribbean students in Canadian schools: Book 2*. Markham, Ont.: Pippin.

Conference on College Composition and Communication. (1974). *Students' right to their own language* [Special issue, Electronic version]. *College Composition and Communication, 25*, 1–32. Retrieved March 13, 2005, from http://www.ncte.org/library/files/About_NCTE/Overview/NewSRTOL.pdf

Crawford, C. (Ed.). (2001). *Ebonics and language education of African ancestry students*. New York: Sankofa.

Crystal, D. (1995). *The Cambridge encyclopedia of the English language*. Cambridge, UK: Cambridge University Press.

Cumming, D. (1997, January 9). A different approach to teaching language. *Atlanta Constitution*, p. B1.

Delpit, L. (1995). *Other people's children: Cultural conflict in the classroom*. New York: New Press.

Delpit, L., & Kilgour J. Dowdy (Eds.). (2002). *The skin that we speak: Thoughts on language and culture in the classroom*. New York: New Press.

Dumas, B. K. (1999). Southern mountain English: The language of the Ozarks and southern Appalachia. In R. S. Wheeler (Ed.), *The workings of language: From prescriptions to perspectives* (pp. 67–79). Westport, CT: Praeger.

Eugenides, J. (2002). *Middlesex*. New York: Picador.

Ezarik, M. (2002, May). A time and a place. *District Administration*, 38–42. Retrieved March 13, 2005, from http://www.districtadministration.com/page.cfm?p=205.

Feagin, C. (2003). Vowel shifting in the southern States. In S. J. Nagle & S. L. Sanders (Eds.), *English in the southern United States* (pp, 126–40). Cambridge, UK: Cambridge University Press.

Fogel, H., & Ehri, L. (2000). Teaching elementary students who speak Black English Vernacular to write in Standard English: Effects of dialect transformation practice. *Contemporary Educational Psychology, 25*(2), 212–35.

Fromkin, V., Rodman, R., & Hyams, N. (2002). *An introduction to language* (7th ed.). Boston: Heinle.

Gadsden, V. L., & Wagner, D. A. (1995). *Literacy among African-American youth: Issues in learning, teaching, and schooling*. Cresskill, NJ: Hampton Press.

Gilyard, K. (1991). *Voices of the self: A study of language competence*. Detroit: Wayne State University Press.

Goodman, Y., & Goodman, D. (2000). "I hate 'postrophe s": Issues of dialect and reading proficiency. In J. K. Peyton, P. Griffin, W. Wolfram, & R. Fasold (Eds.), *Language in action: New studies of language in society: Essays in honor of Roger W. Shuy* (pp. 408–35). Cresskill, NJ: Hampton Press.

Green, L. J. (2002). *African American English: A linguistic introduction*. Cambridge, UK: Cambridge University Press.

Heath, S. B. (1983). *Ways with words: Language, life, and work in communities and classrooms*. Cambridge, UK: Cambridge University Press.

Hughes, Langston. (1994). "Mother to Son." In A. Rampersad (Ed.), *The collected poems of Langston Hughes*. New York: Knopf.

Jencks, C., & Phillips, M. (Eds). (1998). *The black-white test score gap*. Washington, DC: Brookings Institution Press.

Joos, M. (1967). *The five clocks: A linguistic excursion into the five styles of English usage*. New York: Harcourt, Brace.

Kephart, R. (1992). Reading creole English does not destroy your brain cells. In J. Siegel (Ed.), *Pidgins, creoles and nonstandard dialects in education: Occasional paper 12* (pp. 67–81). Clayton, Vict.: Applied Linguistics Association of Australia.

Labov, W. (1972). *Language in the inner city: Studies in the Black English Vernacular*. Philadelphia: University of Pennsylvania Press.

Labov, W. (1995). Can reading failure be reversed? A linguistic approach to the question. In V. L. Gadsden & D. A. Wagner (Eds.), *Literacy among African-American Youth: Issues in learning, teaching, and schooling* (pp. 39–68). Cresskill, NJ: Hampton Press.

Labov, W., & Baker, B. (n.d.). Linguistic component, African American literacy and culture project. Retrieved March 13, 2005, from http://www.ling.upenn.edu/~wlabov/FinalReport.html.

Lado, R. (1957). *Linguistics across cultures: Applied linguistics for language teachers*. Ann Arbor: University of Michigan Press.

LeMoine, N. (1999). *English for your success: A language development program for African American children grades pre-K–8: A handbook of successful strategies for educators*. Maywood, NJ: Peoples.

Macedo, D. (1994). *Literacies of power: What Americans are not allowed to know*. Boulder: Westview Press.

Malcolm, I. G. (1992). English in the education of speakers of aboriginal English. In J. Siegel (Ed.), *Pidgins, creoles and nonstandard dialects in education: Occasional paper 12* (pp. 15–41). Clayton, Vict.: Applied Linguistics Association of Australia.

McWhorter, J. (1998). *The word on the street: Fact and fable about American English*. New York: Plenum Press.

Mickan, M. (1992). Kriol and education in the Kimberly. In J. Siegel (Ed.), *Pidgins, creoles and nonstandard dialects in education: Occasional paper 12* (pp. 42–52). Clayton, Vict.: Applied Linguistics Association of Australia.

Morrison, T. (2000). *The Nobel Lecture in Literature, 1993*. New York: Knopf.

Morrison, T. (2003). *Love*. New York: Knopf.

Nidue, A. J. (1992). A survey of teachers' attitudes towards the use of Tok Pisin in community schools in Papua New Guinea. In J. Siegel (Ed.), *Pidgins, creoles and nonstandard dialects in education: Occasional paper 12* (pp. 13–14). Clayton, Vict.: Applied Linguistics Association of Australia.

Nieto, S. (2000). *Affirming diversity: The sociopolitical context of multicultural education* (3rd ed.). New York: Longman.

Odlin, T. (1989). *Language transfer: Cross-linguistic influence in language learning*. Cambridge, UK: Cambridge University Press.

Ogbu, J. U. (with Davis, A.). (2003). *Black American students in an affluent suburb: A study of academic disengagement*. Mahwah, NJ: Lawrence Erlbaum.

Perry, T., & Delpit, L. (Eds.). (1998). *The real Ebonics debate: Power, language, and the education of African-American children*. Boston: Beacon Press.

Perry, T., Steele, C., & Hilliard, A. G., III (Eds.). (2003). *Young, gifted, and black: Promoting high achievement among African-American students.* Boston: Beacon Press.

Preston, D. R. (2003). Presidential address: Where are the dialects of American English at anyhow? *American Speech, 78*(3), 235–54.

Pullum, G. (1997, March). Language that dare not speak its name. *Currents* [University of California, Santa Cruz]. Retrieved June 1, 2005 from http://www.ucsc.edu/oncampus/currents/97-03-31/ebonics.htm

Pullum, G. (1999). African American Vernacular English is not Standard English with mistakes. In R. S. Wheeler (Ed.), *The workings of language: From prescriptions to perspectives* (pp. 39–58). Westport, CT: Praeger.

Raimes, A. (1996). *Keys for writers: A brief handbook.* Boston: Houghton Mifflin.

Redd, T. M., & Webb, K. S. (2005). *A teacher's introduction to African American English: What a writing teacher should know.* Urbana, IL: National Council of Teachers of English.

Richardson, E. (2002). "To protect and serve": African American female literacies. *College Composition and Communication, 53*(4), 675–704.

Richardson, E. (2003). *African American literacies.* New York: Routledge.

Rickford, J. R. (n.d.). Using the vernacular to teach the standard. Retrieved March 12, 2005, from http://www.stanford.edu/~rickford/papers/VernacularToTeachStandard.html

Rickford, J. R. (1987, January 22). Letter to Senator Arlen Specter, Chairman, U.S. Senate Subcommittee on Labor, Health and Human Services and Education. Retrieved March 12, 2005, from http://www.stanford.edu/~rickford/ebonics/SpecterLetter.html.

Rickford, J. R. (1996, December 26). The Oakland Ebonics decision: Commendable attack on the problem. Editorial. *San Jose Mercury News.* Retrieved March 12, 2005, from http://www.stanford.edu/~rickford/ebonics/SJMN-OpEd.html

Rickford, J. R. (1999a). *African American Vernacular English: Features, evolution, educational implications.* Malden, MA: Blackwell.

Rickford, J. R. (1999b). Language diversity and academic achievement in the education of African American students: An overview of the issues. In C. T. Adger, D. Christian, & O. L. Taylor (Eds.), *Making the connection: Language and academic achievement among African American students* (pp. 1–30). Washington, DC: Center for Applied Linguistics.

Rickford, J. R. (2000). Linguistics, education, and the Ebonics firestorm. In J. E. Alatis, H. E. Hamilton, & A.-H. Tan (Eds.), *Linguistics, language and the professions: Education, journalism, law, medicine and technology* (pp. 25–45). Georgetown University Round Table on Languages and Linguistics 2000. Washington, DC: Georgetown University Press.

Rickford, J. R., & Rickford, A. E. (1995). Dialect readers revisited. *Linguistics and Education, 7*(2), 107–28.

Rickford, J. R., & Rickford, R. J. (2000). *Spoken soul: The story of Black English*. New York: Wiley.

Rickford, J. R., Sweetland, J., & Rickford, A. E. (2004). African American English and other vernaculars in education: A topic-coded bibliography. *Journal of English Linguistics, 32*(3), 230–320.

Rogers, R. (2003). *A critical discourse analysis of family literacy practices: Power in and out of print*. Mawah, NJ: Lawrence Erlbaum.

Rosenthal, R., & Jacobson, L. (1968). *Pygmalion in the classroom: Teacher expectation and pupils' intellectual development*. New York: Holt, Rinehart and Winston.

Schierloh, J. M. (1991). Teaching Standard English usage: A dialect-based approach. *Adult Learning, 2*(5), 20–22.

Secret, C. (1998). Embracing Ebonics and teaching Standard English: An interview with Oakland teacher Carrie Secret. In T. Perry & L. Delpit (Eds.), *The real Ebonics debate: Power, language, and the education of African-American children* (pp. 79–88). Boston: Beacon Press.

Shaughnessy, M. P. (1977). *Errors and expectations: A guide for the teacher of basic writing*. New York: Oxford University Press.

Smitherman, G. (1972). English teacher, why you be doing the thangs you don't do? *English Journal, 61*(1), 59–65.

Smitherman, G. (1977). *Talkin and testifyin: The language of Black America*. Boston: Houghton Mifflin.

Smitherman, G. (2000). *Talkin that talk: Language, culture, and education in African America*. New York: Routledge.

Smitherman, G., & Villanueva, V. (Eds.). (2003). *Language diversity in the classroom: From intention to practice*. Carbondale: Southern Illinois University Press.

Steffensen, M. S., Reynolds, R., McClure, E., & Guthrie, L. (1982). Black English vernacular and reading comprehension: A cloze study of third, sixth, and ninth graders. *Journal of Reading Behavior, 3*, 285–98.

Sweetland, J. (in progress). *Teaching writing in the multicultural classroom: A sociolinguistic approach*. Doctoral dissertation in progress. Department of Linguistics, Stanford University.

Sweetland, J. (2004). The words we choose to use lesson plan. In *Sociolinguistic sensitivity in language arts instruction: A literature and writing curriculum for the intermediate grades, teachers' manual and materials*. Unpublished manuscript, Stanford University, Department of Linguistics.

Taylor, H. U. (1991). *Standard English, Black English, and bidialectalism: A controversy*. New York: Peter Lang.

Thomas, E. R. (2003). Secrets revealed by southern vowel shifting. *American Speech, 78*(2), 150–70.

Troutman, D. (1999). Breaking mythical bonds: African American women's language. In R. S. Wheeler (Ed.), *The workings of language: From prescriptions to perspectives* (pp. 217–32). Westport, CT: Praeger.

Wheeler, R. S. (1999). Home speech as springboard to school speech: Oakland's commendable work on Ebonics. In R. S. Wheeler (Ed.), *The workings of language: From prescriptions to perspectives* (pp. 59–66). Westport, CT: Praeger.

Wheeler, R. S. (2001). From home speech to school speech: Vantages on reducing the achievement gap in inner city schools. *Virginia English Bulletin, 51*(2), 4–16.

Wheeler, R. S. (2005). Code-switch to teach Standard English (Teaching in the World column). *English Journal, 94*(5), 108–12.

Wheeler, R. S., & Swords, R. (2004). Codeswitching: Tools of language and culture transform the dialectally diverse classroom. *Language Arts, 81*(6), 470–80.

Wilson, K. G. (1993). *The Columbia guide to Standard American English*. New York: Columbia UP.

Wolfram, W. (1969). *A sociolinguistic description of Detroit Negro speech*. Urban Language Series, 5. Washington, DC: Center for Applied Linguistics.

Wolfram, W. (1999). Repercussions from the Oakland Ebonics controversy—the critical role of dialect awareness programs. In C. T. Adger, D. Christian, & O. L. Taylor (Eds.), *Making the connection: Language and academic achievement among African American students* (pp. 61–80). Washington, DC: Center for Applied Linguistics.

Wolfram, W., Adger, C. T., & Christian, D. (1999). *Dialects in schools and communities*. Mahwah, NJ: Lawrence Erlbaum.

Wolfram, W., & Schilling-Estes, N. (1998). *American English: Dialects and variation*. Malden, MA: Blackwell.

Index

Accent, 48
Action verbs, 103–4, 122
  be/have plus, 171
Adger, Carolyn, 4, 12, 33, 39, 49, 50, 70, 137, 157
African American English, 16–17
  be understood in, 137–42
  errors in, 13
  habitual *be* in, 36–37, 134–37
  as labeling term, 20–21
  language transfer and, 10–11
  possession in, 33–36, 45–46
  richness of, 5–6, 39–40
  speakers of, 16
  subject-verb agreement in, 105
  variations in, 17
Angelou, Maya, 6
Ash, Sharon, 48
A versus *an*, contrastive analysis chart for, 174

Barth, R. S., 26
Baugh, John, 16, 37, 42
Berko, R., 5
Be understood, 137–42
  contrastive analysis chart for, 169
Birch, B., 31
Boberg, Charles, 48
Bowie, D., 48

Canagarajah, Suresh, 43, 44
Caribbean students, 55–57
Cassidy, F. G., 48
Chesebro, J., 5
Christenbury, L., 32
Christian, Donna, 4, 12, 33, 49, 50, 137, 157
Classroom, attitudes about language in, 14–16
Clothing, formal versus informal, 68–69
Code-switching, 11
  applicability of, 18–19
  contrastive analysis and, 61–62
  justification for, 159–60
  questions about, 159–61
  Shopping List for, 164
  talking to others about, 158–62

terminology for, 57–59
Coelho, E., 55, 56
Community English, 19
Complex patterns, 132–42
  be understood, 137–42
  habitual *be*, 134–37
  multiple patterns in sentence, 132–34
Conferencing, 150–52
Construction paper activity, 69–70
Contrastive analysis, 9, 27
  of past time, 125
  of plurals, 91–92
  of possessives, 81, 82–83
  research results of, 61–62
  of subject-verb agreement, 102–3, 120
  in teaching Standard English, 61–62
Cooper, P., 5
Correction
  code-switching as alternative to, 57–59
  contrastive analysis versus, 61–62
  failure of, 4
  futility of, 30
Cosby, Bill, 39
Creole, 56
Crystal, David, 17, 27
Cumming, D., 62

Day, Alexandra, 74
Delpit, Lisa, 39, 40, 41
Dialect prejudice, 14
Dialect(s). *See also* Language
  defined, 10
  emergence of, 51
  migration routes and, 52
  Standard English as, 50
  standard versus nonstandard, 11–14
  variety in, 47–50
Dumas, Bethany, 14

Ebonics, 161
Editing, 150–52
Ehri, Linnea, 60, 62, 154, 160
English. *See also* Language
  African American. *See* African American English
  formal versus informal, 21–24, 71–72

international variants of, 17–19, 27
standard versus nonstandard, 11–14
terminology about, 19–24
variety in, 47–50
Errors, correcting, 4
Eugenides, Jeffrey, 48
Everyday English, 20

Feagin, C., 48
Felt board activity, 69
Flossie and the Fox (McKissack), 73–74,
    147–48
Fogel, Howard, 60, 62, 154, 160
Formal English, 21–22, 23–24. *See also*
    Standard English
    is/are patterns in, 115–16
    past time in, 124
    plurals in, 94–95
    possessives in, 83–84
    rationale for term, 21
    recognizing, 71–72
    subject-verb agreement in, 104–5
    was/were patterns in, 110–11
Formality, levels of, 67–69
    activities for discussing, 69–70
Fromkin, V., 23, 49

Gilyard, Keith, 5, 31, 38
Gonna/going to, 126–31
    contrastive analysis chart for, 131
    discovering pattern form, 126–29
    reviewing, 129–30
Grammar. *See also specific topics*
    encountering new patterns, 154–57
    equated with Standard English, 32
    top ten patterns for problems with, 59,
        154–55, 163–77
    variations in, 49–50
Grammatical echo, 9
Green, Lisa J., 16, 19, 33, 154, 157

Habitual *be*
    in African American English, 36–37,
        134–37
    teaching, 134–37
Heath, S. B., 31
Herron, Carolivia, 143, 144–46
Hilliard, A. G., III, 41
Hodges, H., 5
Home speech, 5–8, 19

in classroom, 55–57
translating from, 60
Hopson, C., 5
Hughes, Langston, 6–7
Hyams, N., 25, 49

Informal English, 21, 22, 23–24. *See also*
    Formal English; Formality, levels of
    in classroom discussions, 59–60
    is/are patterns in, 115–16
    past time in, 122–24
    plurals in, 92, 95–97
    possessives in, 83
    recognizing, 71–72
    was/were patterns in, 111
International Englishes, 17–19, 27, 55–57
Is/are patterns, 114–17
    contrastive analysis chart for, 120, 176

Jackson, Jesse, 39
Jacobson, L., 14
Jencks, Christopher, 159
Joos, Martin, 32, 50
Journals, student, 148–49

Kephart, R., 56

Labov, William, 5, 13, 14, 27, 48
Lado, Robert, 9, 27
Language. *See also* Dialect(s); English
    assumptions about, 5
    building on existing knowledge of, 8–11
    classroom attitudes about, 14–16
    correcting, 4
    discerning race through, 16
    diversity in, 67–74
    grammar variations in, 49–50
    at home, 5–8
    new ways of thinking about, 58
    setting and, 8
    sound variations in, 48–49
    terminology about, 19–24, 57–59
    variation in, 67–71
    variety in, 47–50
    vernacular features of, 4
    vocabulary variations in, 47–48
Language transfer, 17–19
Language variety, 50
LeMoine, N., 37

Literacy debate, 38–44
Literature
    class discussion about, 147–48
    contrastive analysis lessons and, 146–47
    informal language examples in, 179–84
    language variation in, 72–74, 143–46
    teaching grammar patterns through, 146
Lyric Shuffle Games, 42–43

Macedo, D., 43
Martin Luther King Junior Elementary
    School Children v. Ann Arbor School
    District Board, 63
McKissack, P. C., 73, 143, 147–48
McWhorter, John, 5, 31, 38
Morrison, Toni, 6, 7–8, 39
Multiliteracies, 43–44

Nappy Hair (Herron), 144–46
Negatives, contrastive analysis chart for,
    170
Nidue, A. J., 57
Nieto, Sonya, 5, 14, 54
Nonstandard dialects, 12–14, 52
Noun endings, 175

Odlin, Terry, 9, 10, 27
Ogbu, J. U., 27, 55, 56
Ozark Mountain dialect, 14–15

Past time, 121–25
    contrastive analysis chart for, 125,
      167–69
    discovering patterns form, 121
    in formal English, 124
    in informal English, 122–24
    reviewing, 124
    time/tense contrasts, 122
Perry, Theresa, 39, 41
Personal picture activity, 70
Phillips, Meredith, 159
Piestrup, Anne, 4
Plurals, 91–101
    contrastive analysis chart for, 91–92,
      101, 172
    discovering patterns for, 92–97
    distinguishing from possessives, 99–100
    in formal English, 94–95
    in informal English, 91, 95–97

reviewing patterns for, 97–100
Possessives, 75–90
    activity for, 87–88
    in African American English, 33–36,
      45–46
    applying scientific method to, 76
    contrastive analysis chart for, 81, 82–83,
      90, 177
    discovering patterns for, 83–84
    distinguishing from plurals, 99–100
    grammar rule for, 77
    hypothesis for, 77–79
    lesson plan for, 80–90
    practicing, 84–87
    reviewing patterns for, 99–100
    student questions about, 79
    in student writing, 76–77, 80
Preston, Dennis, 49
Process writing approach, 40–41
Professional English, 20
Publishing, of student writing, 152–53
Pullum, Geoffrey, 47, 137

Race, discerning through language, 16
Raimes, Anne, 18
Reading. *See also* Literature
    language diversity and, 143–48
Redd, T. M., 42, 64, 157, 160
Richardson, Elaine, 27, 43, 71
Rickford, A. E., 11, 42
Rickford, John R., xi–xiii, 11, 16, 17, 20, 33,
    41, 42, 154, 157, 160
Rickford, R. J., 16, 42
Rodman, R., 25, 49
Rogers, Rebecca, 44
Rosenthal, R., 14

Schilling-Estes, Natalie, 10, 49, 50, 51, 52,
    157
School speech, 19
Schroeder, Alan, 143
Scientific method, 34–36
    possessives and, 76
Secret, Carrie, 42
Slang, 47
Smitherman, Geneva, 12, 15, 39, 40, 41,
    63, 154
Sounds, variations in, 48–49
Southern Mountain English (SME), 15
Standard English (SE), 4. *See also* Formal
    English

alternative names for, 13
assumptions about, 5
attitudes toward, 40–44, 52
grammar equated with, 32
as key to participation in society, 41
legitimacy of, 11–12
literacy debate and, 38–39
as prestige dialect, 12
in urban classrooms, 38–44
White supremacist ideology and, 43
written forms of, 51
Standard English as a Second Dialect
(SESD), 10
Stative verbs, 17
Steele, C., 41
Steptoe, John, 144
Student writing. *See also* Writing style
creating characters, 148–49
editing and conferencing, 150–52
language diversity and, 148–53
personal journals, 149–50
possessives in, 76–77, 80
publishing, 152–53
Stylistic variation, 50
Subject-verb agreement, 23–24
in African American English, 105
avoiding correction of, 58
contrastive analysis chart for, 102–3,
113, 120, 165–67
in formal English, 104–5, 110–11
in informal English, 106–7, 111–12
is/are patterns, 114–17, 120
lesson plan for, 104–9
rethinking, 105–6
reviewing, 117–19
subjects and action verbs, 103–4
was/were patterns, 109–113
Sweetland, Julie, 11, 21, 42, 74
Swords, Rachel, 5, 24, 30–31, 35, 161

Taylor, Hanni, 33, 61, 83
Terminology
for code-switching, 57–59
problem of, 19–24
Theory, 25
Thomas, E. R., 48
Tobago, students from, 56–57
Trinidad, students, 56–57
Troutman, Denise, 39

Urban classrooms, teaching Standard
English in, 38–44

Variation in language, 67–71
in literature, 72–74
Verbs. *See also* Subject-verb agreement
action, 103–4, 122
compound, 171
past tense, 121–25
stative, 17
Vernacular features, 4
Vernaculars, 52
Vocabulary, 47

Was/were patterns, 109
contrastive analysis chart for, 113, 177
in formal English, 110–11
in informal English, 111
reviewing, 111–12
Webb, K. S., 42, 64, 157, 160
West Indian students, 56–57
Wheeler, Rebecca S., 5, 19, 31, 161
Williams, Sherley Anne, 144–45, 146, 147
Wilson, K. G., 50
Wolfram, Walt, 4, 10, 12, 13, 17, 33, 49, 50,
51, 52, 137, 154, 157
Writing. *See* Student writing
Writing style, 24–25

Authors

Rebecca S. Wheeler is a research scientist in the Program for Research and Evaluation in Public Schools (PREPS), Darden College of Education, at Old Dominion University. She is on research leave from Christopher Newport University. With a BA from The University of Virginia, MS from Georgetown University, and PhD from the University of Chicago, Wheeler consults with urban schools (K–16) on teaching Standard English and reducing the achievement gap in African American classrooms. She serves the profession as an NCTE urban literacy consultant. Wheeler has published on code-switching in *Language Arts* and *English Journal*. In his *English Journal* column Teaching English in the World, Ken Lindblom says that Wheeler is "becoming one of the most important professional voices in language instruction" today.

Rachel Swords is a second- and third-grade teacher at Newsome Park Elementary School in Newport News, Virginia. She has a BA in English literature and an MA in teaching language arts, both from Christopher Newport University. Swords first became interested in code-switching when she took one of Rebecca Wheeler's graduate courses. As a result of the code-switching strategies she implemented, she was able to close the achievement gap between African American and White children in her classroom. In the year she began creating and teaching code-switching lessons, her African American students outperformed her White students in math and science. In 2003, Swords's action research in code-switching was instrumental in her being named a National Board Certified Teacher. She coauthored an article for *Language Arts* and continues to collaborate with Rebecca Wheeler as they develop materials for professional development and classroom lessons.

This book was typeset in Palatino and Helvetica by Electronic Imaging.
Typefaces used on the cover were Universe and Agramond.
The book was printed on 50-lb. Williamsburg Offset paper by Versa Press, Inc.

Food Webs
Rainforest Food Chains

Emma Lynch

Heinemann Library
Chicago, Illinois

Chicago, Illinois

Customer Service   888–454–2279

Visit our website at www.heinemannlibrary.com

Photo research by Ruth Blair and Ginny Stroud-Lewis
Designed by Jo Hinton-Malivoire and AMR
Printed in China by WKT Company Limited.

09 08 07 06 05
10 9 8 7 6 5 4 3 2 1

Library of Congress Cataloging-in-Publication Data
Lynch, Emma.
  Rainforest food chains / Emma Lynch.
    v. cm. — (Food webs)
  Includes bibliographical references and index.
  Contents: What is a rainforest food web? — What is a rainforest food chain? — What is a producer in a rainforest? — What is a primary consumer in a rainforest? — What is a secondary consumer in a rainforest? — What is a decomposer in a rainforest? — How are rainforest food chains different in different places? — What Happens to a food web when a food chain breaks down? — How can we protect the environment and rainforest food chains?
  ISBN 1-4034-5858-8 (lib. bdg.) — ISBN 1-4034-5865-0 (pbk.)
  1. Rain forest ecology—Juvenile literature. 2. Food chains (Ecology)—Juvenile literature. [1. Rain forest ecology. 2. Food chains (Ecology) 3. Ecology.] I. Title. II. Series.
  QH541.5.R27L96 2004
  577.34—dc22

                    2003026199

Acknowledgments
The author and publisher are grateful to the following for permission to reproduce copyright material: a-z botanicals p. **12**; Corbis pp. **5** (Bob Krist), **8** (Tom Brakefield), **11** (Matt Brown), **13** (Kevin Schafer), **14** (Jack Fields), **15** (Kennan Ward), **17** (Martin Rogers), **19** (Arne Hodalic), **25** (Natalie Fobes), **26** (Alison Wright), **27** (M. Sinibaldi); Heather Angel/Natural Visions pp. **7**, **18** (Brian Rogers); Nature Picture Library pp. **10** (Peter Oxford), **16** (Doug Allan); NHPA p. **23**.

Cover photograph of a toucan eating fruit reproduced with permission of Bruce Coleman/ Staffan Widstrand.

Illustrations by Words and Publications.

The publisher would like to thank Dr Dennis Radabaugh of the Department of Zoology at Ohio Wesleyan University for his comments in the preparation of this book.

Every effort has been made to contact copyright holders of any material reproduced in this book. Any omissions will be rectified in subsequent printings if notice is given to the publisher.

Contents

What Is a Rainforest Food Web? 4

What Is a Rainforest Food Chain? 6

Which Producers Live in Rainforests? 11

Which Primary Consumers Live in Rainforests? 13

Which Secondary Consumers Live in Rainforests? 15

Which Decomposers Live in Rainforests? 17

How Are Rainforest Food Chains Different in
Different Places? 19

What Happens to a Food Web When a Food Chain
Breaks Down? 22

How Can We Protect Rainforest Food Chains? 25

Where Are the World's Main Rainforests? 28

Glossary 30

More Books to Read 31

Index 32

Some words are shown in bold, **like this**. You can find out what they mean by looking in the glossary.

Rainforest Food Web?

All living things, including plants, **fungi**, humans, and other animals, are **organisms**. Each organism is eaten by another organism. Small animals are eaten by bigger animals, and then these animals get eaten by even larger ones. When large animals die, they get eaten by tiny insects, maggots, and **bacteria**. Even mighty trees die and rot, and are eaten by beetles, grubs, and fungi. If you draw lines between the organisms, showing who eats who, you create a diagram called a food web. It looks like a tangled spider's web!

In rainforests, just as in all **habitats**, the organisms that live there are connected as parts of a food web. In food web diagrams, the arrow leads from the food to the animal that eats it.

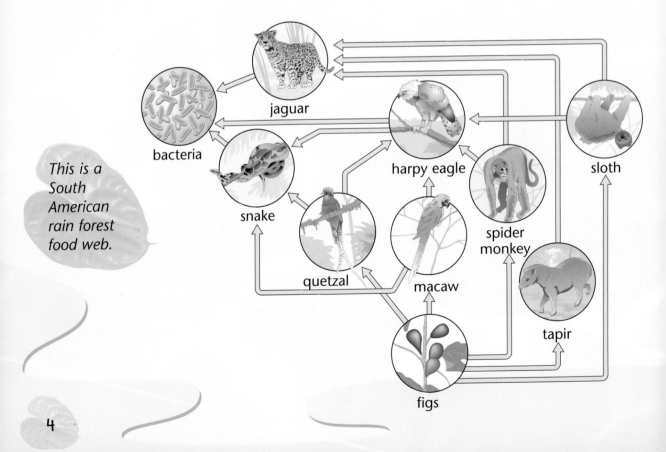

This is a South American rain forest food web.

jaguar

bacteria

harpy eagle

sloth

snake

spider monkey

quetzal

macaw

tapir

figs

What are rainforest habitats like?

This book looks at the food web and food chains of rain forest habitats. Rain forests are found in places with a **tropical climate**, usually near the **equator**. The climate is hot, and there is heavy rainfall all through the year.

Certain plants and animals live in the rain forest because they are especially suited to life there, and because the plants or animals that they feed on live there. Some, like mosses and jaguars, live on the forest floor. Plants such as vines and palms live in the dark **understory**. Animals such as monkeys and sloths live in the trees. Birds such as the harpy eagle fly through the treetops, called the **canopy** level, or above the forest, looking for animals to catch and eat.

This rainforest habitat is in the Caribbean island of Grenada.

What Is a Rainforest Food Chain?

A food web looks quite complex, but it is actually made up of many simpler food chains. These food chains show the way some of the organisms in a food web feed on each other. The arrows in the chain show the movement of food and **energy** from plants to animals as they feed on each other. More than half of the world's animal and plant **species** live in **tropical** rainforests, so the rainforest food web is made up of millions of food chains.

An **organism** can be part of more than one food chain in a food web. Most animals eat more than one type of food, because they have a better chance of survival if they do not depend on just one food source. They will also probably be eaten by more than one kind of animal!

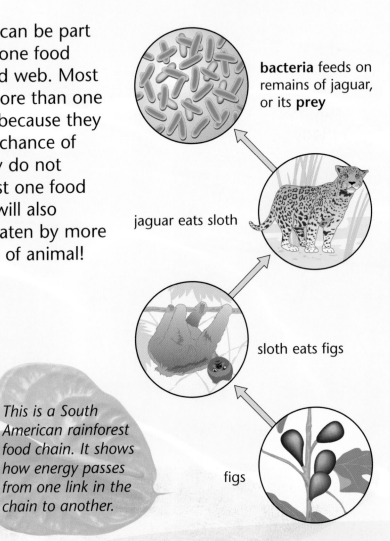

bacteria feeds on remains of jaguar, or its **prey**

jaguar eats sloth

sloth eats figs

figs

This is a South American rainforest food chain. It shows how energy passes from one link in the chain to another.

Starting the chain

Most food chains start with the energy that comes from the Sun. Plants take in water from the soil through their roots and **carbon dioxide** from the air through their leaves. Their leaves also trap the energy from sunlight and use this to change the water and carbon dioxide into sugary food. This process is called **photosynthesis**. Plants use this food, along with **nutrients** from the soil, to grow.

Every part of a growing plant can become food for other organisms in the **habitat**. They can eat the plant's roots, shoots, leaves, nuts, fruit, bark—or even the rotten plant when it has died. Animals cannot make their own food, so they eat the plants to get energy. Plant-eating animals may be eaten by other bigger animals that get energy from them. In this way, the energy flows through the food chain and through the habitat.

*Rainforest trees spread a dense **canopy** of leaves to catch as much of the Sun's light as they can.*

Making the chain

Plants are called **producers**, because they trap the Sun's **energy** and make, or produce, food for themselves and other animals. Producers provide food for plant-eating animals, known as **herbivores**. In food chains, herbivores are **primary consumers**. Primary consumers are often food for other animals we call **carnivores**. In food chains, these carnivores are **secondary consumers**. Secondary consumers catch and eat primary consumers, and they may also eat other smaller secondary consumers.

Animals that eat both plants and other animals are called **omnivores**. Omnivores can be primary and secondary consumers.

Squirrel monkeys are omnivores. They eat mainly flowers, fruits, and seeds, but also insects and other small animals.

More links in the chain

Food chains usually start with producers, and then go on to primary consumers and secondary consumers. But the chain does not end there. All **organisms** eventually die. When that happens, animals called **scavengers**, including worms and maggots, eat their bodies. **Decomposers** such as **bacteria** and **fungi** then eat or break down any dead remains that are left. They also eat or break down rotting trees and plants. The waste from these decomposers sinks into the soil or riverbed, where some of it becomes **nutrients** that can be taken in by plant roots. In this way, the chain begins again.

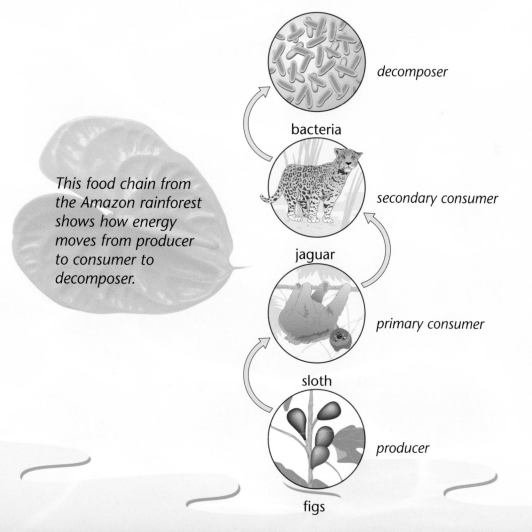

This food chain from the Amazon rainforest shows how energy moves from producer to consumer to decomposer.

decomposer

bacteria

secondary consumer

jaguar

primary consumer

sloth

producer

figs

Breaking the chain

If some of the **organisms** in a food web die out, it may
be deadly for other organisms in the web. Sometimes
natural events can damage a food web, but more often
in the case of rainforests, human activity is the biggest
danger. Rainforests are cut down either for their wood or
to make space for cattle or businesses. This is deadly for
the animals of the rainforest, because they lose their food
supplies, **habitat**, and shelter. **Pollution** from businesses
can also break rainforest food chains and other natural
cycles, with terrible results.

*Forest fires can
sometimes be started
by lightning strikes.
Such natural events
can harm food webs
by destroying large
areas of rainforest.*

Which Producers Live in Rainforests?

Plants are **producers**, and they are at the start of most rainforest food chains. There are many producers in a rainforest **habitat**. Some plants grow on the forest floor, such as shrubs and moss. Ferns, vines, palms, and creepers can grow in the **understory**, since they do not need much light to survive. They provide food and shelter for insects, birds, and small **rodents**. Up in the trees, the leaves, bark, fruit, and nuts provide food for monkeys, birds, and insects. Other plants called **epiphytes** grow on the trees. They get their **nutrients** from air, rainwater, and waste material on the branches where they grow.

decomposer

bacteria

secondary consumer

jaguar

primary consumer

sloth

producer

figs

Mosses and ferns cover the floor of the rainforest and the lower parts of the trees.

Many rainforest **producers** also have brightly colored flowers and fruit that grow high up at the **canopy** level. These are important foods for the parrots and butterflies that live in this part of the rainforest. The insects and birds **pollinate** the flowers.

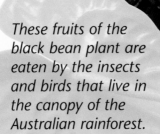

These fruits of the black bean plant are eaten by the insects and birds that live in the canopy of the Australian rainforest.

Breaking the Chain: Producers

Green plants are extremely important to rainforest food chains, but they are in grave danger. It is thought that over 200,000 acres (80,000 hectares) of rainforest are burned down every day around the world—that's 150 acres (60 hectares) of trees, with all the plant life that grows on and around them, lost every minute. Without those trees and plants, there is no food and shelter for the animals that depend on them. Even the soil the trees grow in soon becomes poor. Thousands of **species** are at risk of **extinction**.

Which Primary Consumers Live in Rainforests?

Primary consumers in the rainforest can be small or large animals that live on the forest floor and up in the trees. They feed on the rich plant life of the forest, from the fruit, flowers, and leaves of the trees, to the shrubs and moss that grow at ground level.

On the Amazon forest floor, insects such as leaf-cutting ants and beetles search for food, nibbling the leaves and **fungi**. Ground **rodents** such as agoutis and pacas travel through the forest at night, hunting for plants to eat.

Larger primary consumers include the tapir, a piglike animal with a long, bendy nose. Tapirs spend their days among the low-growing plants, but come out at night to feed on leaves and fruit. They often cover themselves in a layer of mud, as a protection from insect bites!

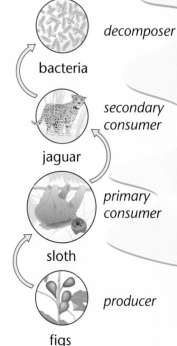

decomposer

bacteria

secondary consumer

jaguar

primary consumer

sloth

producer

figs

This Baird's tapir is munching on Amazon rainforest plants. There are four species of tapirs, and all of them are now **endangered.**

13

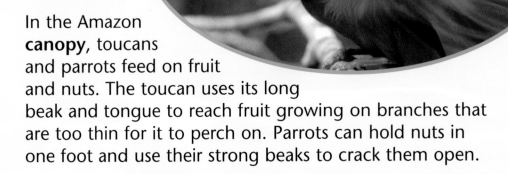

*This male great bird of paradise is from Papua New Guinea, in southeastern Asia. There are over 40 **species** of these birds. Most eat a mixture of insects and fruit.*

In the Amazon **canopy**, toucans and parrots feed on fruit and nuts. The toucan uses its long beak and tongue to reach fruit growing on branches that are too thin for it to perch on. Parrots can hold nuts in one foot and use their strong beaks to crack them open.

Fruit bats sleep all day, then come out at night to feed on fruit, **nectar**, and **pollen**. Brightly colored butterflies flutter through the trees, feeding on the nectar in their flowers. Hummingbirds are also nectar feeders. Their wings move so fast that they are a blur. They hover in midair as they dip their long bills into flowers.

The three-toed sloth is a strange and slow-moving animal that hangs from the branches of trees—even when it is asleep—and grinds leaves very slowly in its teeth. Its hairy coat is green from the mosses and tiny plants that grow on it. It blends in with the leaves, and moves so slowly that **predators** have a hard time spotting it. If a jaguar sees a sloth, it will try to climb up and catch it.

Which Secondary Consumers Live in Rainforests?

Secondary consumers can be **carnivores** or **omnivores**. A carnivore's food is rich in **nutrients** but is not always easy to catch, so predators must put a lot of **energy** into hunting their **prey**. Big cats like the jaguar, ocelot, and margay are rainforest predators.

Jaguars are the largest secondary consumers in the Amazon rainforest. They prowl around the forest floor and will eat any animal they find. Jaguars like to eat tapirs, but they also eat monkeys, water birds, caimans, and tortoises.

The largest flying predator in the Amazon rainforest is the huge harpy eagle. Harpy eagles soar over the treetops, then swoop down to snatch prey with their strong claws, called talons. They also eat other birds, monkeys, and sloths.

bacteria — *decomposer*

jaguar — *secondary consumer*

sloth — *primary consumer*

producer

figs

Jaguars are good swimmers and will even follow their prey into water.

15

The giant anaconda is one of the largest snakes in the world. It lives along the banks of the Amazon River and eats **mammals** and birds that go there to drink. It drags them under the water, where it kills and swallows them. Anacondas can climb as well as swim, and hide from their **prey** in the rainforest trees.

The deep flower of this Madagascar pitcher plant is a deadly trap for careless insects.

Sometimes plants can be **predators**, too! There are some rainforest plants, such as the pitcher plant, that trap small insects and spiders. They invite the insects into their cup-shaped leaves by leaving **nectar** at the top of the "cup." The insects fall into the plant but cannot get back out. The plant takes in the **nutrients** from the insects' bodies to help it grow.

Omnivores hunt for prey, but they also eat many kinds of plants. In the Australian rainforest, the bandicoot feeds on fruits, or may dig its snout and claws into the ground to find insects to eat. It also eats small mammals.

Which Decomposers Live in Rainforests?

Every acre of rainforest is filled with about two tons (about 2 tonnes) of plant and animal waste every year. If this dead matter and waste just stayed on the ground, air and water could not get through to the tree roots, and nutrients would not be recycled for plants to use as food. However, the **decomposers** and **scavengers** on the forest floor help to recycle all the waste matter. When plants and animals die, decomposers break down the decaying matter into simpler substances, such as **carbon dioxide** and water.

In the rainforest, this recycling happens faster than anywhere else on Earth, because of the high temperature and the large amount of moisture in the air. The main rainforest decomposers are **fungi** and tiny **organisms** such as **bacteria**.

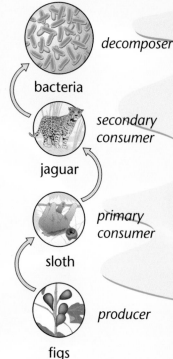

decomposer

bacteria

secondary consumer

jaguar

primary consumer

sloth

producer

figs

These bracket fungi are growing on a tree stump in Costa Rica. The "brackets" are only a small part of the fungus. A network of tiny tubes spreads deep inside the wood.

When a tree falls to the rainforest floor, it is quickly covered with insects and **fungi** that eat the wood and bark. Termites are especially helpful **scavengers** in the rainforest because they are very good wood eaters. The holes and tunnels that termites dig provide a way for **decomposers** such as fungi to get deep into the wood. These insects and decomposers work so well that a dead branch in the rainforest disappears completely in just a week or two.

When an animal dies in the rainforest, fungi and **bacteria** soon decompose it, with the help of earthworms. The animal's body rots and lets out **nutrients**. These sink into the soil of the rainforest floor and are taken in by the plants, making them able to start their life processes all over again.

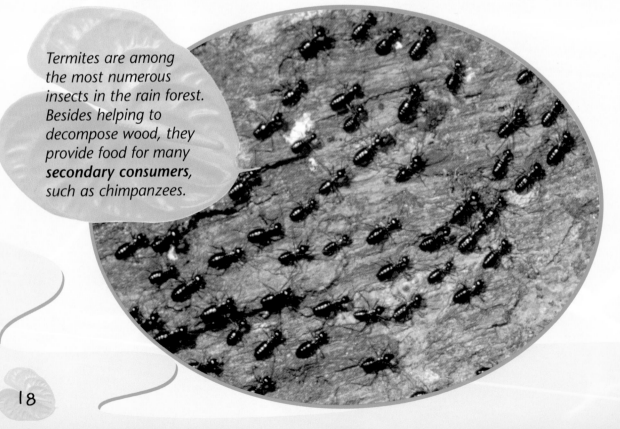

*Termites are among the most numerous insects in the rain forest. Besides helping to decompose wood, they provide food for many **secondary consumers**, such as chimpanzees.*

How Are Rainforest Food Chains Different in Different Places?

There are rainforests all over the world—in South America, southeastern Asia, Australia, and central Africa. Although these rainforests share similar **climates** and thick forests, the food chains can be very different. Food chains depend on the location of the rainforest and the plants and animals that live there. Human activity also affects the food chains.

The Australian rainforest is small, but it is home to some remarkable animals, including this cassowary bird.

The Amazon rainforest

The Amazon rainforest is the largest in the world. It runs through Central and South America and covers approximately 1.6 million square miles (4.1 million square kilometers) in Brazil alone. More than 4,000 **species** of trees live here, some more than 164 feet (50 meters) high. Over 500 species of birds search for fruit and nuts to eat. There are brightly colored toucans, macaws, and parrots, and tiny hummingbirds searching for flowers. Many species of monkeys also live here, from the tiny squirrel monkey to the large howler monkey. Boa constrictors and emerald boas slide along tree branches, watching out for frogs and lizards to eat.

On the forest floor, **predators** hunt in the shadows while huge groups of army ants march across the ground looking for food. Every year, the Amazon River floods across much of the forest, forming the largest river basin in the world. Thousands of freshwater fish swim here, including sharp-toothed piranhas.

The African rainforest

The belt of rainforest that stretches across central Africa is the second largest rainforest in the world. It is home to an amazing variety of animals. Elephants, gorillas, and chimpanzees live at or near ground level. Leopards hunt here, too. Up in the trees, colobus monkeys leap from branch to branch, while hornbills and parrots search for insects and fruit. The crowned eagle hunts up in the **canopy**.

The colobus monkey eats 4.5–6 pounds (2–3 kilograms) of leaves every day. This is about one-quarter of its body weight. To keep this up, the animal has to spend about a third of its day eating.

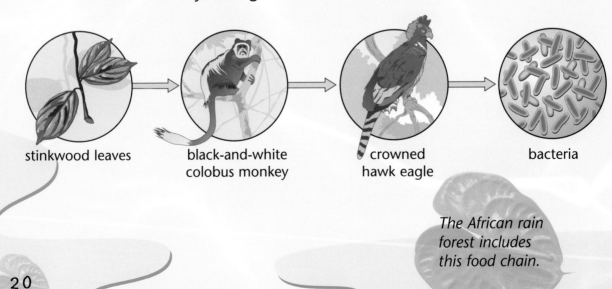

stinkwood leaves

black-and-white colobus monkey

crowned hawk eagle

bacteria

The African rain forest includes this food chain.

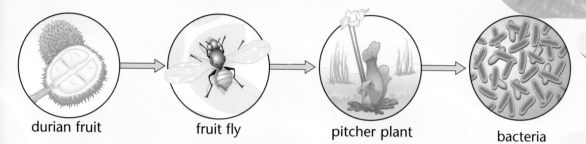

| durian fruit | fruit fly | pitcher plant | bacteria |

The southeastern Asian rainforest

The rainforests of southeastern Asia occur in patches, not in one large area like the Amazon rain forest. They are found in countries like Malaysia and on islands such as Borneo and Sumatra. Borneo is one of the few places in the region where there are still large sections of rain forest that have not been spoiled by farming, wars, or cutting down trees.

These forests have a huge variety of plants and animals. Rain forest trees reach up toward the sunlight, surrounded by vines such as lianas and covered by other **epiphytes**. Many of the insects are big and brightly colored. The stink bug and the atlas moth live among the leaves of the trees. Ants live inside the Malaysian epiphyte *Myrmecodia*. In return for their shelter, the ants protect the plant from plant-eating insects. Durian trees here produce some of the smelliest fruits in the world, and brightly colored **fungi** grow throughout the forests.

Pitcher plants are among the **carnivores** in the southeastern Asian rain forest. Their cup-shaped leaves with **nectar** along their rims invite insects, who then fall into the cup. There they are broken down by the plant.

What Happens to a Food Web When a Food Chain Breaks Down?

All around the world, rainforest food chains and webs are in danger because of humans. Although much work is being done to stop further harm, plants and animals in rainforest **habitats** face many problems today.

Habitat destruction

Rainforests once covered 14 percent of Earth's surface, but they now cover only 6 percent. In less than 50 years, more than half of the world's rainforests have been destroyed, and this pace keeps increasing. Over 200,000 acres (80,000 hectares) of rainforest are lost every day, as trees are cut down to use for fuel or wood, and to provide land where cattle can graze. Cutting down trees, called logging, is destroying the habitat for wildlife. There are fewer animals because there are fewer plants to hide them from **predators** and hunters. Animals are being driven farther into the rainforest to find new homes.

Scientists think that at this rate the last remaining rainforests could be destroyed in less than 40 years. Scientists also believe that about 130 **species** of plants, animals, and insects are becoming **extinct** every single day, often before scientists have even studied them.

Pollution

The Amazon rainforest is also at risk of **pollution** from people digging for metals, an activity called mining. Brazil is rich in metals, and there are many groups doing mining there. However, some of the chemicals used in mining, such as gold, nickel, and copper, run into rivers and streams in the region and are carried hundreds of miles. This pollution poisons plants and animals on and near the river, or drives them away from their natural **habitat**.

Overhunting

Many rainforest animals are at risk from overfishing and overhunting. In the central African rainforest, the western lowland gorilla and the chimpanzee are **endangered** animals. Both have been hunted, and their habitat continues to be destroyed. If they are not protected, they will be gone forever.

In the central African rainforest, the male silverback gorilla is the leading member of his group.

Global warming

Rainforests have been called the lungs of the planet. The trees in the rainforest help us to breathe by giving off the gas oxygen into the air. They also take in large amounts of **carbon dioxide**, a gas that is not good for us to breathe, from the air during **photosynthesis**. This helps to remove some of the carbon dioxide that humans produce by burning oil and coal. When forests are cut down, there are fewer trees to take in carbon dioxide. This could make Earth hotter and cause great harm to all living things.

Breaking the Chain: How We Are Affected

When animals and plants are poisoned, killed, or driven out of their natural **habitat**, it breaks the food chains and affects the entire food web of the region. In the end, breaks or changes to food chains and webs affect humans, too. We can have problems caused by **pollution** and mercury poisoning. When rainforests are cut down, there are fewer plants to keep the air clean, and Earth gets slowly warmer. Humans along the Amazon River have fewer fish to catch and eat. Protecting and caring for rainforest food webs is important for all living things.

How Can We Protect Rainforest Food Chains?

All around the world, scientists, governments, and other groups are working to protect rainforests and rainforest food chains. They want to be sure that no more harm is done to these habitats and the animals and plants that depend on them to survive.

International research and protection

Scientists and **conservation** workers make surveys of rainforest habitats. They keep track of animal and plant life in the rainforests to check that their numbers do not fall. In this way, scientists find the links in the food web that need protection.

Conservation workers will study this Komodo dragon at their research center.

Scientists suggest ways that governments can improve and protect rainforest **habitats** while still making the money they need out of them. Groups like Friends of the Earth, Greenpeace, and the World Wildlife Fund work to make governments take care of rainforests and to make sure people know when problems arise. They try to stop illegal logging and suggest other ways to manage forests.

In the Amazon, scientists, plant collectors, **conservation** workers, and companies that make medicines are studying plants. They want to prove that some rainforest plants can be used for making important drugs and cures. These uses could make more money for countries than they could earn by chopping down the rainforests.

Conservation groups also run projects to teach people living in or near rainforests about how they can help to protect them, now and in the future.

Many groups are working hard to help conserve the world's rainforests. Fifteen percent of the Amazon rainforest is at risk from logging like this.

Research a forest food web in your local area

You can study forest habitats in your local area, even though they are not exactly the same as a rainforest. If you go on a trip to a forest, think about the food chains of that habitat. Here are some suggestions to help you find out about animal and plant life and some tips to help you protect the habitat where they live.

1. What is the habitat like? Is it cold, warm, shady, or light? How is it different from a rainforest?
2. What plants and animals live there? Try to put them in groups that are similar, such as plants, insects, birds, and **mammals**.
3. What do you think each animal would like to eat?
4. Which are the **predators** and which are the **prey**?
5. Can you make a food chain of the animals and plants you see?
6. Think about how the habitat could change. How would these changes affect the wildlife there?

Thousands of plants, animals, and insects live in forest habitats, living on or near the forest trees.

27

Where Are the World's Main Rainforests?

This map shows the location of the major rainforests of the world.

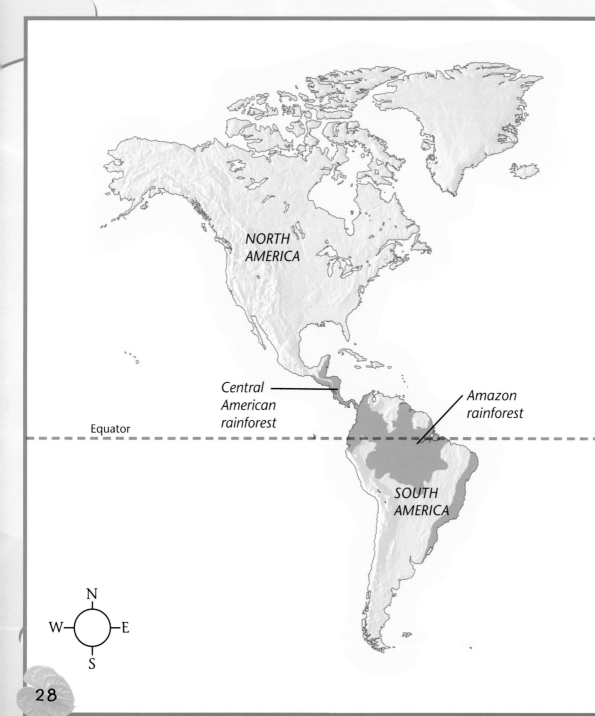

NORTH AMERICA

Central American rainforest

Amazon rainforest

Equator

SOUTH AMERICA

N
W—E
S

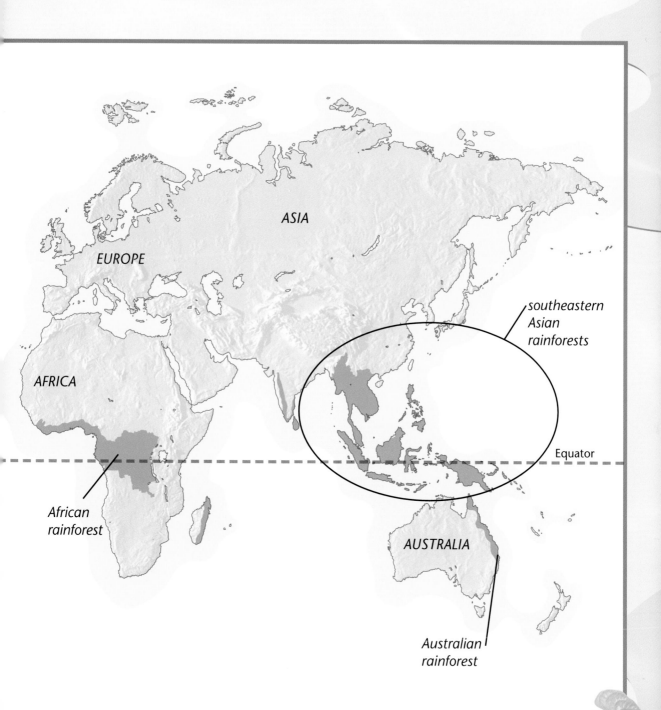

EUROPE

ASIA

AFRICA

southeastern
Asian
rainforests

Equator

African
rainforest

AUSTRALIA

Australian
rainforest

Glossary

bacteria (singular bacterium) tiny living decomposers found everywhere

canopy layer of trees near the top of the rainforest

carbon dioxide gas in the air that animals breathe out and plants use to make food

carnivore animal that eats the flesh of another animal

climate general conditions of weather in an area

conservation protecting and saving the natural environment

decomposer organism that breaks down and gets nutrients from dead plants and animals and their waste

endangered at risk of dying out completely, as a species of animal or plant

energy power to grow, move, and do things

epiphyte plant that grows above the ground, using other plants or objects for support but not harming them

equator imaginary line around the Earth, equally distant from the north and south poles

extinct died out completely

fungi (singular fungus) group of decomposer organisms including mushrooms, toadstools, and their relatives

habitat place where an organism lives

herbivore animal that eats plants

mammal animal that feeds its babies on milk from its own body

nectar sugary substance made by plants to attract insects that eat it

nutrient chemical that plants and animals need to live

omnivore animal that eats both plants and other animals

organism living thing

photosynthesis process by which plants make their own food using carbon dioxide, water, and energy from sunlight

pollen small grains that are the male parts of a flower. Pollen combines with eggs (female flower parts) to form seeds.

pollinate to carry pollen from the male part of a flower to a female part

pollution when chemicals or other substances that can damage animal or plant life escape into water, soil, or the air

predator animal that hunts and eats other animals

prey animal that is caught and eaten by a predator

primary consumer animal that eats plants

producer organism (plant) that can make its own food

rodent mammal with large gnawing front teeth, such as a mouse or rat

scavenger organism that feeds on dead plant and animal material and waste

secondary consumer animal that eats primary consumers and other secondary consumers

species group of organisms that are similar to each other and can breed together to produce young

tropical belonging to a region of the world that is warm all year round but has one or more rainy seasons

understory dark part of the rainforest, above the forest floor but below the canopy, where only plants that do not need much light can grow

More Books to Read

Baker, Lucy. *Life in the Rain Forests*. Santa Monica, CA: Creative Publishing, 2003.

Baldwin, Carol. *Living in a Rain Forest*. Chicago, IL: Heinemann Library, 2003.

Greenaway, Theresa. *Food Chains*. Chicago, IL: Raintree, 2001.

Johansson, Philip. *The Tropical Rain Forest*. Berkeley Heights, NJ: Enslow Publishers, 2004.

Lauber, Patricia. *Who Eats What?* New York: HarperCollins, 2001.

Llewellyn, Claire. *Animal Atlas*. Santa Monica, CA: Creative Publishing, 2003.

Morey, Allan. *Rain Forest Food Chains*. Minneapolis, MN: Lake Street Publishers, 2003.

Morgan, Sally. *Saving the Rainforests*. Danbury, CT: Scholastic Library, 1999.

Pirotta, Saviour. *Predators in the Rain Forest*. Chicago, IL: Raintree, 1999.

Pirotta, Saviour. *Trees and Plants in the Rain Forest*. Chicago, IL: Raintree, 1999.

Index

animals 4, 5, 6, 7, 8, 9, 11, 13–16, 18, 19–21, 22, 23

bacteria 4, 9, 17, 18
birds 5, 11, 12, 14, 15, 16, 19, 20
breaking the food chain 10, 12, 22–24
butterflies and moths 12, 14, 21

canopy 5, 7, 12, 14
carnivores 8, 15, 21
climate 5, 17, 19
conservation groups 26
consumers 8, 9, 13–16, 18

decomposers 9, 17–18

endangered animals 13, 23
energy 6, 7, 8
epiphytes 11, 21
extinction 12, 22

fish 20, 23, 24
food chains 5, 6–21, 22, 27
food webs 4, 5, 6, 10, 22
forest floor 5, 11, 13, 15, 17, 18
fungi 4, 9, 13, 17, 18, 21

habitat damage and destruction 10, 12, 22, 23
   fires 10
   global warming 24
   logging 22, 26
   overhunting 23
   pollution 10, 22–23, 24
herbivores 8

insects 4, 11, 12, 13, 14, 16, 18, 20, 21

jaguars 5, 14, 15

medicines 26
monkeys 5, 8, 11, 15, 19, 20
mosses and ferns 5, 11, 13, 14

nutrients 7, 9, 11, 15, 16, 17, 18

omnivores 8, 15, 16

parrots 12, 14, 19, 20
photosynthesis 7, 24
pitcher plants 16, 21
plants 4, 5, 6, 7, 8, 9, 11–12, 13–14, 16, 17, 18, 21, 22, 23, 26
predators and prey 14, 15, 16, 19, 20, 21, 22
primary consumers 8, 9, 13–14
producers 8, 9, 11–12
protecting food chains and webs 25–26

rainforest habitats 5, 19–21
   African 20, 23
   Amazon 14, 15, 16, 19–20, 22–23, 24, 26
   Australian 16, 19
   southeastern Asian 21
rodents 11, 13

scavengers 9, 17, 18
secondary consumers 8, 9, 15–16, 18
sloths 5, 14, 15
snakes 16, 19

tapirs 13, 15
trees 4, 5, 7, 11, 12, 13, 14, 18, 19, 20, 21, 24

understory 5, 11